John Skelton

Poet of Tudor England

Skelton Poet·

MAURICE POLLET

John Skelton
Poet of Tudor England

Translated by
John Warrington

LONDON
J. M. DENT & SONS LTD

Made in Great Britain
at the
Aldine Press · Letchworth · Herts
for
J. M. DENT & SONS LTD
Aldine House · Bedford Street · London
First published 1971

ISBN: 0 460 03937 7

To Myrtle

Contents

Illustrations

A portrait representation named John Skelton, nearly
contemporary, attached to a copy of *Speke, Parrot*
(?1546).
Reproduced by permission of John Fleming, Esquire,
New York.   *frontispiece*

between pages 62 and 63

Henry the Eighth as a child, the pupil of Skelton. Oil
painting by an unknown artist.
Reproduced from the original by permission of Sir Harry
Verney, D.S.O.

'A Lawde and Prayse made for our Souereigne Lord
the Kyng'.
Crown Copyright. Reproduced by permission of the
Controller of Her Majesty's Stationery Office from the
original manuscript in the Public Record Office, London.

Numerals in small type in the Introduction
and the text proper refer to bibliographical and other notes
grouped in chapter order after the Conclusion

Abbreviations

B.M.	British Museum
CAL. S.P.	Calendar of State Papers
D.N.B.	Dictionary of National Biography
E.E.T.S.	Early English Text Society
EN. RW.	English Review
EN. ST.	English Studies
Eng. Stn.	Englische Studien
ET. AN.	Etudes Anglaises
L.P. H.VIII	Letters and Papers of Henry VIII
M.L.N.	Modern Language Notes
M.L.R.	Modern Language Review
N. & Q.	Notes and Queries
N.E.D.	New English Dictionary
P.M.L.A.	Publications of the Modern Language Association of America
P.R.O.	Public Record Office
R.E.S.	Review of English Studies
R.S.	Rolls Series
Sur. S.	Surtees Society
St. Ph.	Studies in Philology
T.L.S.	Times Literary Supplement
Dyce	A. Dyce, *The Poetical Works of John Skelton*, 1843.
Edwards	H. L. R. Edwards, *Skelton. The Life and Times of an Early Tudor Poet*, 1949.

Gordon	Ian A. Gordon, *John Skelton, Poet Laureate*, 1943.
Lloyd	Leslie J. Lloyd, *John Skelton*, 1938.
Nelson	William Nelson, *John Skelton, Laureate*, 1939.
Ag. C. Coy	Against A Comely Coystron
Ag. Sc.	Against the Scots
V.T.	Against Venomous Tongues
ALB.	Against the doughty duke of Albany
Rep.	A replication against certain young scholars abjured of late
Sc. K.	A Ballad of the Scottish King
B. of C.	Bouge of Court
C. Cl.	Colin Clout
D. of E.N.	Upon the Death of the Earl of Northumberland
E.R.	The Tunning of Elinour Rummyng
G. of L.	Garland of Laurel
Garn. I, II, III, IV	Against Garnesche, I, II, III, IV
Mag.	Magnificence
Ph. Sp.	The Book of Philip Sparrow
Sp. P.	Speak, Parrot
Spec.	Speculum Principis
WCYN	Why Come ye not to Court?
W. the H.	Ware the Hawk

Where no abbreviated source title is given, numerals in parentheses following quotations refer to the work under discussion. Numerals in parentheses throughout are line-number.

FOREWORD

W ITH its undoubted virtues and its glaring faults, the
work of John Skelton, laureate crowned by Oxford University, churchman and tutor of Henry VIII, marks an important
stage between Chaucer and Spenser, between the medieval
spirit and the spirit of the Renaissance. It bridges two generations—that of Caxton under the last Plantagenet, who introduced the printing press from Flanders, and that of Surrey,
contemporary with the Reformation, who brought back the
sonnet from Italy. Between the two, Skelton figures as a
staunchly national poet; as Robert Graves observes, he was
'English through and through'. One may therefore claim that
his interest is more than literary; it is also historical, inasmuch
as he embodies more vigorously than anyone else, at a definite
psychological moment, the national awakening characteristic
of England between the Wars of the Roses and the Reformation.

Long travestied, long defaced by controversy, John Skelton,
himself a man of very strong views, has provoked such passionate
and contradictory reactions that it is impossible to determine
whether truth has suffered more from the hostile or from the
favourable prejudices which have fostered his legend. One of
the most unexpected and most interesting features of the present
study has been to find that certain well-worn theories, bequeathed by a sincere but erroneous tradition, collapse
beneath the weight of contrary evidence. For example, Skelton
was long represented by the Reformers as one of their pre-
cursors, and by German philology as a humanist, whereas in
point of fact he was the very opposite: a fierce opponent both
of Lutheran novelties and of the New Learning.

After more than a hundred years of learned research, inaugurated by Dyce in 1843, the need has lately been felt for a
comprehensive study of the man and his works. America and
Great Britain have led us in this field. It would be unjust not to
acknowledge my considerable indebtedness to works published
by Nelson in the United States, Gordon in New Zealand, Lloyd

xi

and H. L. R. Edwards in England, as well as to the host of scholars who preceded them.

Nevertheless, I considered 'Skelton's case' impossible of solution except by the Cartesian method of systematic doubt, by passing through the sieve of criticism every document we possess. That is what I undertook to do in the course of an exciting investigation which afforded me the pleasure of many finds, ranging from the larger considerations which gradually assumed a fresh significance down to the most trivial points which mean so much to a biographer. It is a pleasure to have something new to say upon such matters as the origins of the poet, whom I have placed in a more clearly defined geographical and social setting than he had previously occupied; his reconciliation with Wolsey, which I trace to a definite political situation; the sources of *Magnificence*; the date of *Elynour Rummyng* or *Against Venomous Tongues*; and many other details which it would be tedious to enumerate here.

For help received in my arduous task I cannot in few words express my gratitude, first and foremost, to the Centre National de la Recherche Scientifique, which provided me with funds that enabled me to work in England on the solution of this enigma.

I am glad to be able to record my heartfelt thanks to my masters and my guides: M. Émile Pons, professor at the Sorbonne, and M. Fernand Mossé, professor at the Collège de France—both unhappily no longer with us.

I am pleased likewise to recall here my fruitful correspondence with the late F. M. Salter, professor at the University of Edmonton, Canada, who was familiar with every problem concerning Skelton and his age.

My thoughts go out to those many, often anonymous, friends who smoothed the path of my inquiries, both in libraries and on the spot in places associated with Skelton's life. In particular I should like to mention the staff of the British Museum, who received me with such courtesy.

I owe a very special word of thanks to those who have allowed me to enrich my book with illustrations—the Director of the Public Record Office, for the poet's precious autograph MS., Sir Harry Verney, of Claydon House, Buckinghamshire, who owns the portrait of Henry VIII as a child, painted at the very time when he was Skelton's pupil, and to Mr John Fleming of New York for the woodcut portrait printed as the frontispiece.

Finally, I must gratefully acknowledge the valuable help received, on the one hand, from the Sorbonne, and on the other from the University of Dakar which made it possible for me to bring my enterprise safely into port in the French edition of 1963, and ultimately in the present translation. I would like also to thank in particular Professor Louis Bonnerot, director of *Études Anglaises*, and the translator, John Warrington.

I ask them to accept these words as token of my utmost gratitude.

MAURICE POLLET.

Dakar,
November 1970.

INTRODUCTION

MODERN Skeltonian studies date from 1843, when *The Poetical Works of John Skelton*, the first critical edition, was published in London by Alexander Dyce, editor of Shakespeare. John Skelton profited thereafter from the steady progress of scholarly research during the nineteenth century, as well as from a revival of interest in old English writers who had heralded the Renaissance.

Dyce's edition, however, was slow to take effect. It resulted in no immediate spate of works; and indeed the author of *Elynour Rummyng* was an unlikely candidate for favour in mid-Victorian times. Apart from two long premonitory articles, one by Robert Southey (1834),[1] the other by Elizabeth Barrett Browning (1842),[2] together with some words in praise of *Phyllyp Sparowe* from Coleridge,[3] it can be said that for about thirty years Skelton had to be content with a few secondary articles, a few cursory and condescending opinions included here and there in manuals of literature.

Nevertheless, a number of small discoveries signposted the road of future studies. While Dyce's edition was still in the press, there was exhumed from the archives relating to Exchequer receipts a hitherto unknown poem by Skelton, *A Lawde and Prayse made for our Souereigne Lord the Kyng*,[4] celebrating Henry VIII's accession to the throne. At Cambridge, in 1873, Mullinger identified the two young heretics of that university whom Skelton had taken to task in his *Replycacion*.[5] In 1878 a unique copy of *A Ballad of the Scottish King*,[6] known to have been published in the author's lifetime by Richard Faques, was discovered in a Dorset farmhouse, included in a volume of *Huon de Bordeaux*, issued by Michel le Noir at Paris in 1513. Next, in 1885, Ernest Law[7] noted that certain tapestries at Hampton Court, once the property of Wolsey, are accurately described in Skelton's *Why Come ye not to Court?* In 1896, Henry Bradley managed with great skill to decipher a couple of Latin puzzles with which our poet had sought to mystify two of his enemies.[8]

Suddenly, the late nineteenth and early twentieth century witnessed a twofold blaze of German scholarship: Krumpholz [9] (1881), Schoneberg [10] (1888) and Flügel [11] (1895) were followed by Koelbing [12] (1904), Thümmel [13] (1905) and, above all, Friedrich Brie [14] (1907), who made the first move to sweep out the aprocryphal poems and undertook an initial (though tentative) chronology of the poetical works. Meanwhile, in the United States, the American edition of Dyce, published at Boston in 1856, gave rise to a few isolated studies, mainly in the field of satire, which led eventually to Berdan's important book on early Tudor poetry (1920).[15] Notable among English contributions were Ramsay's copious edition of *Magnificence* [16] and two penetrating studies (1917) by Dunbabin [17] on the 'humanism' of Skelton and the problem of his birth. In 1912, Dr James [18] had drawn attention to some rare examples of Skelton's handwriting in the dedications appended to the *Chronique de Rains* in the library of Corpus Christi College, Cambridge, and in 1921 Westlake [19] found traces of the apartment occupied by Skelton within the Sanctuary at Westminster in 1518.

Alongside these material discoveries, partial editions helped to nourish the increasing interest in John Skelton's work. In 1902, a small anthology [20] appeared simultaneously in London and Tasmania, and after the First World War a selection of poems was edited by the poet Richard Hughes (1924).[21] In the following year John Lloyd opened a new round of studies with an article in the *English Review* entitled 'John Skelton, a forgotten poet'.[22] Robert Graves then accorded Skelton a place in *The Augustan Book of English Poetry*,[23] while Miss Hammond presented the literary public with a learned edition of the *Garland of Laurel* (1927),[24] thus drawing attention to a less familiar aspect of his work, the poems in *rimes royales*. On the other hand, the unrestrained and burlesque prattle of *Elynour Rummyng* seemed to accord with the uninhibited taste of the post-war period: two luxury editions, with a wealth of illustrations, appeared in quick succession, one in London [25] and the other in California.[26] In London, as if in answer to Lloyd's signal, Skelton received the honour of a long editorial by Edmund Blunden in *The Times Literary Supplement* (20th July

1929),[27] which placed him at the centre of current literary interest. Humbert Wolfe included him in a general work on satire.[28] Finally, in 1931, yet another poet, Philip Henderson, published a complete edition of Skelton's poems, the first in date since that of Dyce; it did much to revive Skeltonian studies, and its modernized spelling helped to enlarge the circle of his readers.

In 1934, in the British Museum, F. M. Salter came across the only known copy of *Speculum Principis*,[29] a prose work mentioned two centuries earlier by Tanner, who had noticed it in the library of Lincoln Cathedral in 1748. Long lost, it had returned through the accident of a sale to enrich the dormant treasures of the Museum.

Also in 1934, there began a series of letters to *The Times*, which were destined for more than two years to open many points of detail to public discussion, thanks mainly to Ian Gordon, John Lloyd and H. L. R. Edwards.

With these three British critics, each of whom devoted a special work to Skelton, it is proper to associate an American, William Nelson, who distinguished himself in a fraternal joust with Edwards in the columns of *P.M.L.A.*[30]

During the past twenty years there have been countless articles and studies, letters to the Press and to the great specialist reviews. Skelton has become part of everyday life. He has been discussed on the Third Programme of the B.B.C., and in 1935 he received an unexpected salute from modern English music, when Vaughan Williams composed a *Choral Suite* on words taken from his poems.[31]

His work has become a familiar bench-mark in the English pre-Renaissance landscape. His name is now commonly used to indicate, as required, either one of the end-products of the Middle Ages or one of the starting points of the Renaissance.[32] Midway between Chaucer and Spenser, John Skelton, along with Barclay and Stephen Hawes, thus dominates a somewhat arid stretch of years that covers nearly two centuries.

The part played by French criticism in the rediscovery of Skelton has hitherto been slight, consisting of no more than a long article by Philarète Chasles,[33] in 1842, a brilliant piece by

Jusserand,[34] another by Taine,[35] and some shrewd comments by Emile Legouis.[36]

John Skelton commends himself to the reader's attention with a body of poetical work of bizarre and disparate character, showing a mixture of traditional metres and facile little verses called by the generic name 'Skeltonics'. But that work over-flows with vitality, tuned to the most varied keys of praise or reproach. It is thus the work of a moralist by turns laudatory and fervent, gracious and courteous, comic and burlesque, jesting and bantering, epigrammatic and puzzling, angry and complaining, severe in judgment and vengeful, loud-mouthed and frenzied, completely unrestrained in his denunciation of the abuses around him. A characteristic common to all his writings is their invariable concern with matters of the hour. Skelton is before all else a man of his time.

There remain, however, only fragments of his earliest work, fragments moreover which have resisted oblivion with unequal success. The satires, for example, whose critical content appealed to the taste of the next generation, that of the Re-formers, have survived in greater numbers than have the didactic treatises or the religious meditations. Fortunately we have at least one specimen of almost every aspect of his talent.

CHAPTER I

Epoch, Origins and Beginnings

IN HIS preface to *The Boke of Eneydes*, translated into English from the French work of Guillaume Leroy in 1490,[1] William Caxton, the aged printer to the royal family at Westminster, has a paragraph in praise of 'Master John Skelton, lately created poet laureate in the University of Oxford', whom he presents to the reader as a skilful commentator, translator of Latin works and a familiar of the Muses:

'. . . For hym I know for suffycyent to expowne and englysshe euery dyffyculte that is therein. For he hath late translated the epystlys of Tulle and the boke of dyodorus syculus, and diuerse other werkes oute of latyn in to englysshe not in rude and olde language, but in polyshed and ornate termes craftely, as he that hath redde vyrgyle ouyde tully, and all the other noble poetes and oratours to me vnknowen: And also hath redde the IX muses and vnderstande theyr musicalle scyences, and to whom of theym eche scyence is appropred. I suppose he hath dronken of Elycons well.'

In accordance with a time-honoured formula, he invites Skelton or anyone else to peruse and correct his book, allowing the corrector full latitude 'to add or cut out whenever it may appear needful'. And such a compliment was all the more flattering inasmuch as the book was dedicated to young Arthur, heir apparent to the throne.

We know, too, that Skelton had recently distinguished himself with a poem on the death of the Earl of Northumberland, and that that poem had been written at the Court of Henry VII in 1489.[2]

From his earliest days at Court, therefore, until his death at Westminster on 21st June 1529, his literary career embraces the new dynasty's first half-century, which was at the same time

(1485–1535) the last half-century of Catholic tradition in England before the Reformation.

In 1489 four years had elapsed since the king wrested his crown from Richard III on Bosworth Field, and three years since his marriage with Elizabeth of York officially terminated the Wars of the Roses. That period, which had begun with a wedding, ended with a divorce. In 1529 Henry VIII's case against Katherine of Aragon began, a case which gradually led to an open breach with Rome. R. W. Chambers has well described the summer days of 1535, when the Act of Supremacy came into force, as 'the great dividing days of English history'. We know indeed that the change of personal status which made the King of England supreme head of his Church inaugurated a most profound spiritual revolution, which did more than anything else to fashion the mentality of the English nation. Thereafter, all history prior to the Reformation wore the colours of an *ancien régime*.

John Skelton's adult life belonged precisely to that somewhat lonely period of the Tudor dynasty which is isolated from the immediate past by a change of political regime, and from later developments by a change of religious regime; a spacious period nonetheless, in which England began groping her way towards Modern Times while looking back to her remotest past.

The young king, brought up as an exile in France and Brittany, never forgot that he had won his realm by the sword. Accordingly, we find that, notwithstanding the union of the Roses, the new reign affected the spirit of a Lancastrian restoration, though with Celtic tendencies, in reliance upon men who had supported Henry in those early days when the Yorkist leaders lay under political interdict. It is thus, for example, that alongside a Percy of Northumberland, who had rallied secretly before the landing at Milford Haven and ranked among the favourites of the new regime, we find a Thomas Howard. His father had perished on the losing side at Bosworth; he himself began the reign in prison, advanced only by stages towards complete rehabilitation, and had to await the reign of Henry VIII before recovering the dukedom of Norfolk after his resounding victory over the Scots at Flodden in 1513.

Conversely there are animosities which do not disarm. The reign of Henry VII is loud with Yorkist conspiracies, often strongly romantic, often extremely dangerous, in which idealism, hatred and fraud are strangely mingled. Yorkshire remained a bastion of opposition to the Tudors long after the kingdom had been pacified. 'Lancastrian restoration' is perhaps something of an understatement. Henry VII's concern was not only to forge links with the might and national glory associated with the reign of Henry V, but also to find for the new dynasty such historical and even legendary roots as would cause men to forget the weakness of his claim. Henry VII traced his origins to the most fabulous past of the Welsh kings. That is why he took care to have his eldest son born at Winchester, cradle of King Arthur, and gave him that illustrious name. That is also why he substituted on his standards the red dragon of Cadwallader, the first Welsh sovereign, for Richard's badge, the boar.

At the same time, he set his new England to feel her way along the road toward her ultimate destiny in the commercial, the maritime, the territorial and even the colonial domain. He did so by creating a merchant fleet, by encouraging the first voyages of exploration in search of the 'island of Brazil', and by marrying his daughter Margaret to the King of Scotland, thus preparing the way for the future unification of Great Britain. Unpopular he may have been in the eyes of his contemporaries, owing to his fussiness and parsimony, to his absurd caprices and his underhand methods. He remains, however, at a more general level, the real father of modern England, though the fact is hardly apparent in the writings of that period.

'It is almost impossible,' remarks Gladys Temperley in this connection, 'to read the reign in the contemporary spirit. It is easy to exaggerate the immediate effect of events which later proved to be of immense importance; there is a constant temptation to read too much of the future into the events of the time. To us the reign appears a time of beginnings, of fresh starts in nearly every branch of human activity; but the points which contemporaries —not being prophets—dwell upon are the details of conspiracy and the incidents of diplomacy. The germs in which the history of modern Europe was hidden escaped them.' [3]

What his contemporaries must in fact have seen—and their view is of peculiar interest to us, since we are starting out to decipher the mentality of one among them—was a conquering monarch who, in difficult circumstances, restored the royal power by relying on the Church in accordanec with a formula not unrelated to French absolutism. The Holy See had recognized the new regime without delay, on the morrow of the royal marriage which united the two Roses. Nor, in turn, did Henry disappoint the papal confidence. His mother, Lady Margaret, endowed the Court with an air of the most fervent devotion. And, of course, Henry VIII, always so prompt to improve upon the ideas of his father, showed the greatest zeal on behalf of the papacy, placing his sword at the disposal of the Holy League and earning for himself the title Defender of the Faith by his ideological struggle against Luther. At that time it was the King of France who set an example of recalcitrance with regard to the Vatican and braved excommunication by Julius II. It can be said, on the other hand, that so long as England remained true to the Spanish alliance sought by Henry VII, and so long as Katherine of Aragon's influence continued, no serious conflict arose to disturb the good relations of the English kings with the papacy. But that was the calm before the storm. The period, indeed, was not altogether exempt from anticlericalism, particularly during its last ten years, after the appearance of Luther. Such outbreaks, however, were mere ripples on the surface of an official conformism attached to an orthodoxy that had endured for a thousand years. Besides, amid the cacophony of voices raised in denunciation of ecclesiastical abuses, it is necessary to distinguish between traditionalist censors, scoffers, reformers and revolutionaries.

Meanwhile, in the domain of manners and fashions, there burst upon England the continental Renaissance which had already long been at full flood in Italy. It can be discerned most clearly on the accession of Henry VIII, when a court intoxicated with youth and pleasure suddenly threw off the morose habits of the previous reign. Symbolically, one might contrast Katherine's angular and starched head-dresses with the free hair-styles introduced from France by Anne Boleyn; or again, the entirely medieval design chosen by Henry VII for his tomb with that straightway substituted by his successor—a model adorned at its four corners with plump little angels in the purest style of the Renaissance.[4]

No less apparent, in the still cloistered courts of knowledge, into which the 'New Learning' had been slowly infiltrating for several decades, is the passionate struggle between old Scholasticism and young Philology, and also the war provoked at Oxford by the introduction of Greek, a discipline that was to prove one of the most active solvents of medieval orthodoxy.

Nor must we overlook the profound changes brought about in the English countryside by advances in the woollen industry since the reign of Edward IV. It was then that the Merchant Adventurers, exporters of cloth, caught up with and overtook the Staplers, exporters of wool, and that the young industry's centre of gravity shifted southward to Norfolk, which had the good fortune to face the commercial outlets of Flanders and the Netherlands. From that period, moreover, date the grievances already being voiced by an impoverished peasantry against the increasing competition of sheep-farming. Those, however, were phenomena that find no spontaneous expression in literature, except perhaps in such remarkable works as More's *Utopia*, which was written in Latin.

It is important, on the other hand, to emphasize one last detail which exerted some influence in the field of letters, and more particularly upon the work of Skelton. I refer to the tense relations that quickly developed between the Tudors, father and son, and the great aristocratic families whose prestige they feared and whose power they sought to weaken: one among several stages in the decline of Norman feudalism which resulted in rearguard actions against the new authority of the State.

Thus, the Catholic half-century of the new dynasty is seen as a period of restoration, expansion and transformation, a period during which, behind the façade of a society still medieval and chivalric, England allowed the entry of continental influences and made acquaintance with all sorts of novelties, but at the same time achieved more and more confidence in her peculiar destiny. Here, before the troublous episode of the Reformation, was what may be called the Little Renaissance.

The childhood and youth of the poet, therefore, were contemporary with the Yorkist governments of Edward IV and Richard III. But that is an obscure fringe of his life. The problem of his origins has caused much ink to flow during the last two hundred years, and it is no doubt because of the uncertainty enveloping this matter that so many different opinions have been advanced concerning a poet without roots, who has always been hard to place in the panorama of his time.

He was long thought to have been a native of Cumberland, related to the Skeltons of Armathwaite.[5] Next, it was believed that he came from Norfolk and that his father's Will survives [6]; then that he came from Surrey and owed his career at Court to the Howards, earls of Surrey and dukes of Norfolk.[7]

But the Cumberland hypothesis has remained obstinately sterile; that of Norfolk collapses when we realize that it is based upon an erroneous document; and that of Surrey is faced with the major objection that the Howards were in disgrace at the beginning of the new reign, at a moment when Skelton was already at Court.

Again, a host of fragile and often ephemeral theories have raised hopes whenever the occurrence of a Skelton in the documents appeared to have some distant connection with the poet. This method of deduction discovers its own weakness when a systematic inquiry reveals about two hundred and fifty Skeltons during the fourteenth and fifteenth centuries, of whom one hundred or so are named John. Some twenty of these are found in London in the poet's time, about half a dozen of them in the neighbourhood of the Court.[8]

Finally, it has even been suggested, mainly on the strength of the wording of the Royal Pardon of 1509, that the poet may have been born in London.[9] Perhaps he was, but that would not solve the problem of his ancestry.

All things considered, there are strong reasons to believe that John Skelton came from the north of England—probably from Yorkshire, in view of the many clues that lead back to that county; that his people belonged to the entourage of one or other of the three great aristocratic families of the North, Percy, Scrope and Neville, who favoured his advancement, unless perhaps he was patronized from the start by the King's mother,

Lady Margaret, who, as Countess of Richmond, had close links with Yorkshire and its higher nobility.

The name Skelton is definitely north-country; the form Shelton belongs to the South.[10]

'Skelton' was long regarded as a contraction of *scale-town*, from *scale*, *shiel* or *skeall*, a temporary shelter or shepherd's hut.[11] Today it is considered to derive either from Anglo-Saxon *scylf* (E. Anglian dialect *scelf*; modern English *shelf*), in which case 'Skelton' would mean *scylf-tun*, 'High Ledge Farm', the *k* indicating Scandinavian influence; or directly from a Scandinavian root related to *skellr* (noise), from Norse *skalla* (to clatter), in which case 'Skelton' would mean 'the farm near the Skell, or rushing torrent'.[12]

The fact is that Yorkshire is the region *par excellence*, the cradle as it were, of Skelton, even more so than its neighbour Cumberland. For a single place called Skelton in Cumberland there are six in Yorkshire, not to mention a crowd of secondary appellations, particularly in the north of the county.

While the poet's name is certainly of northern origin, his work also provides evidence, in its vocabulary, of indubitable nordic influences and particularly a fair number of words of Scandinavian origin.

Many clues, then, taken both from John Skelton's writings and from the known facts of his life, combine to suggest that before his arrival at Court, relations had existed between the poet and the most eminent Yorkshire families. First there were the Percies of Northumberland, great vassals of royal blood, used to independence, governors by tradition of the marches of Scotland, lieutenants-general of Yorkshire, and owners of several castles and manors in that county, where they had their headquarters and normally resided.[13] Hence the importance of the poem on the death of the Earl of Northumberland, written at Court in April 1489, with its Latin dedication to the young orphan, in which the poet vows to remain 'ever at his service' now that the head of the family has gone; with its quatrain of affectionate esteem for Dr Ruckshaw, a distinguished Yorkshire ecclesiastic, born at York and a friend of the Percies[14]; and finally with its numerous details indicating that the poet was closely acquainted with the actors and all the particulars of the tragedy at Topcliffe, the great lord's favourite manor. Now this is a region where Skelton is frequent both as a personal and as a local name. We find one Thomas Skelton at Topcliffe in 1448, twelve years before the poet's birth.[15] He himself shows his knowledge of York by mentioning Bootham Bar,[16] the north-west gate of the city (near which there is even today a butcher named Richard Skelton). He mentions likewise Bamborough Castle, fortress of the Percies in Northumberland, and it is interesting to note that Cockermouth, one of the few places in Cumberland to which the poet refers,[17] was the site of yet another castle owned by Percy. It is said, too, that at Leconfield Castle, a residence of the Percies in east Yorkshire, the walls were adorned with poems by Lydgate and John Skelton.[18] Finally, Skelton speaks of 'pageants' enacted at 'Joyous Garde', and we learn from Malory that Joyous Garde was Alnwick or Bamborough, two castles belonging to the Percies.[19] Knowing the Percies, did he also know the Scropes, another great Yorkshire feudal house consisting of several branches—Scrope of Bolton, Scrope of Masham, Scrope of Bentley near Doncaster? It is among these last that we discover links with the poet, by way of Jane Scrope, the orphan girl of *Phyllyp Sparowe*. Her father was Sir Richard Scrope [20] (younger son of Henry, fourth Lord Scrope of Bolton), who died prematurely in 1485 leaving, with other daughters, Jane, who moved to Norfolk on her mother's remarriage to an East Anglian gentleman.[21] We find, moreover, that the parody of the funeral service which forms the web of the great rhapsody on the sparrow's death follows the rite of York, with one or two variants from that of Lincoln.[22]

The third great family resident in Yorkshire were the Nevilles, lords of Middleham; and they were undoubtedly the greatest, since they had attained royalty by the marriage of Anne Neville with Richard III. Now, it is in the immediate retinue of Anne Neville that we find a maid of honour called Alice Skelton, attending her mistress at the coronation which took place at Westminster on 6th July 1483, a ceremony at which the queen's personal suite included also Lady Margaret, mother of the future King Henry VII. The Wardrobe Accounts [23] show in this connection that Dame Alice Skelton (she is described as 'gentlewoman') and Lady Margaret wore the same rich attire at those festivities. Of course, Percy of Northumberland likewise attended the ceremony, as also did various representatives of the families of Scrope of Bolton and Scrope of Masham.

It is not known whether John Skelton, friend of the Percies, was related to Alice Skelton, friend of their neighbours the Nevilles. But it is very likely that Lady Margaret was acquainted with both; as Countess of Richmond, in Yorkshire, she must have been on intimate terms with the whole of northern society. Thus it is hardly surprising that just when she needed a tutor for the heir apparent (and she reserved to herself all matters concerning education at Court) we find at her side a poet named Skelton, who, moreover, had recently distinguished himself by earning the title of laureate.

In the Privy Purse Expenses of Henry VII there is a single mention of 'My Lady the Kinges moder poete'.[24] It is not unreasonable to suppose that the reference is to the poet John Skelton, especially if we are to believe that he translated for her some long, edifying poems well calculated to please her, such as Guillaume de Guilleville's *Pèlerinage de la Vie Humaine*, which Skelton enumerates as among his works:

> Of my ladys grace at the contemplacyoun,
> Owt of Frenshe into Englysshe prose,
> Of Mannes Lyfe the Peregrynacioun,
> He did translate, enterprate, and disclose.

> (*G. of L.*, v. 1219–22)

We must now state what is known of his studies and of his early academic achievements before his admission to Court.

On the subject of his introduction to higher studies he has left us a number of express declarations which prove beyond doubt that he began as a student at Cambridge:

> Alma parens, o Cantabrigiensis
> ....
> Namque tibi quondam carus alumnus eram,

> (*Rep.* Dyce, i, p. 207)

lines followed by a still more explicit prose commentary: 'Cantabrigia Skeltonidi Laureato primam mammam eruditionis pientissime (*sic*) propinavit.' He sucked the breast of learning first at Cambridge, where Dr Ruckshaw had studied before him; where, rather than to Oxford, a man usually went if he lived in Yorkshire; where one William Percy, a younger son of the Northumberlands, had been chancellor of the University from 1451 to 1456; and where Alan Percy, brother to the orphan of 1489, was to be master of the new college of St John (1516–18).[25]

Unfortunately, the university registers contain no certain record of his sojourn at Cambridge. One Skelton, 'questionist' (i.e. about to take his B.A.) on 18th March 1480, has been considered the nearest approach to our author.[26] To assume that he entered in 1476 at the age of fifteen or sixteen, as was normal at that time, would be to place his birth *circa* 1460 or 1461, the date commonly assigned to it by tradition.

Moreover, in 1480 he would have had the opportunity to associate at Cambridge with two men who seem to have played some part in his life: William Ruckshaw above-mentioned, who had returned to take a rather late doctorate in theology; and John Blythe, already an archdeacon, who had come up to take his M.A. examinations, the prologue to a brilliant career that would lead him to the chancellorship of the University (1493–5) and then to the bishopric of Salisbury (1494–9).[27]

The next significant event in John Skelton's life, one that he always claimed as his chief title to glory and upon which he built his career, was, beyond any doubt whatever, the famous ceremony at which he was crowned poet-laureate of Oxford University:

> At Oxforth the Vniversyte,
> Auaunsid I was to that degre;
> By hole consent of theyr senate,
> I was made poete lawreate.

> (*Garn.*, iv, 81–5)

Attention has rightly been drawn [28] to the curious note of detachment, almost that of an 'outsider', with which the laureate speaks of 'theyr senate', the word senate belonging to the vocabulary not of Oxford but of Cambridge. Hence the conclusion that although Skelton was indeed crowned laureate of Oxford University, it does not follow that he had studied there.

The Oxford diploma [29] was not, properly speaking, the result of passing what are now called Finals; nor was it a purely honorary distinction like a doctorate *honoris causa*. Rather, it was something in between, a sort of free examination in grammar or in rhetoric (which did not as such figure in the Statutes), open to candidates from outside as well as to students of the University, provided that in return they agreed to certain preliminary conditions such as a public and unpaid lecture on one of Cicero's works—*De Officiis*, for example, or the *Familiar Letters*—after which the candidate could undertake the real tests which appear to have included the composition of a hundred Latin lines in praise of the University. One John Bullman, crowned at Oxford in 1511, had lectured on the first book of the *Familiars*, whereas Robert Whittington, a grammarian and friend of Skelton, appears to have received the laurel for having spent fourteen years teaching rhetoric. Between 1470 and about 1513, it seems that Oxford University thus crowned a certain number of eminent men, perhaps with the ulterior motive of attracting the best minds and thereby infusing new blood into its teaching. Such no doubt was the case with Skelton, of whom Caxton spoke as an accomplished latinist and able commentator. The royal printer makes mention of Cicero's Letters as well as of the book of Diodorus Siculus.[30]

Consequently, several years must have elapsed between the end of his studies and the fame which attended his earliest works. This appears to be confirmed on chronological grounds. Indeed Skelton himself comes to our assistance once we are able to interpret a sort of personal calendar, of which we discover furtive traces in his works.[31] That calendar refers to some great event in his life which must have occurred at the end of October or beginning of November 1488. Was it the ceremony of the laurel, celebrated at the opening of the academic year? Was it his admission to Court, coinciding with the young prince's first lessons? Did those two decisive episodes of his life follow hard upon one another? Or again, having been crowned laureate, a merely academic title with small renown outside the University, had he to pave his way to Court with writings of a less restricted character, English translations in the florid style of the new idiom?

This last appears best to explain the translation of Diodorus Siculus,[32] a hurried and exuberant work, written in an affected and ludicrous style, in which the translator ends by no longer following the original except remotely and abandons himself to increasingly more complicated and more personal variations. Moreover, there is absolutely no question at all, as might be thought, of a direct translation from the Greek text; the English is simply a rendering of a Renaissance Latin version.[33] It is limited to the first five books, which deal mainly with events and legends prior to the Trojan War. We read there, for example, paragraphs such as the following, clearly inspired by a wish to attract notice at Court:

'The sixte [Muse] is named dame Erato / whiche thurgh her bounteuous promocioun hir scolers and discyples bryngeth unto so noble auaunsement / than whan she hath enryched theym with the gloryous tresour of connyng & wysedom / he shal stande in faueur of ryal pryncis / and so atteyne unto the spiry-tual rowme of prelacye or other temporal promocioun . . .' [34]

Here we have Skelton already voicing an undisguised ambition to find favour with the King. True, he went on to sketch a shadow into his picture, in the case where 'folly disguised fancifully in the gilded robes of worldly vanity' would bring about the fall of pride, which ordinarily occurs in the 'extreme confusion' into which you are thrown by 'fickle fortune full of duplicity'.

He knew not how well he spoke. At all events, he began by enjoying the prince's favour. And it is probably to that auspicious event that he repeatedly refers by cryptic signs scattered among his works, most often accompanied with the French motto *Bien m'en souvient*.[35] We have every reason to think that by the autumn of 1488 John Skelton had been admitted to Court.

CHAPTER II

A Cleric-Poet at the Court of Henry VII

From Panegyric to Satire

WESTMINSTER, where Henry VII kept court, was at that time the political capital of Tudor England. As a city it was as yet distinct from the City of London, to which it was joined by the long avenue of the Strand. Around the royal palace were grouped the Parliament, the Exchequer and the courts of justice. There too, later, was built the Star Chamber, so called from the decoration of its ceiling.

But Westminster was likewise the home of a great Benedictine monastery [1]: A city within the city and a state within the State— the monastery was exempt from episcopal jurisdiction and depended on Rome only—Westminster formed a veritable urban agglomeration with its parish church of St Margaret and, at the north-west corner, the small rectangle of the Sanctuary, upon whose threshold, by ecclesiastical privilege, the tempest of the outside world was stilled. There indeed was a true Court of Miracles with its Thieves' Alley, its Almonry instituted by the charity of Lady Margaret, and its little, square two-storeyed church, the lower part of which was reserved for criminals and the upper for honest folk. It was at Westminster that Henry VII arranged to build his chapel, which is still ranked among the masterpieces of pre-Renaissance architecture. Westminster was also the rendezvous of many different sorts of men from the world of culture, the Church, diplomacy and big business.

There Caxton had his presses, which were to remain during his lifetime subject to some measure of royal control. But above all, at a time when academic life at Oxford and Cambridge was still lethargic, the Court was the premier international focus of the kingdom, privileged meeting place of the great streams of culture deriving principally from France and Italy.

At the beginning of the reign, French influence remained strong at the Court of Henry VII. There Bernard André, blind poet from Toulouse, exercised the joint functions of official poet, historiographer and also, perhaps, of tutor; Quentin Poulet was keeper of the Royal Library; Etienne Fryon was clerk of the signet and secretary for the French language; while Giles Dewes (or d'Euze?) afterwards taught French to the princes of the blood. Among the numerous Italians who served as officials of the Roman Curia, legates, collectors of Peter's Pence or professional latinists, experienced in the latest novelties of ultramontane humanism, were Pietro Carmeliano, who had been in England since 1481; Cornelio Vitelli, professor at New College, Oxford, since 1475; Giovanni Gigli, and lastly the famous Polydore Vergil, King's Historiographer.[2]

What that cosmopolitan Court lacked, however, was the presence of a first-rate latinist, an Englishman able to hold his own against a crowd of foreigners, to sing the splendours of the new reign in the national tongue and, in due time, to act as tutor to the heir-apparent. That is precisely the threefold duty which appears to have devolved upon John Skelton during his long sojourn at Westminster.

It is easy, moreover, to ascertain his beginnings as official poet with regard to the principal events of the reign. Until about the year 1488, Bernard André and Pietro Carmeliano were practically alone in this field. In 1485 André celebrated the accession of the new dynasty with a long French poem, *Les Douze Triomphes d'Henri VII*[3], which compares the King's exploits to the Labours of Hercules. In 1486 André and Carmeliano hymned the birth of Prince Arthur, which Carmeliano used also as an opportunity to attack the memory of Richard III. In 1487 André extolled the overwhelming victory won by Henry VII over the Yorkist army of Lincoln and Martin Swart. Then, for the first time so far as we know, in the spring of 1489, Skelton's voice is heard along with the court poets lamenting the death of the Earl of Northumberland. Tudor England had at last found her official poet. It may be said that this first English poem by John Skelton is the first poem of a new era which would lead directly to the English Renaissance.

Let us look at the facts.[4] On 28th April 1489, Henry Percy, Earl of Northumberland, lord-lieutenant of Yorkshire and military governor of the central and eastern Marches of Scotland, was killed on active service. The King had ordered the

levying of an extraordinary subsidy intended to provide for a
military campaign against France within the framework of the
recent Anglo-Spanish alliance. The collectors, having met with
popular resistance in Yorkshire and County Durham, had
referred the matter to the local administrator, Henry Percy,
who had tried to obtain from the King some abatement of these
financial measures. But Henry, fearing that any conciliatory
gesture would be interpreted as a sign of weakness, confirmed
the full levy of a tax approved by Parliament, and instructed
Percy to see that his wishes were carried out. A rising ensued,
during which Percy, caught by a hostile mob on his own lands
near the manor of Topcliffe, bravely confronted his assailants;
but his followers gave him inadequate support and he was
finally overwhelmed by sheer weight of numbers.

The King, seriously alarmed, appointed in his place the Earl
of Surrey, Thomas Howard, who was anxious to redeem his
conduct at Bosworth, quickly stifled the rebellion and hanged at
York its leader, John-a-Chambre, with some of his accomplices.
It is said, however, that the man behind the rising, the Earl of
Egremont, a convinced Yorkist and sworn enemy of Henry VII,
managed to escape and find refuge with Margaret of Burgundy,
sister of Edward IV, who was always glad to welcome partisans
of the White Rose. The affair was typical of the new reign, at a
time when the central authority was still not firmly established.
While it reveals clearly a ferment of political opposition combined with a spirit of anarchy still surviving after thirty years of
dynastic struggles, it shows also the Sovereign's intransigence in
money-matters, which was to be so often laid to his charge.

The real gravity of this incident lay not so much in popular
objection to the subsidy as in the fact of its having precipitated
open rebellion against a great feudal and military chief, a direct
representative of the royal authority. Nevertheless, men
whispered one to another—and Skelton alludes to the rumour—
that the rebels had found accomplices in the Earl's own retinue,
persons who had never forgiven him for having rallied secretly
to the Lancastrian cause and thus brought about the Yorkist
defeat at Bosworth.

The affair, a topic of contemporary gossip as far afield as
Danzig,[5] caused a tremendous sensation, partly because of the

importance assigned to the slightest occurrence in the early
years of the dynasty, partly because of the victim's great
renown. For it involved the illustrious house of Percy, whose
legendary conflicts with the Nevilles had enlivened the bloody
chronicle of fifteenth-century England.

Fourth of his name, Henry Percy owned at least a dozen
castles and strongholds, and kept a court that might be considered hardly inferior to that of the King.[6] Like a king, he was
attended by a privy council composed of his principal adjutants,
and was served by an impressive body of retainers, the senior of
whom, such as the chamberlain and treasurer, themselves
belonged to the lesser nobility, sitting at a separate table called
'The Knights' Board'. Hence these words of Skelton:

> At his commaundement which had both day and
>   nyght
> Knygthtes and squyers, at every season when
> He calde vpon them, as meniall household men.

> (*D. of E.N.*, 31–3)

Percy had no fewer than eleven priests in his service, headed
by a doctor of theology. A group of choir-boys, 'the Children
of the Chapel', sang at the religious ceremonies, and there is
mention, at Christmas and Easter, of Nativity and Resurrection
plays, together with interludes composed by one of the household chaplains.

Particulars of that tragedy in the North were no doubt
imperfectly known at the Court of Henry VII, where John
Skelton, familiar as he proves to have been with Percy's
immediate entourage, was therefore the right man for the
occasion, He threw himself heart and soul into his task.

While Bernard André wrote a purely conventional court
poem in Latin, devoting himself first and foremost to eulogy of
the King,[7] John Skelton wrote a poem prompted by indignation, devoted mainly to an account of the tragedy and a eulogy
of the dead man himself. Bernard André, a foreigner, took his
stand on the level of official rhetoric, which was his trade. John
Skelton, an Englishman, took his stand on the level of moral
action, which he considered to be his mission.

He emphasizes the legality of the royal subsidy which gave rise to the quarrel and which had been dictated by the King's concern for the general welfare:

> The ground of his quarel was for his souerain lord,
> The well concerning of all the hole lande,
> Demandyng suche duties as nedes most accord
> To the ryght of his prince, which should not be withstand.

(D. of E.N., 64–7)

He brings out the heinousness of a crime so completely at variance with the feudal code, against a chief who was England's bulwark against the Scots. He flays the demented conduct of the rebels, which can be explained only by some momentary deviation from reason and faith ('God was not in their minds') and which reduces those who inspired it to the level of wild beasts. He flays even more severely the cowardice of the Earl's attendants, who abandoned their master in the hour of peril, defying the most elementary feelings of loyalty and gratitude—unless perhaps their lack of courage is to be explained rather by some sinister complicity.

> But ther was fals packing, or els I am begylde;
> . . . .
> But men say they were lynked with a double chaine,
> And held with the comones vnder a cloke

(D. of E.N., 71–6)

He describes the pathetic way in which Percy continued playing his sword till the end, dealing out 'woundes wyde', and how, exhausted by loss of blood, he ended by losing an unequal fight.

He exalts the memory of that great champion of the North, feared in both France and Scotland, and stresses the royal blood that flowed in his veins and made him equal with the greatest in the land.[8]

He devotes two stanzas to the young orphan, that 'young lion', upon whom he lavishes useful advice on the dangers of flattery, falsehood and calumny, advice which constitutes probably Skelton's earliest denunciation of the vices of Court. He concludes with a long, earnest and most majestic prayer to the Holy Trinity.

For a first poem, the Elegy, or rather the Historical Ode written by Skelton on the death of the Earl of Northumberland, is altogether characteristic of its author's talent at this period, and still more so of his state of mind.

It is first, as one might expect, a piece of eloquence that does not disdain the apparatus of great poetry: the emphasis, the ornate style, the pleonasms imitated from Latin ('I wayle, I wepe, I sobbe, I sigh ful sore'), the solemn invocation of Clio, Muse of History, and, in a more general manner, the ornaments of classical mythology set alongside the sentiments of the Christian religion. There is a striking contrast between Skelton's proud assertion of the divine character of the laureate's poetic inspiration and his conventional protestations of humility based on the uncouthness of the English language considered as a new instrument of poetry.

It must be acknowledged, too, that the poem does not fall so deeply as might have been feared into the tastelessness of aureate preciosity. It is restrained on the brink by the native vigour of indignation; by a liking for strong, sturdy language; by a certain passion for truth; by a rejection of complacency, which is nourished by the springs of clerical independence; as well as by the poet's lofty idea of his mission as laureate, an idea out of all proportion with what that academic title, in that age, could be taken to imply, but one that came, largely through him, to be identified with the task of a court poet fully conscious of his responsibilities. In this exceptional case where his familiarity with the actors in that national drama had no doubt encouraged him to soar at one stroke above the poetry of Court, he had at the same time promoted himself to the office of public prosecutor. He had pronounced a veritable indictment of the guilty, without respect of persons. On his first appearance as a poet at the Court of Henry VII he had let it be clearly understood that he was not a flatterer or one to gloss over the truth.

He had, incidentally, asked some questions relevant to his whole future career:

What shuld I flatter? what shuld I glose or paint?

(*D. of E.N.*, 41)

The poet laureate distinguished himself on at least two other occasions during the winter of 1489–90. On 29th November 1489 we find him, along with Bernard André, celebrating Prince Arthur's creation as Prince of Wales and Earl of Chester,[9] a decisive step towards establishing the line of succession but one that was soon thwarted by the premature death of the young heir-apparent. Not long afterwards he took part in a trifling incident that was quite characteristic of contemporary manners, the chorus of execration unleashed by the tactlessness of the French ambassador and noted humanist, Robert Gaguin.

Minister-general of the Trinitarians,[10] otherwise known as Mathurins (an order founded for the purpose of ransoming Christian slaves in Muslim hands), an erudite latinist, doctor of law, professor of rhetoric, and confidential agent of Louis XI, Anne de Beaujeu and Charles VIII, Gaguin had been sent to London on a diplomatic mission led by M. de Luxembourg. Its purpose was to obtain from the King of England a free hand for France in the marriage of Anne of Brittany, an end to the activities of certain disorders that were a grave menace to peace on the coasts of Brittany and Flanders, and lastly the conclusion of a treaty of peace and alliance between the two countries. However, in 1489 England was about to make the Spanish alliance the pivot of her foreign policy. On the preceding 27th March she had signed the important military, commercial and matrimonial treaty of Medina del Campo. Negotiations, therefore, were going to be difficult and protracted. After the failure in August 1489 of an initial series of talks, notwithstanding a speech by Gaguin described by Bernard André as 'magnificent', the plenipotentiaries returned to the charge in the following month, accompanied by Marigny, Walleran de Saint, bailiff of Senlis, and the herald Montjoie.

The expedition made a bad start. At Calais, an English town where the embassy had been welcomed by envoys of

Henry VII, Gaguin, as Latin Orator, replied to the usual compliments with a piece of verse, perhaps ill-timed, in which he spoke of the English sovereign as 'pastor', a quite inoffensive word in the banal symbolism of the period, but which Giovanni Gigli saw fit to take up by retorting in his master's name:

> *Si me pastorem, te decet esse pecus.*

Gaguin should have been more careful. At all events, no sooner had the embassy reached England than it had to mark time while Walleran de Saint returned to France for new instructions. This delay lasted for months. Reluctantly Gaguin was obliged to spend the winter in company with Sir Thomas Whyting, Chester Herald, who had been appointed to attend him, and he filled in time by writing doggerel such as *Le Passe-Temps d'Oisiveté* or *A savoir dont procède vertu, ou de nécessité ou d'honnêteté*, the latter a treatise in dialogue form, a rhetorical debate with his leader François de Luxembourg.[11]

He waited in vain. On Walleran's return the negotiation collapsed, and when the ambassadors, exasperated by their futile sojourn in England, had obtained their letters of recall, Maître Gaguin, unable to repress his irritation, was so indiscreet as to run off a little rhymed lampoon which referred to the King of England in rather discourteous terms.

Henry VII refrained from comment. But he unleashed against Gaguin the whole pack of his Court's poets, Pietro Carmeliano, Cornelio Vitelli, lately arrived from the University of Paris, Bernard André, who composed a satire of more than two hundred lines, and, of course, John Skelton who penned a *Recule* [12] against the French diplomat. The affair was a mere flash in the pan and was quickly forgotten. Henry VII had the delicacy to send Gaguin a purse of £40 before his departure. And Gaguin, on his side, had the pleasure three years later of signing his name to the peace treaty of Etaples-sur-Mer which was eventually concluded between England and France, much to the annoyance of the Spaniards.

Nor did Skelton bear a grudge against his fellow poet. Later, he would quote a passage from his *Compendium supra Francorum gestis* (on the example of Cardinal La Balue) in the satire against Wolsey *Why Come ye not to Court?* (713–39). And perhaps we should hear a final echo of this altercation in *The Garland of Laurel*, where Skelton recalls

> ... A frere of Fraunce men call Sir Gagwyne,
> That frownyd on me full angerly and pale ...
>
> (*G. of L.*, 374)

At least he did him the honour of including him among the Immortals of his international Parnassus.

Thus, when Caxton made respectful mention of the poet-laureate in his preface to the *Eneydes*, which appeared on 22nd June 1490, John Skelton was already a well-known personage at the English Court, certainly as an official poet but probably also as tutor to Prince Arthur. Since Caxton had dedicated his book to the heir-apparent, it is surely not unreasonable to suppose that when he invited Master John Skelton to correct the errors and explain the obscurities of his translation, he meant to flatter a man whom he knew to have been entrusted with the prince's education. The theory finds some support from a later book, *Speculum Principis*, a didactic work that shows his interest in Arthur as well as in Henry. Indeed, the surviving version, altered so as to address the younger son in 1509, after the death of Arthur, retains features which show that the work in its original form had been intended 'for the princes in their minority'.[13]

Success breeds success. John Skelton, laureate of Oxford University and national poet at the Court of Henry VII, received laurels from overseas in the two years following the Gaguin affair. We learn this from a document belonging to Cambridge University, dated 1493: '*Johanni Skelton Poete in partibus transmarinis atque oxonie laurea ornato ...*'[14] It is generally thought that the reference is to the University of Louvain, decorating *honoris causa* the poet of an allied king at a time when Maximilian of Hapsburg was siding with Henry VII against Charles VIII. But the document in question may equally refer to an honour conferred directly by Maximilian himself, within the framework of a policy intended to isolate England from France. Such an interpretation would explain the fact that no university is mentioned, and would mean that the honour was conferred before the Peace of Etaples (November 1492), which called a halt to that policy.

Cambridge University refused to lag behind. She decided to honour the outstanding merits of her former pupil by granting him the same laurels as he had received from Oxford and from abroad.[15] His friend John Blythe had only just been appointed chancellor of the University, and we are entitled to see this new distinction as one more proof of the active solicitude entertained by the King's chaplain for his young fellow student.

Meanwhile, Prince Henry, younger brother of Arthur, had been born on 28th June 1491. Skelton was to be concerned more particularly with his instruction.

> The honor of Englond I lernyd to spelle.
>
> (*Garn.*, iv–95)

On 1st November 1494, at Westminster, John Blythe attended the ceremony of the royal infant's elevation to the dukedom of York. The occasion had a very definite political significance: it was intended to frustrate once again the Yorkist plans for securing Perkin Warbeck's recognition as the Duke of York and legitimate heir. The intrigues of Warbeck held England in suspense by means of a network of conspiracy and complicity, which spread its meshes into Ireland, Scotland and Flanders, and even among the Flemings of the Steelyard in the City of London. Prince Henry's elevation was therefore meant as a reply to that dangerous imposture.[16]

It was in the turbulent atmosphere of London during the years 1494–5 that Skelton met on several occasions another Cambridge personality, Master Syclyng of Godshouse, who was occupied with very different matters. He was constantly travelling to and fro between London and Cambridge, sometimes in company with the vice-chancellor and sometimes alone, endeavouring to negotiate the settlement of an old dispute between the townspeople of Cambridge and the University. His day-book shows that he invited Skelton to lunch and dinner one Tuesday after Pentecost, because he happened to be in company with the Bishop of Salisbury.[17] Now the Bishop of Salisbury was none other than John Blythe, the ubiquitous John Blythe, who, since he was no longer chancellor, could not do better on behalf of Cambridge than introduce Syclyng to Skelton, an 'old Cantab' who stood so high in the King's household. Skelton and Syclyng saw one another again when they dined together on the following Saturday at Sympson's in Fleet Street.

The bickering between Town and Gown, which had lasted since the thirteenth century, was not settled that year. Some five years later, in 1500–1, we come across Master Syclyng yet again. On his appointment as senior proctor in Convocation he had been obliged to hand over his duties at Cambridge to a deputy and rent a small apartment in London. He made a point of looking up Master Skelton, and his day-book once more provides evidence of several meals taken together.[18] They had become fast friends.

But everybody was not as yet Skelton's friend, especially, one imagines, at Court. His prestige as laureate and royal tutor had protected him to some extent from the mud-slinging of lesser folk. Besides, he had not moved continuously in Palace circles.

Lady Margaret had established the royal children's nursery at Greenwich Palace, adjoining the convent of Friars Observant. Near by at Blackheath, in 1497, a wave of Cornish rebels was halted and thrown back only just in time, on the outskirts of London.[19] The causes of that rising, the last and most important of the reign, are strongly reminiscent of those that occasioned the incident at Topcliffe in 1489: the same opposition to taxation—a war-tax this time, against the Scots—and the same ferment of Yorkist intrigue, in which Perkin Warbeck was once again involved. For Skelton, there was a more personal link between those events and the earlier tragedy, since the young Earl of Northumberland, Henry Algernon Percy, the orphan of 1489 and now aged twenty years, had distinguished himself at the head of the royal troops who had saved the day. Skelton alludes to this episode in *The Garland of Laurel*, where (line 1223), speaking of the *Tratyse of Triumphis of the Rede Rose*, a work now lost, he adds in the margin: '*Notat bellum Cornubiense, quod in campestribus et in patientioribus vastisque solitudinibus prope Grenewiche gestum est.*' The Cornish rebellion marked the final convulsion of the Wars of the Roses. The victory of Blackheath, like Bosworth Field, crowned the triumph of Lancastrian arms (1497).

In the following year Skelton was to receive Holy Orders; but before we reach that momentous stage of his career, let us take a backward glance at the poet-laureate's first decade at Court and see what we can add to our knowledge of his activity.

It must be admitted that, apart from the poem on the death of the Earl of Northumberland and the Gaguin affair, we have very little exact information about that period of his life. Only after the most careful consideration, therefore, can one venture here and there, and with greater or less assurance, to assign an approximate date to one or other of his surviving poems, one or other of the bare titles in the list of his works which he has fortunately bequeathed to posterity.

For example, we may reasonably suppose that it was during his tutorship at Greenwich that he composed the 'New Gramer in Englysshe compylyd',[20] which appears to rank among the earliest Latin grammars exemplifying the new bilingual methods of the Renaissance; as well as a number of didactic treatises which played a part in his education of the princes.[21] But we have reason to think also that his time was not wholly absorbed by his pedagogic duties and his attendance on the King; that by rubbing shoulders with a motley crowd of courtiers he ended by making friends and, not unlikely, enemies; that he had, besides, personal relations with circles of his own choice, at Westminster or in the City of London, among the grammarians and musicians. We catch glimpses of regular contacts with members of the Chapel Royal, Master William Cornish and his fellow Yorkshireman, Thomas Fayrfax.[22] We can guess the considerable part he must have played in the great flowering of religious and profane songs, of motets and of madrigals, which fill the miscellanies of that time. We come upon him sometimes bespattered with the insolence of an upstart, sometimes a target for the vexations of a libertine, sometimes conversing gallantly with a coquette or some great lady, and sometimes even—if we may take him at his word—versifying the secrets of a hopeless love, passing indifferently from the serious to low burlesque, from the elegant style to vulgarity, like the 'Ladies' Champion' described by Gaston Paris: 'He is the very image of his time, intermediate between the Middle Ages and the Renaissance, half pious and half emancipated, mingling erudition with mysticism and interrupting grave moral musings, devout inclinations, amorous genuflexions or solemn reverences with a salty remark, a somersault or a grimace.' [23]

Two miscellanies, though seemingly published (or re-issued?) rather late by Pynson or John Rastell,[24] may well belong, at least in part, to this profane period of his life.

One, entitled *Dyuers Balettys and Dyties Solacyous,* consists of pieces so dissimilar and so indeterminate that the present stage of our knowledge will not entitle us to use them as a biographical commentary.[25]

The other, which lacks a title and begins straightway with the little satire *Agaynste a Comely Coystrowne,* is strongly personal throughout and alludes to events, arguments or feelings that belong rather to the period 1495–9, a little before the *Bowge of Court* and the poet's admittance to Holy Orders.

Agaynste a Comely Coystrowne is a sally against a court musician full of affectation, a mere nobody, a one-time 'holy-water clerk' and former page at Court, who had decided to open a school of singing and organ-playing. As teacher of the aristocracy he assumed pretentious airs and was not afraid to attack his rivals in public. The poet claims to have been provoked by this busybody who neglected his own affairs, and his reply is devastating. The few verses he fires at him, first in English and then in Latin, reflect his utter contempt for a wretched creature who had dared to reprehend the *sacred* person of the poet-laureate.

> *Et violare sacrum desine, stulte, virum.*

(10)

His calculated terseness shows the author's resolve to chastise this impudent fellow without going to the lengths of a full-scale satire, which would do him too much honour. It is not so much a reply to an adversary as the execution of a malefactor.

He ridicules the man in every respect, physical and moral,

stigmatizing particularly his ostentation in seeking to pass as a gentleman:

> For Jak wolde be a jentylman, that late was a
> grome.
>
> (42)

He riddles him with buffoonery, with acid jibes directed at his art, his teaching and his ignorance, taking care to win the laughters to his own side:

> He fumblyth in his fyngeryng an ugly good noyse,
> It semeth the sobbyng of an old sow.
>
> (31–2)

Finally, when the poet-laureate thinks he has played long enough with his victim, he delivers the *coup de grâce*:

> Correct fyrst thy self; walk, and be nought !
>
> (62)

The entire poem, from its very first lines, goes under the standard of folly:

> Of all nacyons vnder the heuyn,
> These frantyke foolys I hate most of all . . .
>
> (1–2)

Hence, no doubt, by way of parting mockery, the author concludes with two absurdities, placing Croydon in Lincolnshire and Candlemas on 1st May:

> Wryten at Croydon by Crowland in the Clay,
> On Candelmas euyn, the Kalendas of May.
>
> (66–70)

This neat little satire may thus be regarded as the first formal denunciation of a court nuisance, as well as the first occasion upon which we learn that the poet-laureate had been personally taken to task and rudely bidden to 'correct himself' (correct first *thy*self).

It can be allowed that Skelton had hitherto been fairly well protected by his prestige as royal tutor and official bard. But skirmishes of this kind seem to indicate that the sacred person of the laureate was not as far removed from outrage as he might have wished. No doubt he disliked lowering himself to such squabbles. But he could no longer entrench himself on the Olympian heights whence he would have preferred to watch over the public welfare with the detachment of a sage. He was going to find himself obliged willy nilly to descend into the arena and wage inglorious warfare. He was going to yield, of course, to provocation from without, but also, it must be confessed, to the irresistible urge of a temperament made for satire, endowed with a matchless spirit of repartee, and perfectly at home in the domain of ridicule and caricature.

The second piece, *Womanhood, wanton, ye want,* is written in the same caustic vein, but the victim this time is one Mistress Anne. *Agaynste a Comely Coystrowne* was an attack upon masculine vanity. *Womanhood, wanton, ye want,* is an attack upon feminine vanity. Mistress Anne poses in vain as a great lady. Proudly she struts, haughty and disdainful, little suspecting that she may one day have need of those whom she now loads with her contempt. And it is an evil tongue that hides its venom under the guise of meekness. She talks too much:

> Though angelyk be youre smylyng,
> Yet is youre tong an adders tayle . . .

> (15–16)

The poet longs to take her down a peg. He does so with a series of rather ponderous puns on her dwelling place, the Quay, in Thames Street, and the key that always hangs on her door for anyone who wishes to enter without knocking.

The third piece in this miscellany is perhaps even more significant, marking maybe a crucial turning point both in Skelton's interior life and in his mode of poetic expression. *Upon a Deadman's Head* is a short meditation on a macabre subject. A lady of his acquaintance has indulged a quaint fancy by sending the poet a skull, and he answers with a little

impromptu note. He describes how the sight of this hideous
present has torn him from worldly pleasure:

> Your vgly tokyn
> My mynd hath brokyn
> From worldly lust;
> For I have dyscust
> We ar but dust,
> And dy we must.

As if bewitched by 'Deth holow eyed', he describes with
truly medieval realism the withered sinews, the worm-eaten
stomach:

> And his gastly jaw
> Grasping asyde,
> Nakyd of hyde,
> Neyther flesh nor fell . . .

(15–18)

These repulsive horrors convey a solemn warning to his
correspondent no less than to himself. Wherever we are, whatever we do, he reminds her, Death will come on the appointed
day 'to deal with us'. On the great board, where he never loses,
he will checkmate us:

> Stoppyng oure breth;
> Oure eyen synkyng,
> Oure bodys stynkyng,
> Oure gummys grynnyng,
> Oure soulys brynnyng . . .

(33–7)

'Our souls burning'! The lesson drawn by the poet from this
horrid image is certainly not that of Ronsard, not the 'Live, I
bid you, wait not till tomorrow' of the pagan Renaissance; it is
not the *carpe diem* of Horace. It is the Christian lesson of the
Middle Ages obsessed with the terror of hell-fire, with the dread
of exile in 'the dark valley of endless woe', in 'the Fiend's black
lake'. Hence, springing from an instinctive need of protection,

the pathetic appeal to Jesus, 'goodly chyld of Mary mylde', that he may be spared those torments. It reminds one of Villon's childlike faith. To the fear of hideous death the poet opposes the hope of contemplating the radiant spectacle of the divine Face, in the heavenly palace 'above the sky that is so hy':

> But graunt vs grace
> To se thy face,
> And to purchace
> Thyne hevenly place,
> And thy palace,
> Full of solace,
> Above the sky
> That is so hy;
> Eternally
> To beholde and se
> The Trynyte!
>> *Amen.*

                    ˅   (45–9)

The poet concludes with a timely but unkind parting shot. By way of a motto he quotes the old French phrase:

> *Mirez-vous-y*

Reading these little verses, improvised with such facility and familiarity, beginning as a simple letter of acknowledgment and ending as a mystical prayer, one is inclined to consider them as the earliest examples of 'Skeltonics'; for they bear no resemblance to his earlier verses, which follow the normal rules of *rimes royales* peculiar to profane poetry. What we have here, on the contrary, suggests that the poet, under the overwhelming influence of the macabre and in the profoundly religious atmosphere created by the sense of death, made instinctive use in English of the short rhythms and bunched rhymes closely associated in the ear of a bilingual clerk with medieval Latin hymns and litanies.

'Skeltonics' have been called by a wide variety of names and have suggested many ingenious explanations.[26] But their clerical affinities are now universally recognized. It is remarkable in this connection that the next time Skelton tried out this new poetic medium was as rector of Diss in works of clerical inspiration, whether epitaphs, trentains or the famous rhapsody *Phyllyp Sparowe*, composed in the rhythms of the funeral service.

Now during those years 1497–8, John Skelton, poet-laureate of Oxford and Cambridge, was preparing to embark upon an ecclesiastical career. If our chronological interpretation is correct, we can discern clearly in the preceding poems the satirical impatience that was beginning to dawn with increasing contempt of worldly vanities in general and of the vanities of Court in particular; while the Meditation on a skull, inspired by a lady's macabre present, reveals the kind of revulsion aroused in him by this hideous confrontation with Death.

He had been at Court for ten years, and the princes' education was drawing to a close. In 1498 his friend John Blythe, chancellor of Cambridge University, was to be appointed Bishop of Salisbury. Was he not showing him the way? Had not Skelton himself, in the distant days of his Oxford laurels, when he was translating Diodorus, dreamed of the honours to which royal favour might lead? 'They shal stande in faueur of ryal pryncis, and so atteyne unto the spirytual rowme of prelacye or other temporal promocioun . . .' He had indeed enjoyed the proud distinction of a royal tutorship, but he was still no more than Master Skelton, poet-laureate. Perhaps he had neglected to lay the modest but indispensable foundations of a career worthy of his talent. We know, on the other hand, that once he had taken the decision to accept Holy Orders, he completed the first three stages within as many months. On 31st March 1498 he was ordained subdeacon in the collegiate church of the hospital of St Thomas the Martyr; on 14th April he received the diaconate at St Paul's Cathedral; on 9th June he was raised to the priesthood in the church of the conventual hospital of Blessed Mary at Elsyng. We find that throughout that period he was attached to the Abbey of St Mary of Graces, a 'free chapel royal' situated near the Tower of London.[27] This connection is explained, no doubt, by his relations with the royal family. Indeed, during November of the same year he had the great honour of celebrating mass in presence of the King, who made him on that occasion an offering of twenty shillings.[28] We are thus entitled to think that it was at about this time that he translated, for Lady Margaret, Guillaume de Guilleville's *Pèlerinage de la Vie humaine*, a long and solemn work haloed in the mystical and imaginative faith of the Middle Ages. 'We have here no abiding city, but seek one that is to come' [29] is his marginal comment in 1523, when he mentions it in *The Garland of Laurel*.

In the light of Pynson's miscellanies, the poetic activity of John Skelton towards the end of his first decade at Court seems to have been confined to small satirical or sentimental subjects without much scope. They show a caustic and jovial vein, delighting to make play with some human weakness, with some particular instance of female misbehaviour or with the intolerable pretensions of some upstart. They betray in this respect a measure of discontent which was inevitably aggravated after the poet's ordination. It was natural that he should then feel a widening of the gulf that separated him from low intrigue, from that whole crowd of conceited parasites who had *Bouche à Cour*. It is true that in the first years of the Tudor dynasty the lower grades of the Court left much to be desired. The new regime had not been able to handle everything at once; a certain amount of disorder prevailed in what we would call today the domestic quarters. It was to grow worse under Henry VIII until Cardinal Wolsey undertook a general re-organization of the Royal Household by means of the Ordinances of Eltham (1525–6).[30]

Skelton, therefore, had occasion to rub shoulders with many picturesque and unattractive types of courtier struggling for royal favour. And he was obliged eventually to recognize that the darlings of Fortune were not always chosen from the best society. Even in his most unassailable positions he felt himself threatened by this rising tide of ambition. What is more humiliating than to find yourself gradually elbowed out by unscrupulous folk who possess neither your talent nor your refinement? Now that he felt his status heightened by the moral prestige of a churchman, he was seized with an intense longing to make full use of his satirical gifts against the whole mob.

Criticism of the Court was a perilous undertaking for a court poet. But he felt himself sustained by the confidence he derived from his clerical independence, as well as by literary precedents which he calls 'the great authority of poets old', who had had the skill to express salutary truths under the veil of allegory. Finally, resolved to devote himself to a great task, he felt himself spurred by the hope of obtaining in his turn the poet's supreme reward—immortality.

'I was sore moued to aforce the same.' It is true that behind the satire of Court circles there lay a strong tradition: Juvenal, his favourite Latin author; Claudian, the merciless painter of the Court of Honorius; Alain Chartier, whose *Curial* had been translated and published by Caxton; King René; Eustache Deschamps; Henri Baude; Michaut, author of *L'Abuzé en Cour;* Aretino; Aeneas Sylvius (the future Pope Pius II); and the Mantuan.

Before taking the plunge, he makes the customary show of hesitation. As a good disciple of Chaucer, he asks himself whether he will have the talent necessary for success in his undertaking. Well, there was one contemporary work to prove the possibility of attaining worldly fame in the field of social satire. That work was Sébastien Brant's *La Nef des Fous*, which was then going the rounds of Europe. It was indeed from *La Nef des Fous* that Skelton borrowed the central theme of his allegory, the image of a Ship of Fools carrying courtiers and named *The Bowge of Court*. Such is the long composition (seventy-seven verses, each of seven lines in *rime royale*) upon which John Skelton deliberately staked his reputation in the autumn of 1498, a date which coincided more or less with the tenth anniversary of his arrival at Court. The prologue, evoking a romantic dream, appeals to the imagination in the (slightly perverted) spirit of courtly and chivalric poetry. It is followed by a parade of court vices, presented in the form of a series of dialogues with the principal character and akin to the morality play.

In the autumn, when the moon smiles 'half in scorn' at human folly and Mars prepares for war, the poet decides to take arms against the vices of Court. Naturally, he understands the full extent of the risk he runs in shouldering such a task, for

What and he slyde down, who shall hym saue?

(28)

He is staying in Harwich at the house of a friend, and there, torn between the contrary feelings of ambition and trepidation, boldness and temerity, he falls asleep. He dreams that he is standing on Power's Quay, whence he beholds

> a shyppe, goodly of sayle,
> Come saylynge forth into that haven brood,
> Her takelynge ryche and of hye apparayle.

(38)

She is awaited likewise by a group of merchants anxious to go aboard and have a look at the treasures in her hold. She is, in fact, the *Bowge of Court*; owner, Dame Sans-Pareille; at the helm, Fortune; cargo, Favour. Like the rest, the poet edges his way forward, jostled by an anonymous crowd in which he can see no friend. Everyone is pushing and shouting, while the master of ceremonies bawls for silence. All are trying to get a glimpse of the owner, who sits like a queen, hidden by a curtain of fine silk, upon a wondrous throne above which is written the French motto: *Gardez-vous de Fortune qui est mauvaise ou bonne.* The trembling poet (who calls himself Drede) finds the throne-room guarded, as in the *Roman de la Rose*, by two very different personages. One, a girl named Danger, who treats him uncivilly, taunts and rebukes him, remarks that he has eaten high-seasoned sauce and asks him whether he is in the habit of drinking from 'saucys cuppe'. The other, more agreeable and named Desire, calls him 'Brother' and encourages him to be bold if he wishes to obtain his share of the cargo, for 'who spareth to speke, in fayth he spareth to spede'. Drede objects that he knows no one in high places and has little money; what can he do in those circumstances? Desire thereupon lends him the precious talisman Bonne Aventure. But, she says, Fortune is a capricious dame: she quickly throws overboard anyone who no longer pleases her.

The vessel weighs anchor and puts to sea. Fortune is at the helm. Drede is congratulating himself upon having come so close to Favour when he notices seven 'subtyll persones'— seven, the number of the deadly sins . . . They often dance with Fortune. Drede is interested and tries to join them, but he is not wanted. Then Favell, the Flatterer, comes and speaks to him, paying pretty compliments, protesting his eternal friendship and good faith. He offers his services all the more earnestly as Drede appears to stand well at Court. However, as he moves away his cloak is seen to be 'lined with duplicity', and he goes to malign Drede to Suspicion. The character of Suspicion is clear, even before he opens his mouth, from his jealous sidelong glances and from the nervous trembling of his hands. He secretly advises Favell to beware of Drede, and just as secretly advises Drede to put no trust in Favell. He believes that every man's hand is against him; he has a persecution complex. As for Harvey Hafter, he is a sharper. He comes leaping up to Drede and fixes him with a hypnotic stare.

> He gased on me with his gotysche berde;
> When I loked on hym, my purse was half aferde.
>
> （237–8）

He is a cunning fellow whose gown is lined with fox-fur. He has one vice, gambling, and one passion, singing. He sings by ear; he cannot read a note of music. He would gladly take lessons from Drede, whom he admires on account of his learning. Impulsive, excitable, he pours out a flood of indiscreet questions. He is a simpleton, 'a homely knave'. But that does not prevent him from immediately plotting against Drede with Disdain, a supercilious snob, wearing gaudy garments embroidered with scorn and a hood lined with indignation. Disdain is a violent man, who takes offence at the poet. He tries to pick a quarrel with him, he swears, he frowns and stamps. Pale with hate, he fumes with rage, bursts into angry complaints of Drede's too rapid advancement at Court at the expense of such veteran servants as himself and his friends. Then he delivers a final ultimatum:

> We be thy betters, and so thou shalte vs take,
> Or we shall the oute of thy clothes shake.
>
> （342–3）

Ryote is altogether different. He is a madcap, an inveterate gamester whose untidy clothes reflect the disorder of his mind.

His head is heavy from sleepless nights, his eyes bleary, his skin
shiny, his nose running, his lips parched, his gown too short, his
hose torn and held up at the knees with a green cord, his
mantle patched with squares of red and blue, his vest of coarse
Kendal cloth, his sword and purse hanging at his side. Heedless,
he 'sings' at the top of his voice, and adorns his hat—full of
holes through which his hair sprouts—with an 'ostrich feather'
borrowed from a capon's tale. He is a debauchee who boasts of
his exploits with the ladies of the red-lamp district, from whom
he derives the best part of his income. His views thereon quite
shocked the laureate's modesty:

> I was ashamed so to here hym prate;
> He had no pleasure but in harlotrye.

(373-4)

This rather shady gallant, who will end sooner or later on
Tyburn Tree, invites Drede to join their company for an all-
night session of food, drink and song, followed by sleep until
noon. He is the embodiment of intemperate amusement, as
opposed to men of science who spend their time 'studying and
musing on the moon'.[31] He asks Drede to dice with him, but
then finds that he himself cannot even put down a stake; his
purse is empty, it contains nothing but a shoe-buckle. So he
decides to go and fill his pockets in the stews, and rushes off
leaving behind his battered old hat as pledge of his return.

Dissimulation hides two faces in his hood, one lean and like a
cheerless ghost, the other darting murderous glances. He has a
knife hidden in one sleeve, upon which is written the word
'Mischief', while in the other he conceals a golden spoon full of
honey 'to feed a fool'. He communes in corners with Disdain.
He is a traitor who affects a dubious commiseration, a hypocrite who pretends to side with the poet against those who envy
his learning or denigrate his virtue, a cheat who laments the
knavery prevalent at Court. He is followed by Desceyte who
appears unexpectedly and frightens you by stealing up behind.
Like Harry Hafter, he has the nimble fingers of a pickpocket.
He wears a straight garment; also a curious hood perforated
and adorned with facings made to resemble the bars of a cage,

He too abandons himself to protestations of friendship and goodwill towards the poet. If he could be taken at his word, he had been ready to rid Drede of his most determined enemy, but for his fear that 'murder will out'.

With this mention of murder, Drede thinks he sees some alarming figures closing in on him. He is clinging desperately to the ship's rail, ready to leap into the sea, when he suddenly wakes up. It has all been a nightmare. But who knows, he asks sententiously, how much truth that dream may perhaps contain?

> Oftyme suche dremes be founde trewe;
> Now constrewe ye what is the resydewe.

(538–9)

Thus the ingenious allegory of the Ship of 'hye apparayle' had re-created the atmosphere of marvel peculiar to courtly verse merely in order to acclimatize the spirit of satire founded upon observation of daily life. It is by the charm of fiction that the poet obtains a hearing, but it is by the vivacity and picturesque character of his description that he sustains the reader's interest. He seems to wish to spare the susceptibilities of his aristocratic public simply with a view to clamping more firmly in the pillory those vile courtiers whom he reckoned among the most determined and perfidious of his personal enemies.

There he was faced with an extremely delicate problem: to suggest that royal favour was the plaything of Chance, not the award of Merit. Royal Majesty, of course, is not the guilty party, Dame Sans-Pareille sits enthroned beneath her damask canopy. It must, however, be acknowledged that notwithstanding her undeniable right to the cargo of Favour, all depends in the last resort upon Fortune, the real mistress aboard, who, at the dictate of caprice, favours her darlings or throws the undesirables into the sea.

Thus he directs attention to a class of dissolute, violent, ignorant, avaricious and quarrelsome courtiers, gamblers, swashbucklers, bandits and debauchees, who entertain ambiguous relations with the daughters of Half Street and the most questionable foreigners. Hence the picture of Ryote (debauchery) and of Harry Hafter (swindling). But the court vices *par excellence* are the most outstanding: Disdain and four different shades of insincerity: Favell (flattery), Suspicion, Dissimulation and Deceit.

These typical vices of the Court, it will be remembered, had already been noticed by Skelton in the warnings he had lavished nine years earlier upon the Earl of Northumberland's young orphan son:

> All flateryng faytors abhor and from the cast;
> Of foule detraction God kepe the from the blast!
> Let double delyng in the haue no place,
> And be not lyght of credence in no case.

> *(D. of E.N.,* 172-5)

We shall meet them again later, treated more fully, in the great morality *Magnificence* under the form of an unforgettable quartet: Counterfeit Countenance, Crafty Conveyance, Cloaked Collusion and Courtly Abusion. In *The Bowge of Court*, the poet-laureate had orchestrated one of the essential themes of his career. Moreover, he understood very well the symbolic value of his choice. He would not confine himself to the official role of a poet writing to order. He declared himself, on the contrary, a satiric poet. He gave first place to the clerk-poet's mission in the sphere of morality upon which he had embarked with his first poem. But he continued in the pleasant and picturesque strain that would, in his opinion, keep the laughers on his side. How far did he succeed? It is difficult to say, although the sequel of his career may perhaps throw some light upon the subject. Assuredly, with *The Bowge of Court* he must have enlarged the circle of his personal and implacable enemies. Nor can we be certain that such freedom of tone, such fierce denunciation of manners at the Court of Henry VII, was looked upon with favour in high places: it was risky for a court poet to employ *rimes royales* in order to disparage the King's courtiers.

While he thus flirted with Dame Fortune, something happened unexpectedly to apply the balm of satisfaction so sorely needed by his self-esteem. What he required was someone to proclaim his merits. That someone was none other than Erasmus, who turned up one day in 1499 at the door of Eltham Palace, accompanied by Thomas More and Richard Arnold.

Erasmus, already half emancipated from his convent at Stein, had been prevented by a series of misfortunes from making the grand tour to Rome. Instead, he had accepted an invitation to stay with his pupil Lord Mountjoy, a young man who had been married for two years and was completing his studies in Paris until his little spouse had attained her majority. In a subsequent work, the *Lucubrations* (1523), Erasmus drew a vivid picture of his impromptu visit to the King's children.

'I was staying at Lord Mountjoy's country house when Thomas More called and took me for a walk to the neighbouring village where all the King's children, except the eldest, Prince Arthur, were receiving their education. When we entered the hall, there were present not only the residents of the palace but also Lord Mountjoy's people all assembled to welcome us. In the middle stood Prince Henry, then nine years old and already with something royal in his demeanour, a mixture of dignity and uncommon courtesy. On his right was Margaret, aged about eleven; on his left played Mary, a child of four. More, attended by his companion Arnold, presented his respects to young Henry (he who is today upon the throne of England), then handed him something he had written. As for myself, not having expected anything like this, I had nothing to offer. I had to content myself with promising that I would do my duty at the first opportunity. Meanwhile I felt most annoyed at More's failure to warn me, particularly in view of a little note from the prince, handed to me during dinner and asking for something from my pen. I went home and, despite long neglect of the Muses, completed my poem in three days.' [32]

That poem consisted of an allegory in which Britannia pronounces a eulogy of her own sovereign. With it went a long dedication in prose, full of commonplaces about the superiority of knowledge to wealth, addressed more directly to Prince Henry. The poem contained a flattering reference to the poet Skelton 'revealing (to him) the sacred springs (of the Muses)'. The dedication included a famous encomium: 'And you have with you Skelton, the light and glory of British letters, who is able not only to rouse but also to satiate your appetite for study.' [33]

Skelton, on the flood-tide of joy, must have answered those two lines of exquisite politeness with one of his own torrential poems, which flowed so readily from his pen. For we possess yet another curious poem by Erasmus in praise of Skelton, which has all the appearance of a hastily written reply to the cascade of eloquence with which the poet-laureate had thanked him: 'Why have you chosen to pour forth the fountains of your eloquence on my behalf, eternal poet Skelton so worthy of the laurel crown, flower of the Castalian springs? I have never frequented the Pierian cave; I have never drunk at the Aonian springs whence poets derive their inspiration. It is to you, rather, that Apollo has given a golden lyre, and the Muses the Plectrum of poesy. Calliope has moistened your lips with the liquor of persuasion that is sweeter than honey. Your songs excel that of the swan. Thracian Orpheus himself yields to the music of your lyre; and when your voice is raised in harmony therewith, you tame wild beasts, sway the hard-hearted oaks, stay the rushing torrents and soften the rocks. What Greece owed to Lydian Homer and Mantua to Virgil, England now owes to Skelton. He was the first to bear away from Latium the Muses' choir; he was the first to teach them a pure and polished language. Under his aegis England need not fear to challenge the poets of Rome. Hail!'

Such extravagances were perfectly devised to flatter the recipient without compromising their author's sincerity. Erasmus had developed the general theme of laureateship without considering the suitability of his words to Skelton personally, whose English poems he could not possibly have understood. He must, of course, have heard a certain amount about him, not only from Thomas More but also from his old friend Robert Gaguin, to whose history of France he had lately

contributed an introduction. But to pretend that the author of
The Bowge of Court and the *Recule* against Gaguin had 'lips
moistened with the liquor of persuasion sweeter than honey',
that 'the tuneful songs of his lyre were able to tame wild
beasts', and so on, was indeed a superlative example of the
backhanded compliment. Incidentally, Erasmus later refrained
from including this *Carmen extemporale* in his collected works.
Skelton, on the other hand, never forgot those passing courtesies
which had added lustre to his name and to some extent regilded
his escutcheon. He never forgot that he had been declared the
Virgil and Homer of English literature, and when he came to
celebrate his own apotheosis in *The Garland of Laurel* (1523) he
took care to parade those flattering comparisons.

It is not unlikely that in 1500 the poet-laureate formed part
of the numerous and splendid suite which accompanied the
English sovereigns on their journey to Calais, where Henry VII
and Queen Elizabeth spent about a month (May–June) dis-
cussing with the Archduke Philip of Burgundy two projected
marriages: that of Prince Henry with Philip's daughter
Leonora, and that of the prince's sister Mary with young
Charles who was one day to be Charles V. At all events, on 1st
June, the King met the Archduke in the church of Saint-Pierre
near Calais, where Skelton, as the prince's tutor, as national
poet and as laureate *in partibus transmarinis*, would not have been
out of place. Moreover, a subsequent poem (*Speke Parrot*),
referring to Cardinal Wolsey's embassy to Calais in 1521, shows
a knowledge of Saint-Pierre de Calais which may date from this
period of Skelton's life.[34]

In 1501, a year marked by the gorgeous wedding of young
Prince Arthur with Katherine of Aragon, we find several
references to Skelton. First, in the Hilary term, the registers of
Cambridge University bear traces of three successive meetings
with John Syclyng. On each occasion the two friends supped
together, the last meal being a mere informal collation in
Syclyng's apartment at Westminster and accounting for only 2*d.*
of the 6*d.* recorded in his ledger as spent on that day:

Item (die Jouis) in camera pro focali et potu cum
Magistro Skelton . . . ijd.[35]

In the same year, on 28th August at Eltham Palace, where the princes' education was almost finished, John Skelton wrote a small didactic treatise entitled *Speculum Principis*,[36] 'for the princes in their minority'—their tutor's pedagogic testament, so to speak. No masterpiece of its kind, it shows how archaic, long-winded and devious some of the poet-laureate's ideas could be. In it, with the massive support of quotations from ancient literature and Scripture, he spins out fatuous commonplaces on the superiority of virtue (here he seems to remember Erasmus's dedication to Prince Henry), the excellence of knowledge and the advantages of self-control. He continues with a parade of practical advice in rhymed, rhythmical and mnemonic prose in the fashion of that age.[37]

He managed, also, to slip in a few pointed words in favour of poets: 'Cherish poets, for muleteers are legion, but Pollios are few.' [38]

The year 1502 brought both joy and sorrow to the royal family. On 25th January Margaret Tudor was married to James IV of Scotland, an event that inspired William Dunbar's poem *The Thrissil and the Rois*.[39] But on 2nd August young Prince Arthur, whose health had always been poor, died at Ludlow Castle in Shropshire. Henry succeeded as heir-apparent to the throne and, it seems, was given a new tutor, William Honne.[40] Skelton's educational duties were virtually ended. On 28–9th April an isolated payment of 40s. 'to the duc of York scholemaster' probably marks a final settlement, a golden handshake telling Skelton that his services were no longer required. We hear no more of the poet until he re-appears one spring day, two years later, as rector of the parish of Diss in Norfolk.

CHAPTER III

The Rector of Diss

From Satire to Fantasy

DISS, a large agricultural township in the Waveney valley, lies on the southern boundary of modern Norfolk, in the diocese of Norwich which at that time extended much farther south. Here, on 10th April 1504, we meet Skelton once again, witnessing, together with his colleague, Sir John Clarke's 'soul priest', the Will of a parishioner named Margery Cowper.[1] We notice that his new duties had not caused him to lay aside his proud academic title: he calls himself 'Master John Skelton, laureate'. Nor, as we shall presently see, had he turned his back on poetry.

At that time the rectory of Diss was in the gift of the royal family. It had previously belonged to the Fitzwaters, until 1494, when their fief was confiscated by the sovereign in dramatic circumstances connected with Perkin Warbeck's conspiracy.[2] The post of rector, at first left vacant, had been conferred in 1498 upon the King's absentee chaplain Peter Greves. Since Lady Margaret had purchased a manor at Diss at about the same date, it is not unreasonable to suppose that she had once again influenced the poet's destiny by helping towards his appointment to the cure of Diss when his tutorship expired.[3]

Skelton's superior was Bishop Richard Nykke (or Nix), a prelate in favour at court, active, worldly, an epicure and a good musician, who had followed the political fortunes of Richard Foxe and had quite recently accumulated a threefold charge as canon of Windsor, Secretary to the Order of the Garter and Dean of the Chapel Royal.[4] He had been appointed to the See of Norwich in March 1500. Here, too, in south Norfolk, Skelton found himself close to the Howards,[5] whose prestige had been rising (while that of the Percies declined) since the appointment of Thomas Howard, Earl of Surrey, as Treasurer of the realm in 1501.[6]

Moreover, Diss, was not far from Cambridge, which, under

the influence of Lady Margaret and her chaplain John Fisher, was taking a new lease of life. The University, in fact, was about to honour her former student. In 1504–5 John Skelton received from his *alma mater* the equivalent of an unspecified academic degree (perhaps M.A.) obtained in the meantime at Oxford, as well as permission to wear the robe granted him by the King.[7]

Skelton at Diss, therefore, was not in disgrace—at least not at this period—but he felt himself nonetheless in a backwater. This was certainly not the high promotion of which he had dreamed, and perhaps the mere fact of not having been retained as tutor to the heir-apparent had already wounded his pride. But who can say that, after *The Bowge of Court* and the ephemeral compliments of Erasmus, he had not found life at Court intolerable, with that pack of courtiers more than ever determined to be rid of him.

Here, he had plenty of time for a change of air and to devote himself to his favourite hobbies. But the demon of satire had not left him. He would soon find numerous occasions for its exercise—at the expense of his parishioners.

His jaunts to Cambridge may have afforded him many an opportunity to slip into the pocket of his cloak some little verses in a lighter vein than his weekly sermons. Indeed two *Epitaphs*, dating from 1506, reached the parish-priest of Trumpington, official copyist to the University, who translated them nearly a year later (5th January 1507) with a note of their origin: 'Auctore Skelton, Rectore de Diss'.[8] They are two macaronic pieces, diverting as well as satirical, which bear the strong academic stamp of parodies in Low Latin as written by the 'Goliardic' poets:

> Frates, orate
> For this knauate,
> By the holy rode,
> Dyd neuer man good:
> I pray you all
> And pray shall,
> At this trentall
> On knees to fall
> To the fote ball;

With, fill the blak bowle
For Jayberdes sowle
Bibite multum:
Ecce sepultum
Sub pede stultum,
Asinum, et mulum!
The deuill kis his culum!
Wit(h), hey, howe, rumbelowe,
Rumpopulorum
Per omnia secula seculorum.

Amen.

(Dyce, i, p. 170–1)

The victims of his coarse fun and facile sarcasm, aggressively burlesque, are two of his parishioners: John Clarke,[9] 'old John Clarke', called 'Jayberd', 'a man of egregious malice, perfidious heart, double tongue',[10] and Adam Uddersall,[11] called 'Adam All (A d-all?)', whom the author's Latin depicts as unclean, rapacious, fat, greasy, revolting, impious, diabolic, a true creature of Beelzebub who has prepared a place for him in the infernal regions.

This is the first time—it will not be the last—that we see Skelton vowing his personal enemies to hell *post mortem*, savaging their corpses with a fury far beyond the range of mild academic lampoon. The theme of the requiem mass (in this case a trental, or series of thirty masses for the repose of a soul) assumes here the quality of brutal derision. Skelton's lines were never intended to evoke mere laughter; they express an attitude of animosity and reprobation which did not cease on the threshold of death. The rector of Diss never hesitated to employ his talents as a rhymster in order to scourge his flock and consign them to eternal flames.

When occasion demanded, however, he found no difficulty in resuming his function as official singer, spokesman of public opinion, which he liked to associate with the dignity of poet-laureate. After two terrible fires in quick succession, on 25th April and 4th June 1507, had devastated Norwich, the capital of the diocese, he composed a short Latin poem, a 'canticum dolorosum', entitled *Lamentatio Urbis Norvicen'*,[12] which voiced the feelings of a whole population in simple and lofty words.

But his professional duties led him back continually to diatribe. He found himself, so to speak, in a position to view humanity in the guise of Good and Evil. And as a poet of action he took up arms against the unruly, the rebellious and the recalcitrant.

Undoubtedly the finest opportunity in his priestly career occurred one day when he discovered that 'a lewd curate, a parson beneficed', who was also a keen falconer, had intruded into the parish church of Diss with his hawks and his hounds.

Ware the Hawk [13] is the indignant diatribe of an honest Christian aghast at the extravagance of that incredible scene: his church invaded by a satanic rabble, one hawk rending a pigeon's crop over the high altar while the other, after flying around for a long time, perched on the rood alongside the figures of the Blessed Virgin and St John; the hunting parson blaspheming in the face of God; oaths and the cracking of whips accompanied with the jingling of his birds; the church turned upside down, the altar stripped of its cloths, the poor-box thrown to the floor together with the lectern, the missal, the processional cross, the lamp and the banner; the pigeons' blood streaking the Holy Table and the hawk's dung falling into the ciborium.

To make matters worse, the curate had premeditated his sacrilege: he had taken care to bolt and bar the church door. Skelton could not have gained admission but for a secret passage. Yet the curate had had the effrontery to answer his angry protest by declaring that he meant to continue his chase 'from the altar to the font'.

That scene took place one summer evening, 28th August, the feast of the Beheading of St John the Baptist. 'It is undoubtedly these good-for-nothing fellows that weaken the authority of the Church', wrote Skelton, adding prophetically: 'It is surely high time to look into such flagrant misconduct.'

The episode of the hawking curate was no isolated occurrence; something similar is mentioned by Barclay in his translation of the *Nef des fous* (1509). But while some of its features, particularly as described by Skelton, may provoke a laugh, it was in no sense a jolly Pickwickian adventure. *Ware the Hawk* ranks among the most vehement satires yet written by the poet-laureate.

Here are no oratorical devices, no allegorical contrivances intended to veil the outlines of harsh reality. *Ware the Hawk* is a forthright censure, punctuated with Latin imperatives: *Observate! Considerate! Deliberate! Vigilate! Deplorate! Divinate! Reformate! Pensitate!* in the tradition of medieval preaching, which was often very close to satire. The narrative is interspersed with some remarkable comments in which Skelton reveals an attitude towards abuses in the Church that he would never afterwards abandon. In the interests of religion itself, he is resolved to denounce the running sores that devour the body ecclesiastic. His anger is directed not against good priests, but against all those who are wronging Holy Church 'which is the rock of our faith'. Applying to the incident his usual comparative method, he draws a parallel between the present sickness and the corruption that reigned in Israel in the first century before Christ. At that time the Pharisees, devout and scrupulous but sluggish and hidebound, dared not raise their voice in protest; they allowed Truth to be outraged and the spiritual Law to be sidetracked into pettifoggery.

Just as the blood of bulls or calves, he ingeniously observes, was offered as sacrifice in religious buildings, so also on the present occasion pigeon's blood has been spattered on the Holy Table. Monstrous profanation! The Church is *polluted* (a word that falls incessantly from his pen). The lesson is clear: in ancient times the Temple was destroyed and Israel passed under the Chaldean yoke; today's abuses open the way to decadence and foreign invasion. But the infidels themselves would never dream of flying their hawks beneath the dome of Hagia Sophia. The most blackguardedly tyrants of history never behaved with less decency than has this 'sporting parson'.

Skelton, therefore, proposes to teach him a good lesson, to crush him under a laureate's contempt. This second part of the poem is quite distinct from the first and was written at a later date. It is a personal invective, crammed with scholastic Latin and hammered home with the refrain 'Doctor Dawcock, Ware the Hawke', which unfolds a succession of insults and subtleties stigmatizing the curate's imbecility. The solution of a Latin puzzle, intended as a parting shot at his ignorance, proves that the author was now setting the debate firmly upon the plane of his own superiority as laureate, for the problem was to decipher the following proposition: 'Just like the phoenix of Arabia, a bird like unto no other, the land of Britain has produced its poet Skelton.' [14] Thus, in his favourite field of animal symbolism he was triumphantly distinguishing a phoenix from a dawcock.

It was a childish triumph: like the *Epitaphs*, it shows us how at that period the laureate eccentrically combined the hounding of malefactors, the most orthodox devotion and the strictest conformity with vagaries of expression belonging to the utmost inordinate fantasy. Yet, he explains in a Latin postscript, 'pious poets enjoy a venerable privilege, that of saying whatever they please and in their own way'.[15] There we have the fundamental *Credo* of his poetic art.

He was about to furnish another proof of it, in a rather different key, with the long and celebrated rhapsody of *Phyllyp Sparowe*.

His duties as rector of Diss occasionally took him to Norwich. In a suburb of that city, at Carrow, there was a Benedictine priory, which had long been the favourite resort of aristocratic young ladies who wished to spend their lives in retreat from the world. It had been governed since 1492 by one Catherine Segryme. She was reputed to be 'rather severe', and the community lived a quiet life. The only grievances of which echoes have reached us concerned the meagre diet and the rapid tempo of the singing in chapel, which the old nuns complained that they could not follow. Twice a year the priory relaxed—at Christmas the members staged a little play; in the spring the young lady-boarders celebrated May and chose themselves a queen.[16]

Now, among these latter was a girl whom the poet knew— Jane Scrope. As we have seen, she was a daughter of Sir Richard Scrope of Bentley in Yorkshire, an old family friend with whom Skelton cannot have been acquainted later than 1485, in which year Sir Richard died prematurely leaving eight daughters and an unborn child whom he earnestly hoped would be a boy. (His Will expresses the wish that 'Thys childe that my wuff is with bee a son'.[17])

Jane's mother, Eleonore, née Washbourne, had married as her second husband a Norfolk gentleman, Sir John Wyndham of Felbrygg, who, having taken a hand in the Yorkist disturbances in Suffolk, had been executed in 1502.[18] We meet Eleonore Wyndham again at Carrow, where she died in 1505. Her Will expressly names 'my daughter Jane Scrope', as well as 'my unmarried daughter by my first husband, Sir Richard Scrope'.[19] There can thus be no uncertainty about her identity. On the other hand, the date of her meeting with Skelton is more questionable. Some think, for reasons of tact, that it cannot have taken place *after* her mother's death. But Skelton's fellow poet and rival, Alexander Barclay, makes no mention of *Phyllyp Sparowe* until 1509, in a passage subjoined to his translation of the *Nef des fous*. Moreover, in his then curious state of mind, the poet himself professed never to have had an evil thought. So we ought not perhaps in his case to lay too much stress upon considerations of tact. It is more reasonable to suppose that he wrote *Phyllyp Sparowe* shortly before Barclay's violent reaction, say about 1508, two or three years after Eleonore Wyndham's death, when the orphan Jane was seeking refuge from adversity in Carrow Priory. She would then have been twenty-three years old at the most, whereas the poet was certainly about twice that age.

The origin of the poem was a trivial incident of convent life—the death of Jane's pet sparrow, victim of a cat's voracity. The poet seems to have composed it at the instance of his protégée. He saw an opportunity to do better than Catullus, Statius or Ovid. Moreover, he had in mind the cadences of the Office of the Dead, which his professional duties rendered ever present to his ear. Hence the idea of a long rhapsody, likely to fascinate the girl who would sing her sparrow's death to the rhythms of the *De Profundis*, punctuated with phrases, taken directly from the funeral service. Then, linking the *Commendations* to the *Lamentations*, he saw the possibility of prolonging this brilliant clerical parody with a second part; he needed only to change Domin*e* to Domin*a* in order to transform the praises of the Lord into a dithyrambic eulogy of the girl herself.

The Boke of Phyllyp Sparowe, therefore, is seen as a twofold amplification in 1382 lines of Catullus's eighteen. It is an unsurpassed medieval *tour de force*, an achievement of consummate virtuosity.

As in *Ware the Hawk*, as in the sarcastic *Epitaphs* on two of his parishioners, the poet chose to use the kind of short, facile lines which he had tried out ten years earlier at Court, when he composed the impromptu note *Upon a Deadman's Head*. In Norfolk, far from Court and free from the tyranny of *rimes royales*, the rector-poet was thus cultivating a sort of semi-clerical verse, daughter of the Latin poetry of the medieval Church, an English equivalent of the French *rythmi gallicani* but less strictly controlled in the matter of rhyme.

At that period, indeed, all France—even her remotest countryside—lay under the spell of an enormous poetic monument, in funeral style: Martial d'Auvergne's *Vigiles de la Mort du Roy Charles VII*. Inspired likewise by the office *pro defunctis*, it is a *Placebo* consisting of nine psalms and nine lessons retracing the whole life of King Charles VII in the form of a great historico-religious rhapsody along with profane interludes. Here we see the people, the nobility, France herself and the train of Virtues singing in unison the praises of that prince. The first part alone extended to nearly 40,000 lines! [20]

Fortunately, the *Placebo* of *Phyllyp Sparowe*, though of substantial length, has nothing near such colossal dimensions. Here, too, Skelton turns his back upon official poetry. The sort of fantasy he cultivates is all the more personal in its inspiration on account of his inability to hide the fact that he has been dazzled by the radiant beauty of his protégée. The winged parody of those musical variations jumps with joy from end to end.

Nothing is more original in this connection than the artistry of the opening measures which covertly combine the discreet introduction of the young woman and that of the elderly poet: first, her wavering, pizzicato-like syllables with the rhythm of a children's ritornello; then, in a voice disguised and with professional solemnity, his announcement of the funeral service of the sparrow, lately dead at the Benedictine priory of Carrow, and of the prayers to be said for the souls of all sparrows 'named in our registers' . . .

> *Pla ce bo*
> Who is there, who?
> *Di le xi*
> Dame Margery;
> Fa, re, my, my,
> Wherefore and why, why?
> For the sowle of Philip Sparowe
> That was late slayn at Carowe,
> Among the Nones Blake,
> For that swete soules sake,
> And for all sparowes soules,
> Set in our bederolles,
> *Pater noster qui*
> With an *Ave Mari*
> And with the corner of a Crede
> The more shalbe your mede . . .
>
> (1–16)

The first movement—the *Lamentations*—is dramatic in conception. It is an apologue attributed to Jane, a kind of interior soliloquy recalling her emotion, her cries, her gestures, as the several stages of the office bring to mind every detail of the tragedy and the picture of her bygone happiness. The treatment is hyperbolical: just as the incident itself is magnified to the proportions of a catastrophe, so the feeling swells to the level of a pathos usually associated with great heroines. Though fundamentally burlesque, it endeavours to outstrip the famous tragedies of legend:

> Neuer halfe the payne
> Was betwene you twayne,
> Pyramus and Thesbe,
> As than befell to me.
>
> (19–22)

Discovery of the loss, tears and groans, grief turning to prostration, prostration to frenzy—all is depicted with the tortured pathos of medieval art, of thirteenth-century sculpture, with its familiar externals:

> Wherewith my handes I wrange,
> That my senaws cracked
> As though I had been racked.
>
> (45–7)

Jane's cries re-echo those both of pagan and of Christian story. Her woe rivals that of Andromache; her mournful utterances are an exact imitation of the Blessed Virgin's sorrow at the Descent from the Cross. Here, for example, is one passage taken almost verbatim from a well-known medieval *Planctus Mariae*:

> O mayden, wydow and wyfe,
> Of what estate ye be
> Of hye or lowe degre,
> Great sorowe than ye myght se,
> And lerne to wepe at me! [21]
>
> (53–7)

Likewise, her imprecations against Gib, the feline murderer, afforded many opportunities for amplification, in which the hell of the ancients, with its fauna so rich in terrifying monsters, is laid under heavy contribution through the medium of Ovid's *Metamorphoses*.

Intermingled with such harrowing scenes, and by way of contrast, a number of more tranquil descriptions evoke the idyllic memory of other days, of a time when the tame sparrow in his little velvet cap would 'seek after small worms and sometimes white breadcrumbs', or perhaps nestle in Jane's bosom:

> Betwene my brestes softe
> It wolde lye and rest.
>
> (125–6)

We see him hopping onto her bed, to wake her with the flutter of his wings; snapping up the fleas he espies 'with his wanton eye'; perching on her finger and sipping her spittle or pressing his beak between her lips. All these pictures are so

many miniatures, produced with brief touches through which
the poet reveals consummate skill as an animal painter. His
refinements of invention go so far as to recall the preciosity of
Alexandrian painting in its decadence. One typical instance is
the passage in which Jane Scrope, embroidering an image of her
sparrow, notices with horror that when she pricks the head a
drop of blood tips the point of her needle.[22]

Now, the whole purpose of all this virtuosity is to astonish us
not only by its originality but also by the teeming wealth of its
inventiveness. Hence the systematic search for topics capable of
development in accordance with the theories of medieval
poetry. Hence that 'Mass of the Birds', a commonplace derived
from the Bestiaries and brilliantly revived by Skelton, who gives
each of his seventy-seven birds a part to play in the sparrow's
funeral, a part suited to each one's physical, moral or
symbolical characteristics. Hence also the composition of the
epitaph, a pretext to display the girl's book-learning.

While the *Lamentations* affect a dramatic note, the *Commendations* are lyrically inspired. The poet is now speaking in his
own name, voicing the heady emotions he experienced in the
presence of that radiant girl, like Petrarch when he first set eyes
on his beloved. He described for posterity the smallest impressions of that memorable interview.

> . . . She made me sore amased
>   Vpon her when I gased,
>   Me thought min hert was crased,
>   My eyne were so dased.

(1102–5)

> . . . And so hath rauyshed me
>   Her to behold and se,
>   That in wordes playne
>   I cannot me refrayne
>   To loke on her agayne.

(1006–10)

> . . . Her eyen gray and stepe
>   Causeth myne hert to lepe

(1014–15)

   ... And with her fyngers smale,
      And handes soft as sylke,
      Whyter than the mylke,
      That are so quyckely vayned,
      Wherewyth my hand she strayned,
      Lord, how I was payned! ...

                     (1118–23)

   ... It raysed myne hert rote
      To see her treade the grounde
      With heles short and rounde ...

                     (1148–50)

A term of falconry best portrays the empire she wields over
him:

   ... Vnneth I me refrayned,
      How she me had *reclaymed*
      And me to her retayned ...

                     (1124–6)

He makes no attempt to deny the agitation he suffered in her
presence, the dizziness that caused him for a moment to confuse
the torments of hell with celestial bliss:

   ... Alas, what shud I fayne?
      It wer a pleasaunt payne
      With her aye to remayne ...

                     (1011–13)

   ... It were an heuenly blysse
      Her sugred mouth to kysse ...

                     (1039–40)

   ... Her kyrtell so goodly lased,
      And vnder that is brased
      Such plasures that I may
      Neyther wryte nor say ...

                     (1194–6)

> ... Yet though I wryte not with ynke,
> No man can let me thynke,
> For thought hath lyberte,
> Thought is franke and fre ...

$$(1197-1201)$$

His morality in this regard is no more than formal and external. As Philarète Chasles observed,[23] it foreshadows the sensuality of the Renaissance. It does, however, recognize certain limits. Having an uneasy conscience and fearing malevolent interpretation, Skelton was at pains to defend himself with a string of rhetorical precautions, to declare the spirit in which he had written his profane hymn to female beauty, the courtly and chivalric sentiments that had inspired him, the frontiers within which he had confined himself: in short, the platonic nature of that fortuitous interlude which had 'made a pleasant break in the monotony of hard work'.[24]

True to the French motto *Rien que Playsere*, with which he concludes his poem, he had 'never given a moment's thought to vice or villainy'.

He hopes thus to be completely exonerated. After so thorough an explanation, none but the most peevish mind would venture to find fault. However, since two precautions are better than one, and since the best form of defence is attack, he thought it advisable to slip in a few lines on the subject of Envy, in order to forestall any criticism that might arise from the jealousy of others who could not equal his own achievement.[25] It is therefore not the lover who has the last word in *Phyllyp Sparowe*, but the poet, the inspired poet, who pleads above all else that he has opened for Jane the road to immortality.

> Wherefore shoulde I be blamed,
> That Jane have named,
> And famously proclaimed?

$$(1255-7)$$

Phyllyp Sparowe thus contained an odd mixture of impassioned language with platonic sentiments; passing frenzy with pious illusions; medieval convention, courtly devotion and literary frolic with mystical belief in the transcendent virtue of Poetry. But in the last resort the thing most likely to hurt certain susceptibilities was his incursion into the profane, especially in view of the fact that his poetic fugue employed the rhythms of the funeral service, that Jane's lamentations echoed those of the Blessed Virgin, and that the commendations in praise of his tender heroine carried overtones reminiscent of the litanies.

Skelton was right: his fears were fully justified. *Phyllyp Sparowe* soon came under fire. Alexander Barclay, the Benedictine monk who never juggled with the liturgy or with liberties of thought—least of all at the expense of a Benedictine convent—ended his translation of the *Nef des Fous* (1509) with some indirectly sarcastic references to those poets 'who sow the sparks and seeds of vice':

> I write no jeste ne tale of Robin Hode
> Nor sowe no sparcles ne sede of viciousnes;
> Wisemen loue vertue, wylde people wantonnes;
> It longeth not to my scyence nor cunnynge
> For Phylyp the Sparowe the (Dirige) to singe.[26]

The rebuke was explicit. John Skelton stood accused both of sacrilege and of licentiousness. But he was not unduly surprised at something he had half expected. He was vexed only by the awareness that all his rhetorical precautions had been so much wasted effort. He consoled himself with the certitude of having written a masterpiece, and thereafter he missed no opportunity to defend his *Phyllyp Sparowe*. The most grievous blow to his self-esteem was delivered, on the contrary, by none other than Jane herself, who had taken fright at the publicity to which her name would be exposed by a poem that indirectly challenged her reputation.

Accordingly, in a florid supplement which betrays his anger and dismay, Skelton undertakes the reply he owes to Jane Scrope and Alexander Barclay.

He attributes Barclay's criticism to jealousy, and stresses the absurdity of finding fault with his parody of the funeral rites, which in his opinion is an altogether harmless and inoffensive trifle. As for Jane, he tries to reassure her by repeating his

favourite argument about immortality. Jane, however, took a
different view; between her and him there was a basic misunderstanding. She was living in the present. Her earthly
'glory' was of more account than the prospect of promotion to
the Temple of Fame along with the most illustrious Loved Ones
of world literature. Intensely annoyed, Skelton then rather
ungallantly threw responsibility for the affair onto her whom he
had lately exalted to the skies, reminding her that he had
yielded to her 'urgent request' for a poem on the death of her
sparrow. After trouncing the pusillanimous Benedictine, he
nearly launched into a diatribe against the beautiful Jane.

This episode of *Phyllyp Sparowe* reveals the impulsiveness and
infatuation that could accompany those outbursts of temper in
which Skelton sometimes indulged. The result was a sort of
blind spot, which caused him to take Barclay's strictures as the
fruit of jealousy, and Jane's indignation as ingratitude. There
was much plain speaking on both sides, but the door remained
open to doubt. Barclay's accusations of irreverence and
indecency were going to stick. Indeed, the monk renewed them
some years later when he published his *Eglogues* (1514), with a
nasty allusion to the poet as a 'graduate of stinking Thaïs'. He
went further, even to the point of declaring that Skelton had
commended the vices to which princes were most prone:

> Another thing yet is greatly more damnable:
> Of rascolde poetes yet is a shamfull rable,
> Which voyde of wisedome presumeth to indite;
> Though they haue scantly the cunning of a snite;
> And to what vices that princes moste intende,
> Those dare these fooles solemnize and commende.
> Then is he decked as *Poet laureate*,
> When stinking Thaïs made him her graduate.[27]

The poem of *Phyllyp Sparowe* was thus the cause of that ill
repute to which the laureate's name was doomed. So too, and
still more than the poem itself, were the hard words it drew
from Alexander Barclay. We know now that within Skelton's
rechosen alm of poetic fantasy those strictures were exaggerated.
But they would remain attached to the memory of his life rather

than to the memory of his work. Skelton had been so imprudent as to speak of Jane Scrope as his 'mistress':

> As my maistres,
> Of whom I thynk
> With pen and ynk . . .

$$(984-6)$$

There, perhaps, we may see the origin of the famous story of his concubine which, however, occurs in no document until after his death, when he had been downgraded to the level of jocular literature.[28]

According to another tradition, related to the first, he was suspended by his bishop on account of his scandalous private life. But nothing we know of him at this period enables us to prove that he was the object of disciplinary sanctions. Such contemporary evidence as we possess tends rather to show that John Skelton performed his duties as parish priest with somewhat meddlesome zeal and that he enjoyed the esteem of his hierarchical superiors.

Thus, on 3rd December 1509, before the ecclesiastical court at Norwich, John Skelton prosecuted one Thomas Pykerell of Diss, 'for the welfare of his soul'. The accused failed to turn up and was declared contumacious. Having put in an appearance on 4th January 1510, he was absolved. However, being required to attend the closing stages of the trial, Pykerell again defaulted and ten days later was for the second time declared contumacious. On 4th February he was suspended and forbidden access to the church until further notice.[29]

On the other hand, there is no proof that during the ten years he spent at Diss the bishop never once had reason to criticize his way of life. In view of his independent spirit, the contrary would surprise us. But there can have been no really serious differences, for in November 1511, two years after the Pykerell affair, we find the Bishop of Norwich inviting his personal arbitration. William Dale, rector of Redgrave in Suffolk, having to answer certain charges laid against him by one of his parishioners named Thomas Revet, appeared before the ecclesiastical court and won his case—except upon one point, which remained *sub judice.* The Bishop then decided to appoint Master Simon Dryver, doctor of laws, and Master John Skelton, rector of Diss, to attempt a settlement of the dispute, subject to the case being reopened before the court on Monday after the feast of St Edmund if agreement had not been reached within eight days. The arbitrators were successful; the rector of Redgrave wrote a letter of apology to the Bishop of Norwich, and order was restored.[30]

Finally, we may note that Skelton remained on friendly terms with Richard Nykke long after his departure from Diss: in 1527–8 we find them both actively engaged in a campaign against two Cambridge students accused of heresy.

Meanwhile, on 24th June 1509, his former pupil Henry had succeeded to the throne of England. Skelton, no doubt, at once read into that happy event the promise of a quick return to favour. He lost no time in writing a poem *In Praise of our Sovereign Lord the King*,[31] one of numerous panegyrics composed for the occasion by Bernard André, Alexander Barclay, Thomas More, Erasmus, Ammonio and others. It is a short poem of forty-two lines in which he rejoices to see the union of the Two Roses finally accomplished in the person of the new monarch. He salutes the dawning of an era of justice 'such as had not been known for a hundred years' (hardly a compliment to Henry VII) and in which Right will at last chase away the foxes, wolves, bears and other malevolent beasts which have caused the country so much unhappiness and unscrupulously stifled the complaints of the people (an allusion to the exactions of Empson and Dudley who were executed soon afterwards on Tower Hill, 17th August 1510). This new 'platonic' era will mark the return of the years of grace and prosperity under the aegis of a 'sage, sober and grave' prince, a 'lusty knight of Mars'. The poet concludes with his old motto *Bien m'en souvient*, linked with the number 21, which becomes curiously significant if we allow Skelton's personal calendar to have begun with his admission to Court in 1488.

It was, however, in another poem, a 'palinodium'[32] of twelve lines, that he expressed more openly his longing to return to favour, to 'resume his plectrum' and 'serve with his songs'. Now a palinode, strictly speaking, is a poem in which the author retracts what he has said in an earlier one, and is also distinguished by a sort of refrain. Skelton's *Palinodium* answers this second requirement, and it may well answer the first too. It may have been written a few months after Henry VIII's accession, though H. L. R. Edwards considered it as a birthday compliment dating possibly from 28th June 1509 or 1510.[33] At all events, the occasion offered Skelton a first-rate opportunity to implore, tactfully and politely, the favour of returning to duty and serving in his rank of poet the heroic enterprises of the new reign.

His hopes of an immediate recall were cruelly disappointed. After the lapse of weeks and months, he had to acknowledge that he must put on the armour of patience; he could do nothing to alter the destined course of events. On 21st October 1509 his name appeared in the general Pardon Roll,[34] an amnesty which was not necessarily intended to efface criminal guilt, but constituted a formality that could extend to many honest folk who might at some time have found themselves at odds with Authority. For Skelton, it was a condition *sine qua non* of his return to favour.

To his profound disappointment, however, the King appeared in no hurry to summon his old tutor. Henry may have feared that Skelton's intemperate language would once again cause trouble at Court. Or he may have regarded him as a little outdated among that team of ardent hellenists who were rapidly altering the intellectual climate of the age. Had not Skelton been forgotten, and in the meantime overtaken by the progress of the New Learning? His removal from Court had certainly done him no good; the absent are always in the wrong. He had been supplanted by Stephen Hawes, a poet of suave and mellifluous speech, a former page of Henry VII, whose *Pastime of Pleasure* [35] was delighting both Court and Town while Skelton kicked his heels in Norfolk.

At this juncture he reappears in London. On 15th July 1511 he ventured to Westminster, where he dined with the prior, William Mane. Their repast was of Lenten austerity, consisting only of plaice, sole, conger, butter and salt fish.[36] Had he come up to further his interests at Court? Or to deliver to some publisher the recent fruits of his vigils? [37] Or perhaps, like his friend Syclyng years ago, to find himself an apartment in the monastic precincts where we know him to have lodged in 1518? [38] Whatever the reason, there was as yet no question of his quitting his post in Norfolk. Blomefield informs us that he was tenant of a house at Diss in 1511, [39] and we have seen him as arbitrator in the case of Revet v. Dale at about the same time.

Since Henry VIII persisted in turning a deaf ear, Skelton resolved to knock more loudly. He would present the King with a work that would revive his childhood memories, a copy (revised for the occasion) of *Speculum Principis* [40] which he had compiled at Eltham Palace in August 1501 'for the princes in their minority'. He considered this the right moment to remind him of those gems of Aristotle's wisdom which he had gathered expressly with a view to the responsibilities of power, and at the same time to repeat that his own satires, like those of Lucilius and Juvenal, were inspired by concern for the Common Good. It was quite in his manner to request with a single utterance the privilege of returning to favour while maintaining his frankness as a satirical poet.

As if to emphasize that he was forging a link with the past, he added to the *Speculum* two poems composed at symbolic dates— the 'Epigram', written at the time of Henry's advancement to the dukedom of York and the 'Palinode' (probably for his birthday), written when he was already King. These he had linked together by means of an identical prayer, repeated in each case: 'May Jupiter Feretrius grant that I languish not by the Eurotas'. [41] He was comparing his sojourn at Diss with Ovid's exile. Still more explicit, a petition in prose completed this cleverly contrived collection: 'Skelton laureate, the King's erstwhile tutor, in a mute soliloquy, as a man utterly doomed to oblivion and, so to say, dead in his heart, . . . By divine and human faith, why should I have been separated from others and condemned to suffer this misfortune? Neither royal munificence nor Fortune's benignity have yet deigned to succour me. O Heaven! O Virgin Mary! to whom shall I impute it. Shall I perhaps accuse the Gods of being wroth with me? Never will I commit such folly. Shall I attribute it to a glaring lack of generosity on the part of a king renowned for his munificence? Perish the thought, Lord God Almighty, who weighest all things in the just balance of thine inexhaustible largess, and likewise dispensest all things with a lavish hand . . .' [42]

He concluded with some advice, brief but heavy with meaning: *Regem te calleas regere non regi(e). Audi Samuelem. Lege Danielem. Tolle Ismaelem. Tolle. Tolle.*

Skelton urges Henry VIII, before all else, to free himself from the tutelage of his ministers, principally from that of Richard Foxe, Bishop of Winchester, who since the beginning of the reign had supplanted the ageing Warham and now wielded such power that in 1510 the Venetian Ambassador, Badoer, said of him '*est alter rex*'.[43]

Audi Samuelem. 'Hear the prophet, hear the voice that warns you against impending danger.' And what voice could be better qualified than the voice of his old tutor?

Lege Danielem. He advises the King to read the Book of Daniel, to heed the writing on the wall, to remember that monarch who became stubborn in pride and was stripped of his glory. There indeed was food for thought, and his voice becomes all the more insistent as clouds gather on the horizon.

Tolle Ismaelem. The lusty knight of Mars has an imperious duty to perform, a military duty in accordance with the needs both of England and of Religion. The fact was that in 1511–12 war was imminent between England, as champion of the Holy Alliance, and France, the professed enemy of Julius II, France in the throes of a Galician schism, mainspring of the dissident Council of Pisa which had dared summon Pope Julius II to its sessions and declare him contumacious! Hence Skelton's categorical imperative *Tolle Ismaelem* (Depose Ismael, or Destroy Ismael), in the sense in which Cicero uses that verb in his *De Officiis: Carthaginem funditus sustulerunt* (Our ancestors razed Carthage to the ground).[44] Thus, in accordance with biblical symbolism, *Ismael*, son of Agar the Egyptian woman, here represents the enemy of orthodoxy, the infidel oppressor, that is to say, in 1511–12, the King of France.[45]

This interpretation is confirmed by the dedication of another book presented by Skelton to Henry VIII at about the same time—perhaps on the very same occasion—and whose martial note is the dominant as it is the dominant of his own minor writings at this period. The book in question was the *Chronique de Rains*, an old French work [46] recounting the exploits of *Richard Coeur-de-Lion* against the *Saracens* or, as Skelton prefers to have them here, '*the tribe of Agareans*'. 'Agareans' is virtually synonymous with 'Ismaelites'. The former name occurs in Psalm LXXXIII, to which Skelton often refers and which is sub-titled 'A Prayer against those who oppress the Church'.

In this way Skelton established a parallel, fully justified by current events, between Richard Coeur-de-Lion, champion of Christianity against the Infidel, and Henry VIII, champion of the Papacy against the schismatics. The subject was one of universal interest, one upon which, it should be remembered, both Barclay and Wolsey, men very different from Skelton, were in complete agreement. Wolsey, who was to be the moving spirit of the approaching military campaign, took care not to overlook the ideological side of the conflict by causing to be published in England, in 1512, the Bull *Universis sanctae matris*,[47] which proclaimed the excommunication of the King of France. Barclay meanwhile wrote a work entitled *Figure of our Mother Holy Church oppressed by the Frenche King*,[48] while Skelton encouraged Henry VIII to assume direction of public affairs and to lead a salutary offensive against the enemies of the Church. At that date his twofold advice could not fail to please the young King. Soon afterwards, Skelton was called from retirement and rewarded with the title *Orator Regius*.

Henry the Eighth as a child, pupil of John Skelton.
Painting by an unknown artist. Oil 12 in. x 10 in.
in contemporary wooden frame.

The Rose both white and Rede
In one Rose now dothe grow:
Thus thorow every stede
There of the fame dothe blow:
Grace the sede did sow:
England now hathe flowrys
Exclude now all dolowrs

Noble Henry the eight
Thy loving subiectis lorde
Of knightis line most streight
His tittle dothe Recorde:
In whome dothe wele Acorde
Algus yonge of Age
Prudens wise and sage:

... from the starry sky
Shall now com and do alight:
This hundard yere stantly
Man knew not ... aspy
That aught dwelt us among
And y was the more wrong:

Right shall the foxes chase
The wolves the bearis alss
That wrowght have moche onre
And browght England in wo
They shall wyry no mo

Nor wrote the ......
by extort ....

Of thes ? noble kyng
The law they shall not breke
They shall com to rekenyng
No man for them shall speke:
The pepull durst not ....
Their grevis to complayne
They brought them in seche payne

Therfor nomore they shall
The comonns overbace
That wont was oves all
Both lorde and knyght to face:
For now the spryt of grace
And welthe as com agayne
That maketh England fayne:

Adornd of fresshe colour
Of yowthe the godely flo?
Our prince of hih hono?
Our peres our ?aroms
Our kyng our Emperour
Our pramour of Troy
Our welth our worldly joy:

Upon us he doth reygne
That maketh o? hartis glad
?? kyng most souerain

That ever England had
Denise felber and sad
And Martes lusty bright
God save hym in his right :

    Amen

Anglicum
Radiant

Bien men souient :

Per me lauruzerum britonu Hettonu Vatem :

A LAWDE AND PRAYSE MADE FOR OUR SOUEREIGNE LORD THE KFNG*

The Rose both White and Rede   Candida,
In one Rose now dothe grow;   punica,
Thus thorow every stede †   &c.
Thereof the fame dothe blow:
Grace the sede did sow:
England, now gaddir flowris,
Exclude now all dolowrs.

Noble Henry the eight,   Nobilis
Thy loving souereine lorde,   Henricus,
Of kingis line moost streight,   &c.
His titille dothe recorde:
In whome dothe wele acorde
Alexis yonge of age,
Adrastus wise and sage.

Astrea, Justice hight,   Sedibus
That from the starry sky   ætheriis,
Shall now com and do right,   &c.
This hunderd yere scantly
A man kowd not aspy
That Right dwelt vs among,
And that was the more wrong.

Right shall the foxis chare, ‡
The wolvis, the beris also,
That wrowght have moche care,   Arcebit
And browght Englond in wo: vulpes,
They shall wirry no mo, §   &c.
Nor wrote ‖ the Rosary ¶
By extort trechery.

* Such (in a different handwriting from that of the poem) is the endorsement of the MS., which consists of two leaves, bound up in the volume.
† *stede*, i.e. place.   ‡ *chare*, i.e. chase, drive away.   § *mo*, i.e. more.
‖ *wrote*, i.e. root.   ¶ *Rosary*, i.e. Rose-bush.

Of this our noble king
The law they shall not breke;
They shall com to rekening;
No man for them wil speke:
The pepil durst not creke
Theire grevis to complaine,
They browght them in soche paine.

Net anti
regis, &c.

Therfor no more they shall
The commouns ouerbace,
That wont wer ouer all
Both lorde and knight to face; *
For now the yeris of grace
And welthe ar com agayne,
That maketh England faine. †

Ecce
Platonis
secla, &c.

Adonis of freshe colour,
Of yowthe the godely flour,
Our prince of high honour,
Our paves, ‡ our succour,
Our king, our emperour,
Our Priamus of Troy,
Our welth, our worldly joy;

Rediit
jam
pulcher
Adonis,
&c.

Vpon vs he doth reigne,
That makith our hartis glad,
As king moost soueraine
That ever Englond had;
Demure, sober, and sad, §
And Martis lusty knight;
God save him in his right!

Anglorum
radians,
&c.

Amen.

Bien men souient. ||

Per me laurigerum Britonum Skeltonida vatem.

---

* *face*, i.e. defy.   † *faine*, i.e. glad.   ‡ *paves*, i.e. shield (properly, a large shield covering the body).   § *sad*, i.e. grave—discreet. || *Bien men souient*. These words are followed in the MS. by a sort of flourished device, which might perhaps be read—*Deo* (2̊1̊) *gratias.*

Text and notes from Alexander Dyce, *The Poetical Works of John Skelton, with Notes and Some Account of the Author and his Writings*, 2v., 1843.

64

CHAPTER IV

Orator Royal

or Poet to the Armies

ACCORDING to the Abbé du Resnil's *Recherches sur les Poètes Couronnez* (1736),[1] the patent declaring Skelton poet-laureate of Henry VIII is dated in the fifth year of his reign, namely 1512 or 1513. These words, written on the authority of Thomas Carte, an English refugee living in France under the name Phillips, obviously cannot mean that Skelton had only just been appointed poet-laureate, a title he had held since 1488. They must mean that the poet-laureate Skelton had just been attached to the household of Henry VIII, an event in full agreement with his presumed return from Diss at about that time and with the first appearance of a new title *Orator Regius*, following that of laureate.

It can be shown, moreover, that Skelton was re-admitted to the King's service in 1513 and not in 1512. For we shall see that the poem entitled *Against Venomous Tongues*, which according to the sub-title was composed in the third year of his appointment as Orator Royal, is proved by internal evidence to be contemporary with the historic interview of Tottenham, 4th May 1516.[2] The date 1513 is likewise confirmed by the *Eulogium pro suorum temporum conditione*,[3] a dithyrambic eulogy of Henry VII and Henry VIII (manifestly written in the euphoria of a return to favour), the martial tone of which suggests an imminent declaration of war:

> Undique bella fremunt nunc, undique proelia surgunt:
> . . . .
> Sors tamen est versanda diu, sors ultima belli: [4]
> . . . .

War was in fact declared on 20th April 1513. Henry VIII embarked at Greenwich on 15th June, and on the evening of

30th set sail from Dover for Calais.[5] It must therefore have been at the very last minute that Skelton was recalled to service, 'in the fifth year of [Henry VIII's] reign'.

Two other poems, contemporary with the *Eulogium*, complete the picture of his return to favour, or rather two versions of the same poem, one in English and the other in Latin, on *Calliope*,[6] the Muse of epic poetry under whose aegis the *Eulogium* also was placed.

The word 'Calliope', embroidered in golden letters, figures on a livery of green and white—the Tudor colours worn by the expeditionary force.[7] This fact appears to indicate that the livery in question was not the 'habit' conferred by the prince in order to enhance the dignity of the poet-laureate's academic lectures, but something entirely new, a uniform indicating that Skelton had been enrolled as poet to the armies.

The appearance of the laureate in this unusual garb puzzled people, while the presence of the word Calliope on that quasi-military attire unleashed a flood of tactless questions: 'Why were ye Calliope embrawdered with letters of golde?' '*Cur tibi contexta est aurea Calliope?*' To which the poet, highly flattered, replied with all good grace: 'Calliope? Well, she's the patroness of poets. She controls the poet-laureate Skelton, in obedience to the orders of his Sovereign. So, you see, I make bold to wear this word embroidered in gold and silk. Although I'm getting on in years, and am even a little hoary, Calliope is kind enough to keep me in her service, and I on my part promise to serve her faithfully, like a queen, to the end of my days.'

To the Latin version of this speech he adds: 'The most sublime, the most admirable, the most radiant of the Muses presides over heroic verse.' Those are words of a veteran, but of one who has retained all the freshness of his enthusiasm and is delighted to find himself part of that great adventure, the campaign of 1513 against a schismatic King of France who has been excommunicated.

We have seen [8] that France under Louis XII, deeply involved in the wars of Italy, had not been content with threatening the papacy in its temporal fief, but had also adopted an attitude of defiance towards the Holy See, a sort of Gallican schism whose earlier symptom had been the Pragmatic Sanction of 1499, whereby the French King arrogated to himself the right to decide questions of internal organization without reference to the Vatican. A national Council, assembled at Orleans and then at Tours, in 1510 absolved the kingdom from obedience to the Pope and voted subsidies for the King. From it there emerged a general Council which sat first at Pisa (11th September 1511) then, when driven from that city, at Milan, where it declared Julius II contumacious for his refusal to obey its summons.

The Pope's reply was not long delayed. He excommunicated the King of France, laid his realm under interdict and summoned the Lateran Council (3rd May 1512), in order to outwit the Council of Pisa and demand, among other things, repeal of the Pragmatic Sanction.

Meanwhile France had lost ground in Italy. By a sudden reversal of fortune she found herself in the spring of 1513 menaced on all her frontiers by the new coalition formed around the Treaty of Malines [9] (5th–18th April 1513) between Henry VIII, Ferdinand the Catholic, the Emperor Maximilian and Pope Julius II. The Pope in turn was threatening all opponents of the League with ecclesiastical censures.

Isolated militarily and morally, France had no ally other than Scotland [10] and—one may perhaps say, for Jean d'Albret had only just lost his throne [11]—Navarre. As for James IV of Scotland, resentment against Henry VIII led him to side with France, his traditional ally. But he would not wholly espouse her ideological quarrel; he did all he could to remain until the last moment on good terms with the Pope, though running serious risk of excommunication.[12]

This propitious moment was chosen by Henry VIII to dream, like Henry V, of recovering his heritage in France. Everything seemed to encourage him towards such an undertaking: Katherine of Aragon,[13] who was urging him to war; his territorial interests; his own glory and the defence of the Church against a mounting tide of schism.[14] His Privy Council, however, was not so enthusiastic, while the Christian humanists—including Erasmus and John Colet, Dean of St Paul's—openly disapproved of this 'war of magnificence' and the policy of Julius II.[15] But Skelton was not among them. He was thrilled with the idea of taking part in a national war that would be no less a holy war against an enemy both of the kingdom and of religion. He made ready to 'unleash the thunder of words', as he had said on another occasion, with a hurling of anathemas that seemed to echo the papal bulls of excommunication. For once, he found himself in agreement with his literary rival Alexander Barclay: both maintained that the Church must be rescued from the oppression of a foreign king. His assiduous persecution of delinquents, non-conformists and atheists in his Norfolk parish must have seemed to him now, as he looked back, like a war of petty skirmishing in comparison with the more weighty tasks that lay ahead. Still, it was nice to think that his patience had not been in vain and that even his humble invectives against the hawking curate had somehow kept him in training and prepared him for his new role.

On 30th June Henry VIII landed at Calais with the Middle Ward, which included, besides a strong contingent of troops, a splendid civil retinue, the Chapel Royal, the minstrels and players, and a whole multitude of secretaries, historiographers and orators royal among whom, we have good reason to think, the poet-laureate John Skelton strutted in his livery of green and white.[16]

Henry left Calais for the front on 21st July. On 4th August he encamped beneath the walls of Thérouanne. Six days later the Emperor Maximilian came in person to place himself under the orders of this twenty-two-year-old prince. Next evening, 11th August, a Scottish herald of arms arrived from James IV, in a final effort to deter Henry from his enterprise—by giving him to understand that if he persisted in his resolution to attack the French, the armies of Scotland would attack his kingdom in his absence. But Henry, more determined than ever, treated this summons with lofty disdain and went ahead. In a written answer, which was fated never to reach its destination, he emphasized his rights as overlord of Scotland and reminded James IV of the example of the King of Navarre, who had just lost his kingdom on account of his decision to ally with France. [17]

On 13th August the French cavalry executed a diversionary manœuvre, an attempt to make possible the revictualling of the besieged town. It failed, leaving the Chevalier Bayard, the

Comte de Longueville and the Comte de Clermont prisoners of the English.[18] On 22nd Thérouanne capitulated. The garrison withdrew next day, and on 24th Henry made his triumphal entry into the city. Then, on the evening of 25th, although clemency had been expected, he suddenly decided, at the request of Maximilian, to raze the fortifications, which was done on the following day.

Now this incident is mentioned in a Latin work written for the occasion, the *Chorus de Dis contra Gallos* [19] which, the poet tells us, 'was solemnly sung on the feast of the Beheading of St John the Baptist', 28th August, less than forty-eight hours later. The fact is rightly accepted as proof that Skelton was indeed present with the general staff of the army on campaign.[20]

This short poem of sixteen lines is a facile and improvised pastiche of the celebrated hymn by Fortunatus, *Salve, festa dies, toto venerabilis aevo* . . .[21] It exults over the capture of Longueville and Clermont, mentions the destruction of the ramparts of Thérouanne and ends with the hope that Henry VIII, soldier of the Blessed Virgin Mary, will reign over France.

Three weeks later, when the centre of operations had moved to Tournai, news arrived from the Scottish border via London that James IV's army of invasion had suffered an overwhelming defeat at Flodden on 9th September.

Skelton thus had the rare pleasure of completing his *Chorus de Dis contra Gallos* with a *Chorus de Dis contra Scottos*.[22] This was another and exactly comparable pastiche of Fortunatus's hymn, composed for the solemn ceremonies that took place on 22nd September, in a cloth-of-gold tent, accompanied by the singers of the Chapel Royal: *cum omni processionali festivitate*. Thus was celebrated in a foreign land the victory of Flodden. There was a *Te Deum*,[23] and a sermon on the death of James IV, preached by John Fisher, Bishop of Rochester. This sermon is echoed by Skelton's poem. He addresses the vanquished king in familiar, sarcastic tones and mocks the royal red lion of Scotland beaten by Surrey's white lion.

Actually, John Skelton had not awaited official confirmation of James IV's death before crowing at his expense. From the beginning of the French campaign the poet-laureate had been collecting scraps of invective, jotted down on the spot and completed as events unfolded. A first surviving fragment, for example, gives a detailed picture of the stormy interview on 11th August beneath the ramparts of Thérouanne, when the Scottish herald came to bid Henry VIII cease hostilities on pain of Scotland's immediate declaration of war.[24] The author highlights the impertinence of such a summons:

> Ye sommnoed our kynge, why dyde ye so?
> To you no thyng it dyde accorde
> To sommon our kynge your souerayne lorde,
> A kynge a somner it is wonder
> Know ye not salte and suger asonder? [25]

He is at pains to stress the superiority of the English King, suzerain of his Scottish vassal, a sovereign king hallowed with sacred chrism in the rite of coronation and standing to James IV as did the priest-king Melchisedech to Amalek. He goes to the length of framing a thinly veiled accusation of parricide against the young monarch:

> Thrugh your counseyle your fader was slayne.

The passage makes much not only of the Franco-Scottish alliance but also of a Danish alliance, the beginning of a counter-league, which was strongly discouraged by the Pope but would remain as a project between James IV and his uncle the King of Denmark, Haakon I (and, after 20th February 1513, his successor Christian II).[26] In this connection Skelton recalls the primacy of the ties which bound James, as Henry's vassal and brother-in-law, to England.

> Before the frensshe kynge danes and other
> Ye ought to honour your lorde and brother.

A month later, the most contradictory rumours began to arrive concerning the battle in Scotland. In France and Italy it was said that the Scots had won a great victory, but that their King had been taken prisoner or had even paid for the victory with his life.

Skelton, on the other hand, though undecided as to the result of the battle and not knowing so much as the name of Flodden, learned at the same time, probably from an English source, that the King's body had been taken to Norham Castle, which was in fact true.

The second fragment which he wrote in these circumstances ignores the military operations but exploits to the full the Scottish King's death, renders homage to St George, Our Lady's knight, and exults over the King's fall:

> For to the castell of norham
> I understonde to soone ye cam,
> For a prysoner there now ye be
> Eyther to the deuyll or the trinite
> Thanked be Saynt Gorge our ladyes knyght
> Your pryd is paste, adwe good nyght.

For having resolved to attack England in her sovereign's absence, James IV has lost his spurs of knighthood. The Danish alliance has been of no avail. Like the King of Navarre, the King of Scotland has lost his realm.

On this note, which recalls the very words used by Henry VIII to the Scottish herald at Thérouanne, the Orator Royal, impatient to diffuse his vengeful and patriotic verses, hurriedly dispatched these two fragments, combined under the title *A Ballade of the Scottyshe Kynge*, to the London printer Richard Fawkes,[27] who published them immediately. During the next few days Skelton was to learn the unhoped-for extent of the great victory of Flodden, where James IV had perished at the head of his troops, involving the flower of Scotland's chivalry in his own ruin.

The first official accounts, based on Surrey's report and forwarded by the queen, arrived from England on 16th September. The poet then learned the whole painful story of the young king's fate—how he had died in the thick of battle, and how his body, abandoned on the field, had been profaned by spoilers. On 20th September, having witnessed the arrival of conclusive evidence—the king's gauntlet and a fragment of the Scottish plaid, eloquent witness of his expiation [28]—Skelton entertained not a moment's doubt that divine retribution had overtaken James at the height of his wickedness, that he had perished

without viaticum, excommunicate for having dared to brave
the authority of the ecclesiastical censures prepared against
him:

> Now from a kynge to a clot of clay:
> Out of your robes ye were shaked.
> And wretchedly ye lay starke naked.
> For lacke of grace hard was your hap:
> The Popes curse gaue you that clap.
>
> (165–9)

Skelton decided, therefore, to revise his *Ballade of the Scottyshe
Kynge* in the light of new facts. He could now enlarge his diatribe
to the national proportions of the Scottish defeat. This second
version was entitled *Against the Scottes*.[29] We are fortunate in
possessing both.

The poet was not content with a superficial retouching. He
altered his first version with a thoroughness and attention to
detail which reveal sound literary craftsmanship.

The *Ballade of the Scottyshe Kinge*—a ballad in nothing but
name—was an anonymous work consisting of bits and pieces.
Against the Scottes is a signed poem, enriched with a preamble
and with an invocation to Melpomene and Thalia. It is
more precise, more affirmative on many points. The poet now
knows the ever-celebrated names of Branston Moor and
Flodden Field. The crushing English victory leads him to
emphasize his declaration of Scotland's vassalage. The accusation of parricide, too, becomes more categorical:

> Thoughe ye vntrully your father haue slayne.
>
> (114)

Scotland is treated, with more disdain than ever, as a poor
country, while the King of England is now likened to Scipio.
The scene of the summoning has been retained for obvious
moral and artistic purposes, as providing a useful starting point,
the act of pride at the root of the monarch's fall:

> Now is your pryde fall to decay . . .
>
> (110)

On the other hand, the references to the Danish alliance have disappeared and the line

> Ye now ranke Scottes *and dronken Danes*

has been skilfully altered to

> The rude ranke Scottes, *lyke dronken dranes*.
>
> (172)

On the whole, it can be said that the second version is more vituperative, more sarcastic, more cruel than the first, and that its style is proportionately more energetic and more concrete. Witness the half-line

> *Your pryd is paste,* adwe good nyght

which becomes

> *Your eye is out*; adew, good nyght!

Events had confirmed the poet-laureate's moral views beyond all expectation. He exulted over the Scottish disaster:

> Continually I shall remember
> The mery moneth of september,
> With the ix day of the same,
> For then began our myrth and game . . .
>
> (65–8)

The north-countryman, the old enemy of the Scots, could now write gleefully:

> *Scotia, redacta in formam provinciae.*
>
> (Dyce i, p. 188)

Scotland reduced to the state of a province. As Jusserand observed: 'The laureate of Oxford speaks of the vanquished enemy with the ferocious exhilaration of the ancient Norsemen.'[30] He did not, however, realize that the prevailing climate had already changed, and that, by a natural reversal of feeling, Scotland on the morrow of Flodden inspired less hatred than compassion.

That campaign of 1513 was peculiar in having been planned during the militant pontificate of Julius II and waged during the conciliatory pontificate of Leo X. At the time of Flodden the French danger was already past, and the Gallcan schism was moribund.[31] It was time to think of matters more serious than wars of ambition between Christian princes, in which so many noble knights had perished. Such was, in effect, the meaning of the complimentary letter sent with a cape and sword of honour to the King of England by Leo X, urging upon him the greater merit of a crusade against the Turks.[32] Henry VIII's prestige was then at its zenith.

But the death of James IV had disarmed hatred. Men were prepared to see only his rash but glorious end in the forefront of his army. Leo X, in turn, refused to confirm the sentence of excommunication passed upon him by the Archbishop of York by virtue of the bulls he had obtained from Julius II.[33] The hour was one of forebearance.[34] Henry VIII himself had to allow his victim a solemn funeral service in St Paul's.

It was therefore not surprising that Skelton's poem *Against the Scottes* was ill received in certain quarters. His raving over a corpse was considered as bad taste. Alexander Barclay, a great friend and admirer of James IV, was certainly not the last to rebuke him for such want of tact, as he had quite recently done also in the eclogue where he describes the poet-laureate as a 'graduate of stinking Thaïs'.[35]

But Skelton held very firm convictions. He would not eat his words. He saw no reason to alter his opinion of James IV, now that he was dead; on the contrary, for the King's death did nothing but corroborate his views on divine retribution. Accordingly, in a supplement intended for his detractors and entitled *Vnto diuers people that remord this rymynge agaynst the Scot Jemmy*,[36] he felt obliged to carry his thought to its furthest extreme. James IV, they had objected, was the King's brother; but could they not see that so unnatural a brother had rendered himself guilty of an impious crime of aggression, the crime of Cain against Abel? People who found his lines objectionable understood nothing of the fundamental reasons that dictated his severity. James was a 'recreant' knight who had perjured the code of chivalry. He was a schismatic, almost a heretic, and

he had died excommunicate. As a king, his fault was all the
more serious, for he was under an obligation to set a good
example proportionate to the dignity of his position in Society.[37]

> And for he was a kynge
> The more shamefull rekenynge
> Of hym should men report,
> In ernest and in sport.

(31–4)

His detractors showed simply that they were not good
Englishmen, that they did not truly love their kind. They were
hollow-hearted folk.

> He skantly loueth our kynge,
> That grudgeth at this thing:
> That cast such ouerthwartes
> Percase haue hollow hartes.

(35–8)

And he ended with one of those emotional utterances which,
at the height of his intransigence, suddenly reveal his candour:

> If I speak the truth, why do you not believe me?

It was not the first time that he had tenaciously pursued the
memory of his enemies with vindictiveness and mockery. But
never more clearly than during that campaign had he given
voice to a mind for which death itself was no barrier against
cheap wit and vile abuse. Henry VIII and the King of Aragon
had regarded the infliction of ecclesiastical censures principally
as means of coercion and propaganda. Leo X and even Julius II
had always been ready to take account of James IV's good will
towards the Holy See. But Skelton was determined to confuse
in a single surge of blind sincerity his chauvinistic and anti-
Scots passion and his propensity to rejoice over the rigour of
expiatory chastisement. His attitude, in short, was that of an
extremist, both in politics and in religion, according to the
Hebrew spirit of the Old Testament.

The French war ended abruptly after exhausting the treasure

so laboriously accumulated by Henry VII. With the return of peace, life resumed its normal course among the King's entourage, and Skelton promptly went back to old pre-war habits, older even than his sojourn at Diss. He resumed without difficulty his role as watchdog, upon which he had always prided himself in his relations with the Sovereign.

The variety of his work during the next three years, from about 1514 to 1517, is very different from the uniformity of interest apparent in his wartime invectives.

To this period we may assign the *Poems against Garnesche* which are, so to speak, invectives of peacetime, transitional poems whose belligerence derives once again from Calliope but whose subject refers to a domestic quarrel which, on the morrow of hostilities,[39] broke out in the King's palace between Skelton and Garnesche, two veterans of the French campaign.

Christopher Garnesche was gentleman-usher to Henry VIII. He was also one of his boon companions at the card-table and in masquerades. Loaded by the Sovereign with gifts both in money and in kind, he had received several manors in Norfolk, Suffolk, Sussex and Shropshire. He had naturally followed his master to the war, and had been knighted after high mass in Tournai cathedral on 25th September 1513, the day upon which the victorious troops had entered that city. Since his return he had lived at Greenwich, not far from the palace where Skelton had once supervised the princes' education.[40] It was there, probably, that there occurred the petty quarrel which, at Henry VIII's suggestion, was to be settled by one of those literary duels, imitated from the Scottish 'flytyngs'[41] in which the adversaries exchanged broadsides of abuse.

The antagonism between the two men was not of recent date. It may perhaps have originated during the late military campaign, or perhaps it dated back to a still more remote period. Garnesche was a native of Suffolk; his maternal grandfather was mayor of Norwich, and certain derogatory allusions to a time when, as a kitchen-boy in Lady Brewse's establishment,[42] he 'sluffered up sowse',[43] take us back to East Anglian persons and places familiar to the author of *Phyllyp Sparowe*.

In this oratorical joust Garnesche acts as challenger, Skelton as defender. As in his wrangles with the Comely Coystrown,

Skelton declares that he has been provoked and called a knave by the King's usher. The insult appeared to him so outrageous, so unsuited to his dignity as laureate, that he has no fear in throwing it back at its author by taking as refrain some stanzas in *rimes royales* which constitute the first stage of the flytyng.

> . . . What auctoryte ye have
> In your chalenge, Syr Chystyn, to cale me knave?
>
> (6–7)

He is almost glad to be dealing with an adversary who lends himself so well to caricature as does Christopher Garnesche: a big ungainly fellow, with powerful torso set up on straight spindly legs, his swarthy face topped with sparse black hair, his profile like that of a bird of prey, with round eyes like agates protruding from a brightly coloured doublet; a drawing-room braggart, boastful and vain, *miles gloriosus* of amorous and irascible temper, rebuffed by the weaker sex.

Upon this unflattering portrait the poet constructs an ingenious system of attack, based on analogy. It consists in comparing this tawny giant, 'Sir Chestnut' (Chystyn), to the most unattractive figures of history and legend, beginning with the Saracens, enemies of Christianity, and continuing with the wicked men of the Bible and the sworn foes of his country, French and Scottish. It is not the first time we find the poet discrediting his personal adversaries by representing them as enemies of the human race. Nor does he neglect the resources of animal symbolism, likening Garnesche to beasts and birds of prey.

A second series of stanzas in *rimes royales* opposes Garnesche's reply (now lost) with new variations on the same themes and according to the same methods, but in a more lofty tone. The poet-laureate, who had affected until then a haughty and contemptuous detachment, begins to lose patience. His comparisons become more offensive; birds of prey, chosen for their striking physical resemblance, give place to swine and vermin, chosen for their denunciatory value. To the images of braggarts drawn from the romances of chivalry there is added a biblical allusion to the Gabaonites (famous for having betrayed Joshua), which throws a cruel doubt upon Garnesche's loyalty to the

King. Menaces also appear, with spiteful predictions: 'Beware of checkmate!'—the very words in which the poet had prophesied the King of Scotland's downfall. The conflict grows more envenomed, and at the same time more extensive. This second piece introduces into the lists a new character at Garnesche's side: 'Greasy, Gorbellied Godfrey'. There has been much discussion as to this man's identity. It has been discovered that at about the same time Barclay took to task a certain Godfrey Gormand,

> Godfrey Gormand lately did me blame
> And as for him selfe, though he be gay and stoute,
> He hath nought but foly within and eke without,

a figure who fits quite well the description of *Gorbellied* Godfrey and who may have been a sort of professional pamphleteer.[44] Some have likewise noted the resemblance of names between Gorbellied Godfrey and Godfrey Gobelive, the dwarf in the *Pastime and Pleasure*, companion of Sir Grand Amour. And it has even been suggested that Godfrey was Stephen Hawes himself, as if Stephen had deliberately chosen as his pen-name that of the most unattractive character in his works.[45]

It is possible that Godfrey really existed and that he was the professional pamphleteer who had attacked Barclay. It is possible that Skelton perceived the artistic value to be derived from the name Godfrey by suggesting the contrast of a fool and a giant comparable to Godfrey Gobelive and Grand Amour. It is possible, on the other hand, that Skelton's Godfrey never existed at all, except as a poetic fiction in accordance with the current usage of the flytyng. Thus, in the quarrel between Marot and Sagon, the protagonists introduced their respective men-servants. Marot allows Frippelippe to speak for him, and Sagon does the same with his page Matthieu de Bontigny, both purely fictitious characters. 'There was no more a page involved in the affair than there was such a person as Frippelippe; it was simply that under those borrowed names the two adversaries found it easier to hurl the vilest insults at one another's head.'[46]

The third and fourth rounds mark a new phase of the combat.

The poet discards the too ponderous pattern of stanzas in *rimes royales* and makes use of distichs in *rimes plates*, short and supple lines which his pen turns into the yet shorter and more supple lines now known as Skeltonics. Henceforward the flytyng proceeds on the ground of personal argument. The two adversaries dig up each other's past and fling mud in each other's face.

Satire becomes invective

> Thou tode, thow scorpyone,
> Thow bawdy babyone,
> Thow bere, thow brystlyd bore,
> Thou Moryshe mantycore,
> Thou rammysche stynkyng gote,
> Thou fowle chorlysche parote,
> Thou gresly gargone glaymy,
> Thou swety slouen seymy,
> Thou murrionn, thow mawment,
> Thou fals stynkyng serpent,
> Thou mokkyshe marmoset,
> I wyll nat dy in thy det . . .

(III, 162–73)

There indeed Skelton displays astonishing imagination, a wealth of words worthy of Rabelais. But much of the artistic savour of the initial diatribes has vanished beneath the overwhelming torrent of insult and personalities.

What emerges above all from these invectives is the fact that the two adversaries were struggling in the last resort for the King's confidence—a sensitive point with the laureate, whose jealous and pretentious nature was most unwilling to share it.

A short satire *Against Dundas*,[47] a Scot who had revived the old joke about Englishmen having tails and had drawn upon himself a withering but coarse reply from Skelton, shows analogies of form and expression both with the diatribes against Garnesche and with the invectives against the Scots. Written, as usual, in Latin and in English, it is of the same type and doubtless of the same period, though not of the same quality, as the preceding.

CHAPTER V

Magnificence

A Moral Interlude

THE DIATRIBES against Garnesche had resulted from trivial circumstances, a momentary altercation which had degenerated into poetical exercises in which buffoonery found no less prominent a place than the spirit of satire. It all led virtually nowhere.

Subsequent works, on the contrary, from the year 1516 onwards, mark a turning point in the laureate's career. For while continuing to shelter beneath the signature 'Orator Regius', they inaugurated his first clashes with Cardinal Wolsey.

In 1516 the former royal almoner, who in 1513 had distinguished himself by organizing the campaign in Picardy, had just completed his spectacular rise to power. Within a space of two years, and in quick succession, he had been promoted Bishop of Lincoln, Archbishop of York, Cardinal, and Chancellor of the realm. The infant prodigy, who had graduated at the age of fifteen, had managed, when hardly forty, to concentrate in his own hands the greatest measure of power imaginable at a time when the office of prime minister was as yet unknown. He needed only to be appointed legate *a latere* of the Pope in order to obtain authority over the Archbishop of Canterbury himself.

Great determination and an enormous capacity for work, combined with a dauntless enthusiasm for administration, had enabled him to win the confidence of a youthful king who appeared, anyway at first, to prefer the pleasures and splendour of government rather than its responsibilities.

So while the Court abandoned itself to a carefree life of brilliant festivities and masques, altogether different from the cross-grained parsimony of the preceding reign, King Henry VIII's factotum, faithful to the methods of his former master Henry VII, ensured the continuity of the Tudor despotism.

In 1516 his grand designs—complete remodelling of the royal administration,[1] reform of the ecclesiastical establishment [2] and an ambition to make England arbiter of European affairs—were still obscure. They revealed themselves only when put to the test or in the light of projects not all of which he had time to carry out in full. It could, however, already be seen that, with regard to the nobility, he had decided to adopt a policy similar to that of Henry VII, who, in order to strengthen the central power, had never missed an opportunity to clip the wings of his great vassals. But what the nobles, weakened by the Wars of the Roses and the sudden changing of regime, had been willing to endure from a reigning monarch, they were hardly prepared to accept without flinching from an upstart. The result was a secret war, a war of attrition, in which Wolsey won most of the points until one day a quick turn of Fortune's wheel brought about his fall.

The struggle was particularly fierce in the King's Council. Thomas Howard the elder, who had withdrawn from Court in September 1512, repeated his gesture in 1516, from weariness as well as by way of protest against the sumptuary laws of Henry VIII and the Chancellor.[3] His son Thomas had married as his second wife Elizabeth, elder daughter of the Duke of Buckingham and of Lady Elinor Percy, daughter of the Earl of Northumberland; and in 1513 that alliance between the Howards, the Staffords and the Percies had helped to strengthen the opposition to Wolsey. But Wolsey, now Archbishop of York, found himself in a position to control from near at hand the acts and gestures of the Percies in their own domain.[4] As for the Earl of Surrey, he was very soon at loggerheads with the Cardinal. We learn that on 31st May 1516 'the Lord Marquis, the Earl of Surrey and Lord Abergavenny were excluded from the Council Chamber'.[5]

Thus in 1516, anxious to assert his recently acquired authority, Wolsey began to put more and more pressure on the nobility. In particular, he took advantage of the historic meeting between Henry VIII and his sister Margaret of Scotland, at Tottenham on Saturday 4th May, to accuse certain noblemen of having violated the regulations limiting the number of servants in livery. A letter of 8th June, addressed by

Thomas Allen to his master Lord Shrewsbury, gives us the details of this affair:

'The King's solicitor told me that the Lord Marquis, the Lord Hastings, Sir Richard Sacheverel, Lord Abergavenny and Sir Edward Guilford, by information put into the King's Bench, are like to be in great danger, for retaining of servants. At the reverence of God, my lord, take heed to it; for Bulkley, which is commander to the Fleet, at his first coming (unto such time as some of . . . spied it, and gave him warning of the same) ware your badge upon [him]. There is great trouble between the Marquis, Lord Hastings and Sir Richard Sacheverell. Both parties are bound to appear in Star Chamber, and, as they say, will be bound to be of good bearing. Hastings and Sacheverell are examined, because they had so many men in livery at the meeting of the Scotch Queen. Heard the Cardinal command them to bring in every man's name who was with them in livery at that time. I hear some things which are not to be written. Coldharbour, 8 June.' [6]

These stories about liveries, intimidation, spies and strange rumours are echoed in Skelton's poem *Against Venomous Tongues with sclaunder and false detractions*,[7] where the meeting at Tottenham is evidently referred to in the line:

What tidings of Totnam, what newis in Wales.

(9, p. 135)

It is a curious, irregular poem, comparable to a series of chromatic variations on the theme of calumny, with a Latin gloss inspired by the Psalms and some ancient authors. Certain informers have reported that Skelton wished to 'control' the emblems of certain noble lords, and a widespread rumour credits him with the authorship of an anonymous pamphlet. One choleric individual 'of vertibilite, and of frenetyke folabilite, and of melancoly mutabilite', is threatening to prevent him from writing, although the fellow himself invariably parades with lackeys wearing on breast and back emblazoned and interlaced roman letters that make them look like walking alphabets.[8]

Dimly, through his veiled sarcasms, we discern our poet accused of upholding the cause of the aristocrats in defiance of the Cardinal's hostility. Hence the poem's two different notes: vehement refutation of the dangerous calumnies that have sought to defame him and, in spite of all, robust irony springing from the absurd contrast between Wolsey's ostentation and the restrictions he imposed so severely on all but himself. In this respect the poem *Against Venomous Tongues* foreshadows the raillery of *Speke Parrot*.

But it likewise heralds, in a Latin postscript, a work nearer at hand, 'a holy work, praiseworthy, acceptable and memorable',[9] a phrase that must surely be understood as referring to the morality *Magnificence* because the subject appears to be sketched in the following lines:

> Such tunges, vnhappy hath made great diuision
> In realmes, in cities, by suche fals abusion
> Of fals fickil tunges suche cloked collusion
> Hath brought nobil princes to extreme confusion...

> (p. 134, 22–5)

There we see dawning, as it were, the outline of the Court vices called in *Magnificence* 'Courtly Abusion' and 'Cloked Collusion', as well as the idea of the prince's fall which forms its central theme.

Now that idea, which is related to the concept of the *De Casibus* so familiar to the Middle Ages, had just been illustrated, in spectacular fashion and at about the same fateful date (Ascension Day, 1516) upon which the meeting at Tottenham occurred, by the personal misfortune of Skelton's old friend Percy, Earl of Northumberland, called 'the Magnificent', who had incurred Wolsey's displeasure and been sent to the Fleet, where he remained for nearly a month. On Tuesday 15th May he was again received in private audience by the King.[10] According to Holinshed, Wolsey had the consummate artfulness to claim credit for his release.[11]

Here, beyond any doubt, material for a literary work lay ready to the hand of a poet-laureate convinced of the importance of his poetic and moral activity. But since at that date Skelton had not begun openly to defy Wolsey, he could not as yet tread the paths of satire. The morality play, however, favoured his purpose. With its strict conventions, its traditional allegories and its associations with sacred art, it afforded both the intended dignity and the needful security, provided that the various factors borrowed from real life underwent a thorough thematic and formal transfiguration. In this respect, it can be said of *Magnificence* that the necessity of veiling the satire combined with the needs of poetic transfiguration to preside over the elaboration of a work that was, in the poet's own words, both 'acceptable' and 'memorable'.

The traditional theme of the morality—a struggle between Virtues and Vices for the destiny of Mankind—thus became, by a bold and none the less simple transposition, a struggle between good and evil influences for the conscience of the hero, Magnificence, or rather, of the Sovereign, upon whom depends the ultimate happiness or unhappiness of the Realm, that is to say, in theological terms, its salvation or damnation. The plot properly so called is intended to illustrate in striking and picturesque manner the lesson of a logical and inexorable chain of events, namely that the exile of Measure leaves the field free to Folly and Fancy, grotesque buffoons who strive to introduce the Court Vices. Disguised as Virtues (in accordance with the hypocrisy of courts) these last ensnare the prince's good faith and bring about his fall. He is ultimately saved only by the intervention of divine grace.

The composition is commendable for the almost classical regularity of its proportions. At a time when division into acts and scenes was still something quite unknown,[12] Skelton's *Magnificence* is found to divide naturally into five phases of an entirely logical process, which reveals not so much the early influence of Terence (though that is not to be completely excluded) as a framework already peculiar to the morality. Originally, it seems that the morality set itself the ambitious but hardly dramatic task of retracing the story of the human soul, from a man's birth to the hour of his judgment, just as the mysteries retraced the story of the world from the Creation to the Redemption. (This purpose is apparent at least in the archetype of the category, *The Castle of Perseverance*.) Next, it felt urged to simplify its themes and its plot, thus gaining in dramatic abridgment what was lost in epic dimensions, in order to concentrate upon the representation of a symbolical crisis, susceptible indeed of variation but always reducible to the five fundamental phases: 1. Innocence; 2. Temptation; 3. Fall; 4. Repentance; 5. Redemption.

It is this traditional composition that reappears in *Magnificence*, adapted to the court morality but still constituting five phases or parts: I. Prosperity; II. Conspiracy; III. Error; IV. Chastisement; V. Restoration.

The characters are divided into two camps: the forces of Good and the forces of Evil contending for the fate of the central figure, Prince Magnificence, who here takes the place of *Humanum Genus* or Mankind. Another personage occupies a middle position together with the Prince—Liberty, a vice or virtue as the case may be:

> For I am a vertu yf I be well vsed,
> And I am a vyce when I am abused.

> (2101–2)

The Virtues and the Vices are balanced in pairs (allowing for dimidiation in the case of Felicity, a unique character who actually represents two concepts, that of happiness and that of wealth). Thus Felicity-Wealth is opposed to Adversity-Poverty; Measure-Circumspection to Fancy-Folly; Goodhope-Redress to Despair-Mischief. There remain two rather important exceptions: the group of four Court vices, without counterpart in the balance of human and divine affairs, and consequently justifying the poet-laureate's personal conduct in regard to the Sovereign; and Perseverance, a gift of God, the Christian quality *par excellence*, which, all things being equal, ensures the final victory of Good. Hence this table showing the distribution of the roles in *Magnificence*:

MAGNIFICENCE

LIBERTY

Felicity-Wealth	{ Adversity { Poverty
Measure	Fancy
Circumspection	Folly
	(Counterfeit Countenance { Crafty Conveyance { Cloaked Collusion (Courtly Abusion
Goodhope	Despair
Redress	Mischief
Perseverance	

Reduced to its logical data, Skelton's play manifests a scholastic bias fully justifying the form of the debate which it adopts at the outset. It is not only a piece intended to illustrate in striking fashion the fall of a prince, after the manner of a medieval *exemplum*; it is, in the full sense of the word, a morality, intended to prove the falsity of a logical argument, to demonstrate by A+B that the spirit of liberty should be subordinate to the spirit of measure, and not the spirit of measure to the whims of imagination.

I. PROSPERITY. The play begins with a storm of aphorisms on the relations of reason and wealth, of wealth and wisdom, of wisdom and destiny, which serve as a kind of prologue to the drama and introduction to a short but lively debate between Felicity and Liberty on the question as to whether the spirit of Liberty should tolerate the chain of continence, or should be free of every impediment in accordance with the very meaning of his name.

Enter Master Measure, a counsellor of State who, recalling Horace, shows with much learning that the spirit of Measure is equally necessary to Wealth and to Liberty. Those are the indis-

pensable conditions of good government, which Liberty sums up
as follows:

> There is no prynce but he hath nede of vs thre,
> Welthe, with Measure, and plesaunt Lyberte.

$$(161-2)$$

At this opportune moment, Prince Magnificence arrives to
take part in the debate. He declares his indefectible attachment
to Measure, going so far as to promise that he will never be
separated from this counsellor whom he appoints 'chief ruler'
(line 204).

Encouraged by so much virtue, Measure describes his happy
fellowship with Liberty and Wealth on the one hand, and with
Nobility on the other, as 'this chain of love with links so strong
that no flatterer, no scoundrel will be able to dissolve it'.
(202–3)

Liberty, however, takes the first opportunity to dangle before
the eyes of the young prince the pleasures of unbridled sensuality, a move at once suppressed by Measure, with the
approval of Felicity. Magnificence realizes the danger of the
suggestion and bids Measure 'take Liberty with you and rule
him after the rule of your school'. There lies the secret of perfect
equilibrium; for one brief moment there is absolute harmony.
Then, Fancy bursts upon the scene, sweeps aside all that has
been said and rudely opposes the decision of the prince. Fancy
is a giddy young fellow posing as Largess, a person of good birth
who favours Wealth, upholds Religion (he buys pardons by the
gross) and increases Fame, in fact (thinks Felicity, touched on
a sensitive point by the mention of gain) a very suitable companion for the prince. But the latter does not agree: he will not
forgive Fancy's insulting arrogance and unseemly language.
However, just as he is preparing to dismiss him, Fancy-Largess,
by one of those sudden reversals so characteristic of his ways,
produces a letter of recommendation signed by Circumspection,
a man high in the prince's esteem and a colleague of Measure,
who is at present on a journey. The prince then starts to take a
better view of Fancy, never for a moment suspecting that the
letter is a forgery, though a trivial incident comes very near to

rousing suspicion. Noticing the repeated calls of a mysterious personage, Counterfeit Countenance, who from a distance is trying to attract Fancy's attention, he asks:

'Did I not hear someone call "Fancy, Fancy"?'

'No, no,' Fancy quickly replies, 'it must have been someone in the street calling a Fleming: "Hansy, Hansy".'

Then, changing the subject, Fancy explains to the prince that he has just returned from Pontoise, whence his letter is dated, and that he received some very rough treatment at the frontier, where he would still be had he not greased the palms of his tormentors. For Largess, he remarks, opens every door.

'But Largess is not suitable for everyone,' the prince objects, rather shocked by this behaviour.

'Far from it,' replies Fancy. 'Largess is the mark of nobility. Measure is a bourgeois quality. But Largess befits the royal state.'

Charmed by this flattery, the prince at length becomes friendly towards the young page and takes him into the palace.

II. CONSPIRACY. After an interval devoted to Counterfeit Countenance's confession, a monologue that was probably sung, Fancy returns to the palace in lively conversation with a new acolyte, Crafty Conveyance, a sort of medieval Mercury dressed as a postillion, who immediately recognizes Counterfeit Countenance as a very old friend. Fancy has obtained lodgings at Court, where he will have room for his associates. The conspiracy has made an excellent start, thanks to the letter from Pontoise, which, we learn, was indeed a counterfeit skilfully devised by Counterfeit Countenance. The gang—for they are in fact a gang of swindlers—decide to adopt false names under which to operate at Court. Fancy has already passed himself off as Largess; Crafty Conveyance will call himself Sure Surveyance. The three colleagues plot to get rid of Measure, 'who reigns over everyone like an eczema spreading over a man's face'. Their comments are interrupted by the arrival of a fourth rogue, Cloaked Collusion, the brains of the gang, affecting the most lofty airs and draped in his mantle. He is not a man to waste time in chat, but comes straight to the point. What is their aim? To bring off a masterly 'scoop'. Magnificence has great wealth? Yes indeed, but he spends it with Measure, who has Liberty under his thumb. First of all, then, they must liberate Liberty. After that, the dismissal of Measure will follow for certain. The whole gang decides to go and live at Court. Fancy and Crafty Conveyance have already assumed false identities. Counterfeit Countenance will now call himself Good Demeanance; Cloaked Collusion will be known as Sober Sadness. 'Here begynneth the game' (192).

Enter yet another character, Courtly Abusion, the dandy who makes such an impression that Cloaked Collusion starts addressing him in French, only to be answered in pure cockney:

> Decke your lofte and couer a lovce.
>
> (759)

He is a good candidate for membership of the gang, having already made his way at Court, thanks to his worldly ways. So he too is enrolled in the conspiracy. Meanwhile, Fancy rushes back and directs Courtly Abusion to the palace, where the plot is slowly hatching and where he will find Crafty Conveyance waiting for him in the street. But this coxcomb too will need a false name; he will be known as Lusty Pleasure . . .

Fancy, left alone, then meets Folly, a professional buffoon who makes his entry like a clown, playing an instrument and waving his bauble .Fancy carries a hawk on his fist, Folly is followed by a mangy cur. A dialogue ensues:

'Is that an owl or a kite?' asks Folly. 'What a big head she has.'

'Can't you see,' replies Fancy. 'It's a French butterfly.'

'Ah! I see,' answers Folly; 'but she's a great deal smaller than those in our country!'

Fancy then observes that Folly's dog seems very mangy.

'My dog mangy?' echoes Folly. 'Ah! yes, I sold his coat to Mackmurr as a lambskin.' (1059–70.)

The two jolly fellows eventually decide to exchange pets: 'I'll take your poultry and you take my cattle,' says Folly. Then they amuse themselves recalling snippets of Latin and composing macaronic verses in memory of their schooldays. Meanwhile, Crafty Conveyance overhears enough to realize Folly's hidden talents. It is true that he possesses a remarkable gift of repartee; that he knows how to enflame men's imagination and inspire them with lascivious cravings. He could make a very useful member of the conspiracy. Folly is enrolled under the name Conceit, but, he insists, upon the sole condition that he be employed at Court in some job connected with brewing, 'for he hathe a full dry soule' (1337). That can be easily arranged; once Measure is gone, it will not be difficult to make the purse strings jingle.

III. ERROR. This third act is the act of error, which corresponds to the episode of Life-in-Sin in the traditional moralities. The prince is now disposed to withdraw Liberty from the control of Measure, despite the repeated objections of Felicity who knows well what awaits him if Liberty becomes Licence. But Magnificence has made up his mind: Felicity himself will now be under the thumb of Liberty and Largess. A formal contract will clarify the prerogatives of each partner in the new association. Magnificence is delighted with this new arrangement:

> For nowe, Syrs, I am lyke as a prynce sholde be;
> I have welth at wyll, largesse and lyberte.

> (1475-6)

His monologue is typical of the pride that precedes a fall. Henceforward he speaks as a spoilt king. Unawares, he is already moving towards the abyss.

Courtly Abusion-Lusty Pleasure helps to drive him deeper into sin, firing his concupiscence with the description of an ideal mistress, a young lass whose favours he will easily be able to buy. There follows a scene worthy of *Volpone*, in which Courtly Abusion introduces the prince to seduction by means of utterly cynical advice, a true devil's breviary which finds an all too ready response in that perverted soul:

> Thy wordes and my mynde odly well accorde.

> (1624)

'Follow your inclinations,' continues the Tempter; 'let your desires have the force of law':

> Let your lust and lykynge stande for a law.

> (1628)

'And when someone importunes you, say you're not feeling well and pretend you're on the point of vomiting. There's nothing like it for getting rid of undesirables.'

These perfidies rouse the monarch's brutality so successfully that he now recalls having had more than one offender flogged for mere enjoyment.

Soon afterwards Cloaked Collusion comes to plead hypocritically on behalf of Measure, whom he has in fact determined to ruin. But the words he whispers in the prince's ear concern the payment of a certain annual rent he has extorted from Measure. When Measure tries to argue in his own defence, the monarch feigns indisposition. He accuses Measure as the cause of his feeling unwell and dismisses him roughly without more formality.

'Now Measure is gone,' sighs Magnificence, 'I feel much better.'

'True,' echoes Cloaked Collusion, 'there's no pleasure to be had when the stomach is compressed' (1765).

Cloaked Collusion now achieves his purpose. He obtains from the prince the guardianship of his purse. He has, moreover, some excellent economic principles. 'It is easier,' he urges, 'to satisfy three persons than a whole crowd. So confiscate the fortune of a hundred rich men and distribute it among three good friends' (1798). The prince, completely suborned, yields to this argument. He delivers Largess and Liberty into the charge of Cloaked Collusion, Courtly Abusion and Crafty Conveyance.

Magnificence, free from all financial cares, thinks of taking a mistress. His interest in the rubbish talked by Folly shows the depth of depravity to which his mind has fallen. It is the very symbol of a topsy-turvy world in which 'the hounds run before and the hare behind' (1847). At this exact psychological moment, when the prince's mind seems to touch the nadir of baseness, Fancy rushes in to announce that the swindlers have made off with the treasure. Fancy in turn vanishes on the appearance of Adversity.

IV. CHASTISEMENT. The prince, trembling with fright, is beaten to the ground and despoiled of his goods and raiment. Adversity reads the lesson of his fall. It is an apocalyptic vision,

full of sickness, abscesses, sores, torments, suicides, endless
calamities heaped upon the innocent to try their patience; of
incurable evils attacking children in order to punish their
fathers, or striking the fathers to punish their children. Adversity is God's monitor, the great Master's deputy, brandishing
the rods of chastisement. By him the prince is delivered into the
hands of Poverty ('He dined with Delight, with Poverty he
must sup'), a filthy old man, the colour of dried grass, covered
with running sores, riddled with aches and pains, crippled with
sciatica and greeted at every door with the barking of dogs.

Poverty proceeds to lift up Magnificence, who is now a pitiful
sight. He, Fortune's darling who believed himself forever secure
against want, the spoilt child of yesterday, used to sleeping on a
featherbed and to feeding on egg-flip, is the victim of cold and
nakedness. He would rather be dead than endure such misery.
Step by step, Poverty endeavours to lead back this errant soul
to the paths of contrition. He speaks to him of God, reminds him
of the example of Christ who suffered far more in order to atone
for the sins of men, although He was innocent. The prince
begins to recognize the folly of his past conduct.

Liberty then reappears and, regardless of the prince's
presence, sings a very gay love song, an indication of the
shamelessness to which he has fallen since the dismissal of
Measure. He finishes by recognizing the prince in beggar's rags.
Following Liberty, the four scoundrels come to parade their
insolent delight, their admission of barefaced robbery, their
cruel laughter—and their quarrels too. They in turn recognize
the prince and load him with sarcasm and coarse merriment.

And now Magnificence, bowed down beneath the insults of
the wicked, is visited by Despair, that evil genius who comes
upon the scene in moments of great distress, to burden the heart,
to close the eyes, to extinguish the torch of fervent Charity, to
oust Faith and Hope, and to present confidence in God's grace
as the ultimate absurdity. Despair overwhelms Magnificence,
drives away his thoughts of repentance, persuades him that he
cannot be saved, confirms his distress and implants in his mind
the idea of suicide. Despair is followed by his acolyte Mischief,
the executor of dire deeds, whose business here is to help the
prince take the fatal step. He offers him a rope with which to

hang himself, or, if he prefers, a gleaming dagger. Just as the prince is about to seize the dagger, Mischief's hand is disarmed by the intervention of Goodhope. The demons, frustrated of their prey, disappear in a cloud of sulphur. 'Hell burneth' (2352).

v. RESTORATION. The prince, on the brink of eternal damnation, has been saved. Goodhope utters words so gentle that they soothe his hardened heart better than all the unguents of Arabia. He is the spiritual apothecary whose duty is to present the prince with the rhubarb of Repentance, seasoned with a few drops of Devotion, together with the pastilles that restore gaiety to the heart and mind.

Goodhope's colleague, Redress, comes in turn to administer his remedies. He is the soul's physician, the confessor who leads the sick man to convalescence. When Magnificence has recovered the state of grace, Redress gives him back his princely garments and summons Circumspection, the good counsellor whose absence had been at the root of the whole tragedy. Circumspection helps to elucidate the mystery of the letter of recommendation used by Fancy. The prince, learning it to have been a forgery, has no more reason to doubt that he was the victim of an evil gang of wicked courtiers. Finally, Perseverance offers to vouch for the healing of the prince who is now restored to power and prosperity. He is there in order to prepare him for salvation by reminding him of the shortness and the vanity of life.

The overall dramatic action of *Magnificence* is thus seen as a movement of descent towards the abyss, followed by a movement of ascent towards the light. In detail, those two movements are cleverly graduated by numerous intermediate stages the effect of which is to render both more plausible and more exemplary the extent of the fall and the merits of the redemption.

Thus, for example, in the first act, before starting to bend towards evil, the curve of the play rises in the opposite direction towards a peak of virtue and well-being which is reached when the debate establishes the ideal relations between Felicity, Measure and Liberty, and when, in addition, it is learned that the prince has just promoted Measure to the office of prime minister. Likewise, Act IV marks a gradual sinking into distress, a sort of Calvary in reverse, which leads the prince from material ruin to the brink of suicide and damnation. This fourth act is particularly interesting as a zone of conflict where the consequences of evil continue to unfold inexorably although the prince is already, though unconsciously, on the road of rehabilitation, thanks to the saving grace that springs from suffering and chastisement. It is the metaphysical act *par excellence*, in which the combat around the prince becomes nothing less than a duel between the Devil and God.

To this general design of the drama there corresponds an internal structure which reveals the interlocking of a twofold mechanism. On the one hand we have the mechanism of imposture, which highlights the treacherous perfidy of Court vices, and tends thereby to diminish the prince's moral responsibility. First, the chance absence of Circumspection, leaving Measure deprived of his normal safeguard, favours the initiative of Fancy, who poses as his corresponding virtue, Largess, and deceives the prince's good faith by showing him a forgery (the height of cunning consisting precisely in attributing this forged letter to Circumspection, the most suspicious of all counsellors). Second, Fancy, once established at Court, introduces into the royal palace, disguised as virtues, those vices who ultimately secure the freeing of Liberty and then, as a consequence, the dismissal of Measure and the luring of the prince to extravagant projects which bring about his ruin. On the other hand we have the mechanism of temptation, which highlights the prince's weak points, and tends to emphasize his moral responsibility by keeping the drama in the atmosphere of religious spirituality characteristic of a morality. Thus he allows himself to be beguiled by the flatteries of Fancy, who skilfully plays upon his sense of class distinction (measure is a bourgeois, largess an aristocratic virtue); he yields to the lustful temptations awakened in him by Courtly Abusion; he allows Liberty to be withdrawn from the control of Measure; he permits the exile of Measure, libelled by Cloaked Collusion; he yields to the sophisms of political economy expounded by the latter. In a word, the prince's fall, both material and spiritual, is brought about inevitably by the perfidy of the Court vices combined with the culpable imprudence of the prince deprived of Circumspection. To this twofold mechanism of the fall there corresponds the twofold mechanism of final damnation or final salvation, representative of the Devil and of God.

Hence the dramatic and at the same time necessary character of the two great surprises, the two great theatrical strokes which counterbalance that determinism, one relating to the prince's fall (when Fancy tells him he is ruined, at the end of the third act), the other relating to his salvation (when Goodhope disarms the hand of Mischief in the nick of time, at the end of the fourth act). The first is in fact no more than the visible result of a long series of errors; the second, the miraculous result of a long expiation.

The characters do not really exist except by virtue of the parts they play in this moral demonstration. Their physical nature is determined largely by their symbolic nature; ideas are treated here with an altogether medieval (and Aristotelian) attention to the nuances and secondary senses gravitating around the first and principal notion. It cannot, however, be said that the *dramatis personae* of *Magnificence* are mere abstractions. They are concepts embodied in human types borrowed from the society of that time and affording a glimpse of how the comedy of humours developed from the morality. It may be that through the accident of too emphatically satiric a trait, or of too evocative a model, these waxen figures recalled for a moment some well-known portrait, but the author would have been the first to deny having intended any resemblance to one or other of his contemporaries.

The central character, Magnificence, who gives his name to the play, is a princely and even royal figure. About that there can be no doubt whatever. He is 'a noble prince of might' (1681), 'prince royall' (175). He lives in a royal palace: 'Home to your paleys with ioy and royalte' (2591). He is called 'your grace', a title applied in those days not only to bishops but also to the English sovereign. He is, moreover, a young and candid prince (here perhaps the author has in mind some earlier examples, *The Castle of Perseverance*, *World* and *Youth*), endowed with good principles but susceptible to bad ones. Surrounded with good counsellors he gives proof of virtues and sound sense, but left to himself he yields to temptation. As soon as evil gets a grip on him, he is no longer the same: the pure gold turns into base lead. Step by step he shows himself imprudent, boastful and blustering. He speaks of governing fortune. He lulls himself into false security. He behaves imperiously. His orders are accompanied with thumps on the table:

> I dryue downe these dastardys with a dynt of my
>   fyste.
>
> (1504)

He is even brutal—

> What man is so maysyd with me that dare mete,
> I shall flappe hym as a fole to fall at my fete—
>
> (1524–5)

with the sadistic and alarming side of a sick man, subject to sudden indisposition. He is a spoilt child, used to pampering and dainty dishes, a coxcomb, accessible to the decadent charms of florid rhetoric (1547–8) and even more responsive to the solicitations of sensuality. He has the defects and vices of a Roman emperor, and is justly likened to Nero (1527).

Meanwhile, he continues pliant. He does not plunge headlong into sin until he finds himself separated from Measure and Circumspection. Once he has suffered the ordeal of pain and chastisement, and been reunited with his good counsellors, his good qualities will flourish again as in the past.

Those two counsellors, Measure and Circumspection, are indispensable and at the same time complementary. If Circumspection is absent, Measure is in danger. That indeed is the starting point of the play.

Measure is an attorney, prudent, cultured and sententious. He quotes Horace. He speaks in similes:

> Your language is lyke the penne
> Of hym that wryteth to fast.
>
> (91–2)

He has the quirks of his profession. When he talks he invites the approval of his hearers. He is rectitude itself, and gravity personified. Before serving as victim in the knavery of the *captatio*, he plays the part of a mere concept in the scholastic debate, along with the two necessarily more abstract characters, Liberty and Felicity.

Felicity, as we have seen, embodies the double notion of happiness and of prosperity, manifest signs of wisdom:

> Welth is of wysdome that very trewe probate.
>
> (4)

It is to Wealth, brother of Largess, that he feels attracted, although he places his trust in Measure and fears the excesses of Liberty, a sentiment which he voices in words of prophetic irony:

> Than waste must be welcome and fare well thryfte!
>
> (1461)

Those are his last words, for he does not reappear after Act III; the end of the play takes on a more specifically religious colouring.

Liberty is a young and very famous man, but timid as a hare. Mere trifles scare him, because, despite his youth, he had already experienced fetters, stocks and dungeons. He prefers to regard himself as above the reach of laws, for to live under laws is only another form of captivity. He does not like taking second place. He is loath to submit to the control of Measure and be put to school, like an Aliboron. Once freed from that tutelage, he is overjoyed. He talks volubly about his unbridled loves. He lives as he pleases, utterly carefree, a pupil let out of school, a goliard, who styles himself 'President of Princes' (2018).

After the characters of the academic debate, we turn to those of the imposture, the Court Vices, among whom the leading role belongs of right to Fancy. He is an impudent and insolent page, a busybody who moves to and fro between the utmost politeness and utmost rudeness, the depths of sadness and the heights of gaiety. Unstable, irresolute, harebrained, he acts and goes back upon what he has done, causes trouble and scribbles, tirelessly occupied with countless trivialities; he goes from one caprice to another, he dances to the point of intoxication; he is the image of buzzing and frivolous activity, who, with a mixture of pirouettes, flattery and indelicate behaviour, will open the door to the vices and lead the prince to perdition. His complement and antithesis, both physically and morally, is Folly. Fancy is dwarflike in stature, Folly is as tall as a giant. Fancy is lively and inconstant as quicksilver, Folly is placid and phlegmatic. But they are of the same stamp as well as of the same age; brothers in unreason, they recall having been at school together. Some have justifiably seen in them the characteristics of two court fools, Fancy the natural fool, Folly the professional fool, the buffoon by trade, who flaunts the attributes of his employment—cap and bells, rattle and mangy dog. Folly pours forth a continuous stream of drollery. He exploits an inexhaustible source of comedy by affecting a touch of deafness, which makes for misunderstanding. He respects neither God nor Law, his wit is corrosive. He excels at misleading others, driving them to theft, corruption, luxury. Fancy lures his victims, and Folly destroys them. Both enjoy close relations with the four Court vices, Counterfeit Countenance, Crafty Conveyance, Cloaked Collusion and Courtly Abusion.

The enigmatic and extravagant quartet certainly constitutes one of Skelton's most original creations in *Magnificence*. It expresses the obsession with conspiracy common to the poet and to the English sovereigns in the first decades of the Tudor dynasty. Clearly formulated in the *Elegy on the Death of the Earl of Northumberland* (1488), denouncing the 'vilane hastarddis'—

> Fulfylled with malice of froward entente,
> Confetered togeder of common concente—

(24–6)

and resumed under a mysterious and semi-dramatic guise in the picture of the seven scoundrels in the *Bowge of Court* (1499), it is in *Magnificence* that it attains its full development.

It has been regretted that these four personages, so closely linked by the alliteration of their names, are in practice hard to distinguish from one another. Nevertheless, they denote differences of function and character certainly more marked than between, say, Rosencrantz and Guildenstern, each being depicted for us not only by his conduct in the play but also in a monologue-programme which fixes his portrait still more clearly.

Counterfeit Countenance is the great simulator, the specialist in forgeries of every kind; he is the supreme hypocrite, the Tartuffe, the masked man who poses as what he is not. Crafty Conveyance is the quartermaster of the gang, the recruiting sergeant, the talent-spotter, who discerns the cleverness of Folly and enrols him in the conspiracy. He makes claims to command—

> In fayth, I rule muche of the rost—
>
> (813)

and thereby confronts an extremely dangerous rival in Cloaked Collusion.

Cloaked Collusion is, indeed, the superior intelligence, disdainful, abrupt, wrapped in his voluminous black cloak. He is the brain, the persuasive speaker with forked tongue, who delights in doing evil. He is the businessman who can embroil his clients and ruin them even while he pretends to help them. As financial adviser to the prince he makes him accept the worst sophisms.

Finally and somewhat apart, the fourth swindler, Courtly Abusion, represents the dandy, dressed in French fashions, corrupter of youth, who manages to impress the prince with his flowery rhetoric. He is a depraved cynic, brother of Riot in *The Bowge of Court*, who talks as a connoisseur of loose women and who recites in the presence of Magnificence a frightful catechism of evil.

Last of all come the characters of the religious morality, symbolic figures each representing a particular aspect of the general idea of chastisement or of salvation: Adversity, the instrument of divine retribution, appearing as a *prepositor*, rather like a school prefect whose duty is to keep order in the master's absence; Poverty, in the guise of an aged beggar, riddled with aches and pains; Despair and Mischief, like diabolical executioners, resolved to distort the meaning of divine chastisement in order to work against God; then, by way of contrast, Goodhope and Redress, figures reminiscent of Confession and Shrift in *The Castle of Perseverance*, one the apothecary and the other the physician of the soul, the confessor dispensing absolution. Finally, Perseverance, playing rather the part of spiritual director, of chaplain watching over the spiritual health of the prince and appointed to remind him of the brevity of life, the certainty of death and the vanity of human affairs.

Skelton, in fact, places the old morality within a new framework of Court life, surrounding the prince (Magnificence) with characters borrowed from various classes and categories of society: counsellors (Measure and Circumspection), a page (Fancy), a Court fool (Folly), a middle-class type (Felicity), a clerk (Liberty), a group of swindlers (the four Court vices), a monitor (Adversity), a beggar (Poverty), executioners (Despair, Mischief), an apothecary (Goodhope), a doctor (Redress) and a chaplain (Perseverance).

Magnificence, then, appears as a kind of medieval *exemplum* on the theme of a prince's fall, intended to serve both as a salutary warning to Henry VIII and as a thinly veiled satire against Wolsey. It showed the necessity of making a decisive choice between the spirit of moderation and extravagance, between wisdom and folly, a choice upon which depended nothing less than the happiness or misfortune of the prince, and consequently the prosperity or ruin of the kingdom. On the one side are the followers of reason and faith, the advocates of God; on the other, the followers of foolishness and evil, the Devil's advocates. That is why a play which starts from a problem concerned, so far as we can see, chiefly with moral conduct, rises eventually to the level of a drama of Christian virtue, in the traditional spirit of the moralities.

In approaching thus the general problem of Good and Evil under the particular aspect of Wealth and Poverty, Skelton was following a precedent. His morality *Magnificence* offers striking analogies with an earlier work, *Le Chemin de Povreté et de Richesse* or the *Livre du Chastel de Labour*, composed in 1342 by Jehan Bruyant of Paris, 'notaire du Roi au Chatelet',[13] of which

Pierre Gringore made use in 1499 under the title *Château de Labour*, a poem most probably known to Skelton, if not in the original, at least in the English translation of which four editions were published between 1503 and 1510, and traditionally attributed to his great literary rival Alexander Barclay.[14]

Bruyant's work, however, is not a morality. It is a long allegorical poem, prolix and sinuous, much more free and easy than the theatrical type, inspired both by the *Roman de la Rose* and by Prudent's *Psychomachia*, which, in the form of a dream, presents the married state as a cause of ruin and perdition. It is a gentle mockery of that institution, bearing a truly Parisian stamp and containing four principal episodes. The bridegroom or *nouveau mesnagier* is haunted in the nuptial bed by the spectres of Misery: Dearth, Lack, Want, Need, Thought (a hideous old hag), Care (a vile hunchback), Discomfort and Despair. He is comforted by the voices of Reason and Understanding who strengthen him against the vices by teaching him the Christian virtues; seduced by the perverse counsels of Barat, a treacherous lawyer, accompanied by his clerk Tricherie and his manservant Hoquellerie; and finally conducted to the Castle of Labour, a busy hive of one hundred thousand workmen, where he discovers the benefits of toil and frugality. It is not difficult to perceive the poem's overall similarity to Skelton's play: the theme of poverty resulting from foolish behaviour; the pair of good counsellors, Reason and Understanding in Bruyant, Measure and Circumspection in Skelton; the party of wicked counsellors, Barat and his attendants in Bruyant, the crowd of Court knaves in Skelton, both groups endeavouring to seduce their victim with speeches full of cynicism.

Pierre Gringore followed the general outline of his model slightly altering its spirit. He gave the appeals to Reason a more serious tone.[15] He turned this transparent satire on marriage into a more learned and more sententious work, a kind of long, edifying poem for the use of young people; witness the interminable digression (dropped in the English rendering) on the dangers of 'Bad Counsel' and 'Foolish Company', characters strongly reminiscent of Fancy and Folly in *Magnificence*. Lastly, he elaborated the episode of Despair by imagining the bridegroom driven almost to the point of suicide and saved by the providential intervention of Reason, in a manner not at all unlike that in which the prince is urged to suicide by Adversity and Despair but saved *in extremis* by the intervention of Good-hope.

Skelton, in turn, considerably enhanced the interest of this theme by writing a political play on the ruin or prosperity of the prince, an agonizing dilemma upon the outcome of which depends the happiness or unhappiness of the realm. He brought together those scattered and ill-co-ordinated episodes to form a straightforward plot, well articulated and strengthened with the solid armour of logic. He went even further than Gringore by emphasizing the religious spirit of the principal drama, that of the temptation, thus bringing back the composition of his play to the norms of the traditional morality.

On 16th August, in that same year, 1516, Skelton, still firmly established at Court, wrote a Latin *Elegy* [16] of twenty-six lines in memory of his protectress Lady Margaret, Countess of Richmond, Henry VII's devout mother who had died seven years before, in the dawn of the reign of her grandson Henry VIII.

This *Elegy* was a pendant to that composed in 1512 on Henry VII, at the request of John Islip, Abbot of Westminster, who had always shown affectionate esteem for Skelton. Consequently it went to join the epitaphs set up in the royal chapel at Westminster, the mausoleum of the Tudors, where a visitor reported having seen it in 1631.[17]

The poem in question, then, was a work written to order, hyperbolical and impersonal. Good taste required that its author should discover in the great benefactress (Maecenas) Tanaquil's nobility of mind, Penelope's chastity, Esther's courage and the prudence of Abigail.

It is curious to find, however, that while remembering the days of yore, dominated by the highly characteristic tone of fervent piety which she had managed to breathe into the ceremonial of the Court, Skelton inclines, by way of contrast, to denounce the impiety of modern times, revealed by two alarming symptoms: a weakening of the awareness of death and the ravages of the libertine spirit, of indecent lust, 'stinking like a billy goat'. In thus opposing *decus* to *hircus*, the satiric poet did not hesitate to fire a shaft which, in its crudity, recalls the coarseness of ancient Latin satire. It is therefore not surprising to hear him invoke the spirit of Juvenal, from whose first satire he quotes a phrase at the end of his own piece.[18]

Elynour Rummyng

A Profane Interlude

THE EPITAPH on Lady Margaret sounded the knell of a bygone age; but Skelton quickly proved that his old gaiety was still very much alive.

Some words in the poem *Against Venomous Tongues*—'what newis in Wales . . .'—appear to be echoed by two lines from *Elynour Rummyng* [1]:

> And she was full of tales
> Of tydynges in Wales.

> (352-3)

This coincidence affords reason to think that *Elynour Rummyng*, long assigned to the Diss period, may well belong to the post-war years at Court. It is indeed, at first sight, a work whose coarse joviality is unlikely to have been produced in the solitude of exile. Its opening, modelled upon that of a *fabliau*, recalls rather the art of a minstrel addressing a merry audience. One can certainly imagine Henry VIII begging his old tutor to lay aside for a moment his moral precepts and write something more spicy, more picturesque, displaying that virtuosity in the use of words which had delighted His Majesty in the diatribes against Garnesche.

Now, *The Tunnying of Elynour Rummyng* contains descriptive themes common alike to the diatribes *Against Garnesche* and to the satire *Against Dundas*, both of which belong to the period 1514-15.[2] Moreover, H. L. R. Edwards has pointed out similarities of style between *Elynour Rummyng* and *Colin Clout*, composed in 1521.[3] Contemporary allusions to the 'great war' in the City 'between Temple Bar and the Cross in Cheapside', suggest in this case the year 1517, when the violent agitation against foreigners, Flemish and French, culminated in the riot of 1st May, the famous Evil May Day of sinister memory.

That year was marked also by a renewed outbreak of sweating sickness with which Wolsey, among others, was seriously affected. The King moved his Court to Richmond in Surrey, and on 10th May he gave audience to a Portuguese ambassador, who had managed with great difficulty to escape safe and sound from the disorders in London.[4]

We find an echo of those events in the lines:

> Than thyder came dronken Ales,
> And she was full of tales,
> Of tydynges in Wales,
> And of sainct James in Gales,
> *And of the Portyngales;*
> *Wyth, Lo, gossyp, I wys,*
> *Thus and thus it is,*
> *There hath been great war*
> *Between Temple Bar*
> *And the Crosse in Chepe,*
> *And there came an hepe*
> *Of mylstones in a route . . .*

(351–62)

All the evidence, in fact, points to the ribald fantasy of *Elynour Rummyng* having been composed outside London, during the year of the sweating sickness and the xenophobia of 1517, for the amusement of a jolly gathering of people who were nevertheless idle and ready to cry with Elynour's customers

> . . . Now away the mare
> *And let us sley care*
> As wyse as an hare!

(110–12);

in short, under conditions very like those in which the *Decameron* was born.

At such times, as we know, it was extremely unwise to travel, and still more so to visit such sordid places as the 'Running Horse' tavern at Leatherhead. Several details suggest that

Skelton wrote his poem from memory, or perhaps rather from someone else's account:

> And this comely dame,
> *I vnderstande, her name*
> Is Elynour Rummynge,
> At home in her wonnynge;
> And, *as men say*
> She dwelt [5] in Sothray,
> In a certayne stede
> Bysyde Lederhede.

(91–8)

The realism of time and place must not deceive us. It is partly derivative. The portrait of this *vetula* is in line with a characteristically medieval development of the theme of ugliness, of which the Leatherhead tavern provided only the starting point. In his treatment of the gossips, Skelton relied on an old fifteenth-century poem, a 'Gossips' meeting',[6] which no doubt explains why the poet introduced none but women.

Be that as it may, *The Tunnyng of Elynour Rummyng* affords, after an interval of ten years, a remarkable contrast to the book of *Phyllyp Sparowe*. The praises of Jane Scrope were a variation on youth and beauty. The portrait of Elynour Rummyng is a variation on ugliness and old age. The former exalted the irresistible attraction of sensuality. The latter may fairly be considered as a rejection of sensitiveness. It is a composition 'full of unlust', calculated to discourage amorous desire, a feature which the author stresses on more than one occasion. While he showed to some extent an artist's complacency with regard to the sordid, there was to be no ambiguity about that complacency. Indeed, the poet harps upon the fascination of the ugly; his heroine is 'ugly fair'. He produces a new shudder from that favourite theme of the Middle Ages, but in full accord with the well-established custom of turning to ridicule the stigmata of vice and profligacy. The spitefulness of *Elynour Rummyng* by no means foreshadows the racy gauloiseries of Rabelais. It heralds much more surely the ferocious comedy of Ben Jonson.

Intended to be read, and better still to be heard, this work takes advantage of the freedom of 'Skeltonics' in order to achieve the tone and rhythm of the *fabliaux*. But it remains a *genre* piece, in which the author employs his virtuosity, not to tell a story but to sketch a series of little pictures, a gallery of portraits after the manner of Chaucer in the Prologue to the *Canterbury Tales*. In fact, he returned to the method of composition which had made *The Bowge of Court* so successful, but without the dialogues or the elements of scenic effect reminiscent of a marionette show or the rather stiff motions of a ballet.

But where Chaucer is an amused observer of mankind, Skelton is mordant and dynamic. His search is not so much for studied accuracy as for the accumulation of peculiar and picturesque details. Here the overtone of the picturesque replaces the overtones of the pathetic, which dominated the first part of *Phyllyp Sparowe*.

Accordingly, this grey-haired *vetula* has a repulsive face, a muddy complexion, wrinkles, an unhealthy skin bloated with too much drink and bristling with tufts of hair like the ears of a piglet. From her lips falls a coil of glairy liquid. Her eyes are bleary; her hooked nose runs continuously; she has a long pointed chin and toothless gums. The skin of her body is 'loose and slack, grained like a sack'. Her back is hunched, her hips look as if they were held with buckles. She has feet like a duck, legs like a crane, and yet she will strut 'in her furred flocket and grey-russet rocket'! Her hood of Lincoln green, which she has worn for forty years, is quite threadbare: the wool looks like dried weeds, 'withered like hay'. And yet, on holidays, she thinks herself gay when she dresses in her pleated gown, red kirtle, and all the scarves she piles on her head in heavy wreaths like a Saracen. When she goes out to show herself thus arrayed, she 'driveth down the dew with a pair of heels as broad as two wheels'. She hobbles like a goose, her shoes smeared with tallow and greased with the dirt that befouls her skirt. Elynour Rummyng is something of a gipsy. She is a creature of the Devil:

The deuyl and she be syb.

(100)

The tavern where she lives is an isolated building, perched on top of a hill, and of evil reputation. There she herself brews and sells her beer to passing customers—travellers, tinkers and labourers—and also to regular female customers who come, unknown to their husbands, to drink the famous ale. By 'ale' was meant an infusion of fermented barley, a malt, sometimes flavoured with aromatic plants such as ginger or juniper. At that time there was no such thing as beer; only barley-brew lacking the flavour of hops which were not introduced from Flanders to England until the sixteenth century.

The brewing industry was long a monopoly of religious houses. Then it gradually passed into the hands of private persons, especially women. A hundred years before Skelton, Lydgate had devoted a piece of verse to an 'ale wife'; nor must we forget the celebrated tavern described by Langland in *Piers Plowman*. Elynour Rummyng is a typical *cervisiaria*.

She may be judged by the prevailing atmosphere of her tavern. It is a noisome den where men and beasts rub shoulders in repulsive promiscuity. Swine go in as if into their own home, the sow followed by her piglings and the boar, who wriggles his tail and rubs his rump against the high wooden table. They have to be cudgelled off the premises, for not satisfied with drinking up the contents of the swilling tub, they leave behind them malodorous tokens of their call. So too with the poultry, which roost on the ale joist and let fall their droppings into the tuns. But Elynour is not the least worried. She can always give the mash bowl a little shake, tip the dung to one side and skim it into the yeast tray with her mangy fists. Sometimes she even blends the muck with the ale. 'There's nothing like a little hen's dung for aiding fermentation,' she brazenly assures her gossips. The old hag had the recipe from a Jew in her young days when she was learning the trade. The liquor thus obtained, she declare, possesses astonishing powers of rejuvenation. It is a regulasr youth-restoring elixir:

> For ye may prove it by me;
> Beholde, she sayde, and se
> How bright I am of ble [colour]!

And she goes on to expatiate on her sordid love-making with her husband when they are together in bed 'like two pigs in a stye'.

Those tosspots, who come to drink on the sly in that place of perdition, a forerunner of the nineteenth-century 'gin-palaces', furnish the poet with an inexhaustible theme for amplification, whether he describes them individually or in groups,

> With theyr naked pappes,
> That flyppes and flappes;
> It wygges and it wagges,
> Lyke tawny saffron bagges.

$$(135-8)$$

There is lame Joan, exacting and ill tempered; there is the unnamed slut whose mouth foamed while her belly groaned; drunken Alice, who 'pissed where she stood, then began to weep, and forthwith fell asleep'; there is mad Kit, a half-wit; Margery Milduck, 'crook-necked like an owl', who liked to display her short, sturdy legs, 'white as the foot of a kite'; there is the witch who knows how to stop a stitch and could fly to Bordeaux on a quail's feather; there is dropsical Maude Ruggy, dumpy, swollen, crippled with gout and subject to fits of palsy; there is sorrowful Sybil, her face covered in pimples, her belly swollen with enormous draughts of ale (she can swallow two pints at a go); there is the 'prick-me-dainty', short of breath, who panted as though she were about to faint.

All these clients of the Devil, marked with the stigmata of a vice that no doctor could fail to diagnose, seldom pay in coin; almost always they do so in kind, each one bringing Elynour some sort of pledge: a rabbit, a jar of honey, salt, a spoon, a pair of hose or shoes, a small saucepan, a pot, some Leominster wool, malt, wheat, a peck of rye, flour, a girdle, a wedding ring, a man's hood, flax, a bobbin, a hatchet, a needle, a dice, a thimble, beans, peas, a brass pan, a ham, a flitch of bacon, a tippet, a ladle, a cradle, a saddle, a cloak of grey coney-skins, a pitcher, a barrel, a bottle, a hunk of Essex cheese, walnuts, apples, pears, clipping shears, a man's cap, sausages and pudding, tripe, two goslings, an egg, a duck, heads of garlic, jet beads, a whimple, a silk lace, a box of pins, a man's gown, a pillow of down, linen, eggs and butter, a brace of pigeon, a young boar, a pincushion, a string of amber beads.

There surely we have a wealth of detail whose picturesque character forms a happy counterpoise to the sordid nature of the clinical observations, as well as producing a mechanical effect of irresistible movement by making Elynour Rummyng's tavern a mysterious storehouse of so many different kinds of object, so many strange evidences of the craving for drink. For indeed it is movement that constitutes the mainspring of this poem. In default of action, it seethes with vitality.

We see and hear the tosspots running, shouting, drinking, talking, swearing, foaming at the mouth, snivelling, weeping, trembling, taking a beating, swooning away, or even lying stretched out, legs in the air, on the doorstep, while beasts and humans, united by the great animal promiscuity of elementary needs, relieve their entrails amid the general confusion. A tremulous rhythm animates this diabolical display, a veritable *danse macabre* under the auspices of alcohol, degradation and sickness.

Incidentally, Skelton was well aware that by exploiting the sordid he would once again incur the strictures of cheerless people like the sombre Barclay, who would not fail to accuse him of sacrificing upon the altar of 'stinking Thaïs'. He therefore took the usual precaution of adding a postscript to his poem, a sort of parting memorandum *in despectu malignantium*, in which he let it be known, not without a touch of insolence, that he was resolved to disregard the advice of malevolent and jealous censors; that while his work, as he was first to recognize, gave out a somewhat 'raucous' sound, it deserved to be taken in good part, for it had been conceived under the sign of joviality: '*Haec loca plena jocis*'.[7]

It was perhaps the last poem of a mainly happy period of his life, during which, more than at any other moment, the poet-laureate had enjoyed the privilege of living, writing and striving in the orbit of his beloved sovereign. He had served him with his whole soul, in war and peace, justifying his two-fold title of laureate and orator royal by a rich variety of works composed

eyther for delyte
or elles for despyte

(C. Cl., 7–8)

sometimes in order publicly to defend the King's cause against his enemies, sometimes in order to put him on his guard against insidious dangers, and sometimes purely and simply in order to amuse him with the fireworks of his inexhaustible fancy.

One threat, however, never ceased to grow in the King's entourage, very close to Skelton. The time was not far off when his loyalty, his foresight and his courage would be severely tested. He was not blind to the fact that his duel with Wolsey had begun with the composition of *Magnificence*. The period of veiled opposition, carried on behind the façade of official poetry, was soon to be followed by a new period of direct opposition, the period of the great satires written away from the Court.

CHAPTER VII

Freelance

The Satires against Wolsey

AT THIS turning point of his career we lose sight of the poet-laureate to find him again, on 3rd August 1518, lodging within the Sanctuary at Westminster,[1] in an apartment 'south of the Great Belfry'[2] a few yards from the church of St Margaret and the Old Palace. The rent of lodgings in this neighbourhood was high, because of their legal advantages, although Skelton's presence on the threshold of this Court of Miracles may have originally had no motive other than its proximity to the royal palace and the neighbourhood of old friends, Prior William Mane and Abbot John Islip. This is confirmed to some extent by their continued relations, of which the dinner of 15th July 1511 and the epitaph for the tomb of Lady Margaret on 16th August 1516 are certainly landmarks. But in the hour of danger Skelton probably had every reason to congratulate himself upon having chosen to reside in the precincts of the Sanctuary.

In that same year, 1518, he distinguished himself with another epitaph, of a kind less orthodox than its predecessors, the *Devout Epitaph on Bedel*,[3] which reminds us rather of the goliardic and irreverent strain of the epitaphs written at Diss. This time he elected to stigmatize (*post mortem*, as usual) William Bedel, formerly Lady Margaret's treasurer and comptroller, whom he charged with anticlericalism.[4] The violence and brutality which adorn this piece of obituary are all the more startling when we consider that the dead man had received the honour of burial in the Abbey, at the entrance to Henry VII's Chapel.

Apart from these unworthy sallies, in which the burlesque note is always a sign of contempt, Skelton retained, despite his years, the reputation of being 'the glory of English poets'. It was with these very words that Robert Whittinton, one of his young colleagues in the Order of Laureates, dedicated to him in the following year (1519) a long dithyrambic Epigram of one hundred and thirty-six lines, *In Clarissimi Scheltonis Louaniensis poetae Laudes Epigramma*,[5] full of mythological allusions in accordance with contemporary taste. This poem stands, in a *Collection of Minor Works*,[6] alongside panegyrics addressed respectively to Henry VIII, the Duke of Suffolk, Thomas More and Cardinal Wolsey.

Robert Whittinton had been crowned laureate by the University of Oxford on 14th July 1513. A grammarian by profession, he was not averse from blowing his own trumpet by styling himself 'protovates of England'. Author of numerous manuals for the teaching of Latin, he had access to Court. He neglected nothing that might attract Wolsey's good graces, for it appears that in the same year (1519) he had dedicated to him two works, one entitled *De difficultate justitiae servandae in reipublicae administratione*, and the other *De quatuor uirtutibus cardineis*.[7]

However, the determination with which he set about winning the favour of the great—and it is curious to find him associating Skelton with the most eminent personages of the realm—was not entirely disinterested. He had, indeed, just involved himself wholeheartedly in a violent quarrel—the quarrel of the *Vulgaria*, which raged in the City from about 1519 to 1521.

The introduction of printing had given rise to a new harvest of Latin text-books for schools, which, with improved techniques, continued the great pedagogic tradition of men such as Neckam and Jean de Garlande. One pioneer of the printed manual had been John Stanbridge, a learned contemporary of Skelton, who died prematurely in 1510. He had succeeded Anwykyll as headmaster of St Mary Magdalen's School, Oxford, where Robert Whittinton had been his pupil.[8]

One of Stanbridge's most popular works was a Latin vocabulary with translations into the vulgar tongue, whence its name *Vulgaria*.[9] It was re-issued in 1519 by Wynkyn de Worde, but in that same year was abandoned at St Paul's School in favour of a rival work by William Horman, likewise entitled *Vulgaria* [10] and published by Pynson.

The irascible Whittinton straightway took the view that this substitution was an insult to the memory of his old headmaster, and he decided without more ado to compose a third manual of the same name.[11] Then, taking the offensive, he had the audacity to go and affix to the railing of St Paul's School a placard written in Latin hexameters which boasted the advantages of his own manual over that of his competitor.[12] His gesture marked the beginning of a ferocious war, a war of epigrams and of pamphlets loaded with ridicule, during which William Horman was seconded by William Lily,[13] headmaster of the school, while Robert Whittinton managed to win the backing of John Skelton both as a grammarian [14] and as poet laureate.[15]

In fact, behind the screen of commercial rivalry we discern a pedagogic emulation showing divergent tendencies in conformity with one of the period's main lines of demarcation.

Whittinton represented the traditional type of grammarian, a staunch supporter of rules and precepts. Horman, on the contrary, a humanist educator after the heart of John Colet, advocated a systematic intransigence against non-Ciceronian Latin in the matter of vocabulary, which marked a break with tradition.[16]

The two *Vulgaria* reflect those differences. Whittinton's method consists of a strict alternation of rules and examples. Horman's method consists of Latin sentences classified under headings and intended to lead the pupil quickly, by means of imitation, to the reading of good authors. Whittinton, despite the intrusion of English as a medium of instruction, which he tolerated rather by way of a concession to the march of time, continues in point of fact to treat Latin as a living language in current use, which, before it can be spoken, needs above all a strong casing of syntax. He remains liberal as regards vocabulary. Horman, on the contrary, makes no secret of his design to bring back Latin to its Ciceronian purity. In an appendix to his work he sets out a double list of Low Latin words classified as dubious or as frankly detestable. Whittinton remains attached to the traditions of the past; his manual is printed in gothic characters. Horman is a modernist; his is set up in roman type. Whittinton deplores the hardness of the times, and ends on a note of bitter pessimism:

'Alakke this heuy world! Wo is my herte to remembre ye felycyte and wealth yt hath be! Poore men cryeth out of this scarsyte of al thynge! O ye felycyte of olde tyme! O this newe

mysery! O good lord! refourme our maners: yet the old wealth
maye renewe.' [17] Horman, on the contrary rejoices in the
smiling prospects afforded by the advance of science. He
declares with satisfaction: 'I reioyce in the encresse of cun-
nynge: that is now a dayes.' [18]

In this dispute Skelton, by supporting his young colleague,
took a firm stand against the humanists. For he fully shared
Whittinton's ideas about Latin. He also shared his pessimism in
view of the increasing misery and moral decadence. We have
already noticed an echo of that pessimism in the epitaph composed for Lady Margaret's tomb. [19] It is unfortunate that there
has survived only one unimportant scrap indicative of the part
he played in the quarrel of the *Vulgaria*. It is the first line of a
Latin invective in sixty-four verses against Lily:

Vrgeor impulsus tibi Lille retundere dentes. [20]

We possess, on the other hand, Lily's reply, a devastating
epigram which ends with the two oft-quoted lines:

... Et doctus fieri studes poeta,
Doctrinam nec habes, nec es poeta. [21]

Thus, by decree of Fortune, within the space of twenty years
John Skelton received from two humanists and mutual friends,
Erasmus and Lily, the most splendid commendation that courtly
language could inspire and the most inexorable condemnation
that polemic could arouse to the confusion of posterity.

To speak the truth, the quarrel of the *Vulgaria* was only one
incident in the general conflict raging at that time around the
New Learning, a mere ripple in the great tide of the Renaissance which threw up on either hand supporters of the new
movement and partisans of the established order. Greek, that
powerful solvent of medieval culture, was in process, after a
long subterranean course, [22] of winning its place in the broad
light of day. Erasmus had not actually introduced it into
England, for he acknowledged his debt to such pioneers of
hellenism as Grocyn and Linacre; but he had become the life
and soul of that small English élite grouped around St Paul's
School and the circle of Thomas More. [23]

It was Erasmus who introduced Greek to Cambridge when he was called by Fisher (1510–11) to the chair of theology created by Lady Margaret. But he had no time to do more there than the work of a precursor. Not until two years later do we see a sudden expansion of the New Learning in English academic life. In 1516 Bishop Richard Foxe, when founding Corpus Christi at Oxford, provided for a course in the Greek as well as in the Latin classics. That was a great novelty in the bastion of medieval theology, and it resulted two years later in the student unrest which was nicknamed 'the War of the Trojans and the Greeks'. But in 1518 Wolsey asked Thomas More to damp down the excitement, and instituted with royal approval a chair of Greek in that University. In 1519 it was the turn of Cambridge to receive its first official Reader in Greek, Richard Croke. The new discipline triumphed all the more easily because, thanks to Cardinal Wolsey, it could count on the active support of Government.[24]

The New Learning, however, still had determined adversaries, not so much on account of old prejudices attaching to Greek, the language of heretics, not so much on account of an instinctive fear of seeing the dethronement of Latin upon whose supremacy Western Christendom had rested for hundreds of years, but rather because of the new philosophy's daring in the field of biblical exegesis. The Latin translation of the New Testament, published by Erasmus in 1516—the *Novum Instrumentum*—had alarmed many men who, in spite of its dedication to the humanist Pope, Leo X, were troubled at seeing the authority of the Vulgate thus called in question by a private individual. In 1519 appeared the second edition, considered as even more radical than the first. Its publication embittered the dispute between Erasmus and Edward Lee, Dean of Colchester, chaplain to the King and a personal friend of Thomas More, a learned man who was familiar with both Greek and Hebrew, and whose strictly orthodox convictions rallied to his side the general opinion of conservatives, notably of the Dominicans who regarded Erasmus as a kind of heretic.[25]

A significant incident occurred in December 1519, when Thomas More received a letter from a monk who wished him well, warning him against the jeopardy in which he placed his

soul by associating with so suspect a man.[26] Further, on 31st
July 1520 a rival of Lee, Henry Standish, Bishop of St Asaph
and *persona grata* at Court, preached a sermon at Paul's Cross
against the second edition of the New Testament, and attempted
on the same day to discredit its author at the Palace, where the
bishop had been invited to dine.[27]

Erasmus, then, was opposed in England by men who were far
from manifesting equal relentlessness against his friends who
represented the New Learning there. Like Louvain, London
had its die-hards, its *Lovanienses*, among whom of course was
Skelton. The epithet *Lovaniensis*[28], conferred upon him by Robert
Whittinton in 1519, at the height of the quarrel between
Erasmus and Edward Lee, was perhaps intended to emphasize
the firm convictions that ranged him on the side of tradition in
the current strife, rather than the close relations he had long
since enjoyed with a particular continental university.[29]

In fact, Skelton did not hesitate to direct his sarcasm at the
author of the *Novum Instrumentum* in the poem *Speke, Parrot*,
where he takes exception to the New Learning. Witness the
disdainful couplet which sums up his opinion of the new
philology:

> For they scrape out good scrypture, and set in a
>   gall,
> Ye go about to amende, and ye mare all.[30]

(158–9)

This poem, *Speke, Parrot*, contains some curious stanzas on his
objections to Greek[31]; commonsense rather than theoretical
objections of a man completely satisfied with his Latin culture,
and who is annoyed above all at seeing the sacrosanct *curriculum*
of medieval studies jostled by the intrusion of a second living
language which he considered untimely, to say the least.[32] Not
that he harboured prejudice against Greek in itself, but he
accused it of monopolizing the attention of students at the
expense of Latin, although those hellenists could not even say
in the language of Plato: 'Hi, ostler! bring my horse a load of
hay!'[33] Again echoing the quarrel of the *Vulgaria*, he complains
that students are being introduced straightaway to Latin texts

that are much too difficult, and taught fine Ciceronian phrases to the detriment of instruction in grammar.[34] See how textbooks are discarded that have proved their worth for centuries— Donatus and Priscian, for example; see the abandonment of exercises in formal logic and debate, which used to train men to the art of speaking and temper their minds. The whole fine system of traditional education is imperilled.

> And syllogisari was drowned at Sturbrydge fayre;
> Tryuyals and quatriyuyals so sore now they
>   appayre,
> That Parrot the popagay hath pytye to beholde
> How the rest of good lernyng is roufled vp and
>   trold.

$$(170\text{--}3)$$

Briefly, Skelton opposed 'Good Lernyng' to 'New Learning', and 'Good Scrypture' to the new philology of the humanists against whom he stirred up the rhetoricians and orators 'in freshe humanite'.[35]

But where the new movement threatens him personally and most directly is, undoubtedly, in his relations with the Court. He is fully aware that every advance of the New Learning in official circles entails *ipso facto* a diminution of his influence with the King. Skelton's tragedy is that the New Learning threatens to alienate his old pupil from him. Not that Henry VIII's attitude towards the humanist revolution was altogether clear at this date. It is true that generally speaking he showed sympathy with the English representatives of the New Learning, and even admiration for Thomas More. But he did not, on the other hand, forget that his relations with Colet had not always been unclouded. He did not forget the resistance he had met in those quarters at the time of his war in 1513. Nor, finally did he make any effort to keep Erasmus in England. He actually manifested some solicitude for certain of his declared enemies, such as the Dean of Colchester and the Bishop of St Asaph. In short, he looked favourably on everything connected with academic reform, but remained orthodox in the matter of religion. From 1517 he was seriously worried by the growth of the Lutheran schism, and Queen Katherine's influence remained a trump card for the conservatives.

Such an ambiguous attitude left Skelton perplexed and suspicious, all the more so because there stood between him and his King the person of Cardinal Wolsey. He reacted quite naturally by venting his spleen on one whom he considered to be the active and redoubtable agent of those novelties. The more power obtained by that ex-schoolmaster, the more precarious became Skelton's situation. Henry VIII's official poet, champion of the established order, felt himself driven irresistibly to become an enemy of the Government. This uncompromising conservative was transforming himself into a rebel.

In the desert of intellectual and moral isolation into which the poet-laureate found himself thrust, he began to devote more attention to those aristocratic circles where questions of pedagogy were seldom if ever debated, but which shared to the full his rancour against the Cardinal. The policy of systematic vexation practised by the latter against the nobility—of which we had several instances during the crisis of 1516—had created among their leaders a spirit of latent rebellion in which the poet found his own sentiments reflected.

It is not, as might have been expected, with the Earl of Northumberland that we meet Skelton again at this juncture; for since the affair of his imprisonment, Percy the Magnificent, three-quarters ruined and deeply depressed, had remained secluded in his northern castles, away from active life.[36] Instead we find him with the Howards, at whose place in Norfolk the Countess of Surrey, descendant of the Percies and granddaughter of the Duke of Buckingham, always made him welcome.

There were many ways of opposing Wolsey. There were those who bowed beneath his rod and fretted in secret; there were those who criticized his acts but recognized the ability of his administration; those who sulked in a corner like Percy; and those who, for the sake of peace, were on the best of terms with him, like the old Duke of Norfolk.[37] But undoubtedly the most hostile to the Cardinal were the Duke of Buckingham,[38] and the young Earl of Surrey who boiled with indignation. With them Skelton found himself at the very heart of the opposition.

The Earl of Surrey was not invited to the Field of the Cloth of Gold in May 1520. Nor, most probably, was Skelton. It was his rival Alexander Barclay who was invited 'to devise histories and convenient raisons to florrishe the building and banquet house withal'.[39]

Some months later the conflict between the nobles and the central authority took a tragic turn with the summary execution of the Duke of Buckingham.[40] It was not the first time that Henry VIII rid himself of someone whose principal offence was his undesirable nearness to the throne. And in order to favour his design, he had previously taken care to remove Surrey, under the pretext of a mission to Ireland. The opposition was frozen stiff by this gesture. Skelton could no longer doubt that the King's subjection to the detestable influence of his first minister would lead both the Sovereign and his realm to disaster. Since acquiring the functions of chancellor and cardinal-legate, Wolsey had become absolute master of the temporal and spiritual affairs of the kingdom. In the autumn of 1521 Wolsey's thirst for power was proclaimed by his pomp and aloofness on the occasion of the meeting at Calais, whither he had travelled in style (taking with him the great seal, indispensable for payments from the Treasury) [41] in order to confer on an equal footing with Charles V and François I. His driving ambition reached its climax in the following year, when he presented himself as a candidate for the papacy.

Such, in brief, are the events and the resentment that lie behind the great satires which the poet-laureate, more than ever imbued with his prophetic mission, wrote at that period against Cardinal Wolsey.

Speke, Parrot, can by no means be considered as a homogeneous poem. It is rather a 'collection', as the poet himself called it, a mosaic of fragments laid according as current events and the reaction of his readers happened to dictate, for the earliest fragments were in circulation before the whole poem was completed. The total forms a kind of hotch-potch or, if preferred, 'satire' (in the etymological sense of the word), akin to the log-book, the newspaper editorial, the ballad-book or the philippic. The artistic unity derives mainly from the purpose which had inspired it. It is a network of disparate themes,

woven on the loom of satire against the contemporary dictator.
The poet certainly had no intention of producing an anonymous
poem. He signed his work, and even appended to his signature
the title 'Orator Royal'. He merely entrenched himself behind
a parapet of obscurity which was meant to veil the audacity of
certain criticisms rather than the author's identity, the protec-
tive cloud becoming thicker, it seems, when the satire might
possibly reflect upon the person of the Sovereign. Nevertheless,
it is easy to see that the poet was less and less concerned with
taking those precautions which, while ensuring his own safety,
would hinder the achievement of his purpose. When the satiric
urge reached its full extent, as in the closing lines of *Speke,
Parrot,* or attained the summit of its violence, as in *Why Come ye
not to Court?*, he resolutely laid aside all subterfuge, all 'sophisms',
and expressed himself plainly with an unprecedented freedom
which no dyke, no artistic discipline, no fear could any longer
stem.[42]

By putting into the mouth of a parrot the daring thoughts
which he decided were too risky to speak openly in his own
name, the author had recourse to a procedure that was both
ingenious and fertile in artistic effects. The medieval parrot
afforded him three priceless advantages: its nonsensical babble
could benefit by the indulgence granted to the remarks of
fools and clowns, those convenient channels of free speech
under a regime of orthodoxy; its notorious addiction to wine
would confer on its ramblings the gift of prophetic intoxication
(*in vino veritas*); and since, according to one tradition, it came
straight from the Earthly Paradise, somewhere between the
Tigris and the Euphrates, it was well suited to the idea of
embodying the immortal voice of Poesy.[43]

Others before Skelton had made use of the fine-speaking bird.
In 1505 Jean Lemaire de Belges had written *La Première Epître de
l'Amant Verd* [44] in order to pay court to Margaret of Burgundy.
Skelton was no doubt acquainted with that precedent; but he
may also have wished to take the opposite course to a sally by
Erasmus against the upholders of traditional education, those
'old parrots' (*vetuli psittaci*) who opposed the foundation of the
trilingual college at Louvain.[45]

The fact is that Skelton's parrot is offensively polyglot, as if he in turn were employing his malice to mock the rage for new languages and for polyglot translations of the Bible.

Finally, this bird of infinite resource and sagacity is a drawing-room bird, pampered by the grandest ladies—he had found a refuge with the Countess of Surrey—a frail, timid and defenceless little bird, at the mercy of a great big tom-cat, just as his brother Phyllyp had fallen victim to Gib:

But ware the cat, Parrot, ware the fals cat!

(101)

From his precarious retreat, the parrot banters with astounding volubility. He rattles off odds and ends, mingling the obscure with the intelligible, like an oracle. He pours forth veiled metaphors with an almost oriental profusion of images. Memories of the Bible play a large part in this deliberate secretiveness.[46] Wolsey is by turns Moloch and Aaron, he sacrifices to the Golden Calf. He is Og, the big-bellied king of Bashan, while Moses, leader of peoples, and Melchisedech, the priest-king, stand for Henry VIII. The first is distinguished by his devouring, impious and senseless activity, by dark duplicity and by sacrilegious brutality. The second is above all reproach, although he shows an excessive and inexplicable complacency towards that lunatic, who in the domain of education alone—a fief dear to the poet—has managed to deface the true countenance of traditional culture by the untimely favours he grants to the New Learning. But the prophetic bird does not lose heart, for, thanks to a reversal of roles in accordance with natural justice, he already sees in the bosom of his Gehenna a day at hand upon which the proud will return to dust while the voice of Poesy soars into Eternity.[47]

Then the bird's mistress, Galatea, asks the parrot point-blank to recite for her the lament sung by Pamphilus when his beloved deserted him. (Here, it seems from the marginal comment, we have a reference to the celebrated medieval Latin poem *Pamphilus de amore Galatheae*.[48]) The parrot then pronounces a sort of popular ritornello, which appears to mark a break with the style and atmosphere of the preceding mystical flight:

My proper Besse,
My praty Besse,
   Turn ones agayn to me.
For slepyst thou, Besse,
Or wakest thou, Besse,
   Myne herte hyt is with the . . .

                    (240–5)

This curious interlude is quite inexplicable if taken in its literal sense. But the ritornello is not as irrelevant as it appears. To H. L. R. Edwards belongs the credit of having shown that it derives from an old moralistic ballad

   Come over the burn, Besse,
   Thou little pretty Besse,
   Come over the burn, Besse, to me

in which the burn represents the World, Besse erring Humanity, and the Lover who invites her with his incessant calls, Christ the Redeemer:

   The burn is this world blind,
   And Besse is mankind,
      So proper I can none find as she.
   She dances and leaps
   And Christ stands and clepes:
      'Come over the burn, Besse, to me!' [49]

Skelton-Pamphilus, deserted by errant humanity, and urging her to take him back in return for a promise that he will be firm, useful and a good counsellor, affords a true picture of the situation in which he found himself *vis-a-vis* the Court and his Sovereign:

   I will be firm and stabil
   And to you serviceabil
   And also prophitabil,
   If ye be agreabil
   To turn again to me.

                    (251–5)

The poet was all the more drawn to liken erring humanity to the symbolical figure of the sovereign, in that he had already substituted Magnificence for Mankind, the traditional character of the moralities. It remains to ask why he associated the old moralistic ballad with the story of Galatea. He had no doubt an excellent reason for doing so, by stealth, when we consider that in setting the reader on the false trail of the Latin *Pamphilus* (which was supposed in his day to be by Ovid) he had in mind that other story about Galatea, in the *Metamorphoses*, where her lover, Acis, has a powerful rival, Polyphemus, the monstrous cyclops by whom he is crushed under an enormous rock.[50] Now Skelton's rival with the Sovereign, Cardinal Wolsey, was suffering at about this time from an ocular affection which obliged him to wear a black patch over his right eye.[51] This second Polyphemus is the subject of a postscript to *Why Come ye not to Court?*

> Sequitur Epitome
> De morbilloso Thome
> Necnon obscoeno
> De Polyphemo . . .

Thus, in a roundabout way, the ritornello to Galatea may be taken as the quintessential expression of Skelton's show of jealousy with regard to the King in *Speke, Parrot*. It is in secret harmony with the contrast between Henry VIII and Wolsey upon which the previous passage is built, as well as with the mystical symbolism of its inspiration.[52]

The allusions to Juvenal's Sixth Satire show that the poet was still thinking of the ravages committed by the vogue for Greek, which had come to compete with Latin even in the intimate language of love. Such were the consequences of that rage for innovations, which, as Juvenal had so vigorously declared, is the death of ancient virtue.

With *The First Envoi* we enter the domain of exact chronology. On 30th October Wolsey was on a mission to Calais, busy offering to mediate in the armed conflict between Charles V and François I. He had been away since 1st April, and the time passed slowly for those who awaited his return and had only the vaguest notion of the obscure negotiations conducted by the Chancellor on his own authority.

At the same time a new theme appears: the Parrot's witticisms had not been to everyone's liking, and in some quarters had been strongly disapproved. The poet again awoke to find himself the target of ignorant men who did not understand the veiled sagacity of his metaphors.

The Second Envoi (November) and *The Last Envoi* (17th November) repeat, with variations, the subject of the Cardinal's return and that of slander.

Finally, *The Royal Envoi*, abandoning for a moment the satire against Wolsey, asks the great lords and ladies among his friends to excuse the vigour of his outspokenness and to protect him, if necessary, against his old enemy Detraction.

The fragment entitled *Le Popagey s'en va complayndre* voices the poet's deep-seated bitterness and points out his detractors, the dignitaries of the Church, who do not understand his activity as a satirist, frown upon it or, through cowardice, dare not follow him in his struggle with the Cardinal, whose return (28th November) is painted in the darkest colours.

The second Dialogue between Galatea and the Parrot comes back to the central theme of satire against Wolsey who, on the death of Leo X (2nd December), presented himself as a candidate for the papacy, hoping for the Emperor's support in accordance with the agreements reached at Calais. Galatea, in the role of a sorceress, espies the Cardinal's special envoys, Richard Pace and his colleague Thomas Clerk,[53] hurrying to Italy. She asks her oracle the reason of this scurry and promises him a date as his reward. The parrot surpasses himself in sarcastic comments strewn with puns, earns his date and, encouraged by this beginning, launches into a burst of general satire denouncing all the evils of society at every level, a 'State of the World' in true medieval style [54] which forms a worthy conclusion to *Speke, Parrot*.

The passages in *Speke, Parrot*, which first declare the poet's astonishment, bitterness, contempt and righteous indignation at the lack of understanding and the hostility encountered by his satires, introduce a theme which he develops in *Colin Clout* [55] under a significant headline quoted from the Psalms: *Quis consurget mecum adversus malignantes, aut quis stabit mecum adversus operantes iniquitatem? Nemo, Domine.*

The poet-laureate, indeed, is the victim of a painful misfortune. Having marched straight against the most powerful man of the day, he finds that no one follows him, that there are even minds so myopic or so feeble as to criticize what he does. That disturbing fact leads him naturally first to turn back upon himself, then to listen more closely to what is said around him:

> As I go aboute
> And wandrynge as I walke
> I here the people talk.

(288–90)

As a result, he determines no longer to veil his personal opinions under the irresponsible chattering of a bird, as in *Speke, Parrot*, but to acknowledge his responsibility by allowing public opinion to speak with his own voice. So he creates a character named Colin Clout, a relative of Piers Plowman and Jacques Bonhomme. In some 1,300 lines he inveighs against the three great scourges of the established order: the shortcomings of the ruling class, the recent spread of the Lutheran heresy and the misconduct of Wolsey.

The first accusation is principally, and rightly, directed at the social group upon whom falls the chief responsibility: the prelates who do nothing to stem the danger, the prelates who should be 'lanterns of light' but who, through their unworthiness, communicate to the rest of the body ecclesiastic those glaring faults that do the Church so much harm and are called Ignorance, Apathy, Worldliness, Cowardice and Immorality. As a conscientious and respectful critic of sound doctrine, he takes care to distinguish the healthy from the corrupt members. He criticizes neither good bishops, nor good priests, nor good friars, nor good canons, nor good nuns, nor good monks, nor good clerks. On this point he is quite definite and shows himself particularly anxious to avoid any misunderstanding:

> Of no good bysshop speke I,
> Nor good preest I escrye,

Good frere, nor good chanon
Good nonne, nor good canon
Good monke, nor good clerke
Nor yette of no good werke:
But my recountyng is
Of them that do amys,
In speaking and rebellyng
In hynderyng and dysauaylyng
Holy Churche, our mother . . .

(1097–106)

He speaks only of the others and he has some hard things to
say. He has left us in *Colin Clout* a striking picture of the complaints lodged by his contemporaries against the various
religious categories: the prelates, the secular and the regular
clergy, the contemplative and the mendicant orders.

It is mainly the prelates that he takes to task, not only because,
through them, he aims to strike at Wolsey, but also because he
accuses them individually of being too feeble to dare oppose the
Cardinal's dictatorship and whims. They are yes-men who can
only nod assent.

They are made for the becke . . .

(167)

They have forgotten the example of Thomas Becket.

How be it they are good men
Moche herted lyke an hen:
Theyr lessons forgotten they have
That Becket them gaue.

(168–71)

They are intolerably insolent, and at the same time neglect
their most elementary duties. They preach no sermons. They
abandon their flocks in order to busy about their own advancement. They try to worm their way into the royal circle so as to
grow fat and solicit the favours of the Court; or else they spend
their time in such amusements as falconry and skirt hunting.

They eat meat in Lent. They drink hypocras and their behaviour is less than chaste:

> *Viventes parum caste.*
>
> (449)

Mitres are bought and sold. Bishops oppress the people, the towns, the cities; and while their mules eat gold their neighbours starve to death:

> Their moyles golde dothe eate,
> Theyr neyghbours dye for meate.
>
> (321–2)

The rest of the clergy follow suit, for bad shepherds make bad flocks. Ignorance is rife among churchmen. Some cannot even spell their names, others can hardly read. They are scheming, negligent and dissolute:

> The money for theyr masses
> Spent amonge wanton lasses.
>
> (425–6)

Monks desert their monasteries to go wandering and singing from one place to another like apostates. Nuns do likewise; they lay aside the veil—a deplorable consequence of the policy of dissolving smaller convents.[56] The friars, finally, are accused by the laity of being gluttons and hypocrites, of feigning the utmost piety for selfish motives, of begging in order to buy delicacies. They are unwilling to obey their bishops.

He has much to say, also, on the subject of the nobility who should have the courage to withstand Wolsey but who excuse themselves on the plea of too much business and do not understand the importance of what is at stake:

> . . . noble men borne
> To lerne they have scorne,
> But hunt and blowe an horne,
> Lepe ouer lakes and dykes,
> Set nothyng by polytykes.
>
> (621–5)

They have no proper pride; they swallow without flinching
the most outrageous insults:

> This is a pyteous case
> To you that ouer the whele
> Grete lordes must crouche and knele,
> And breke theyr hose at the kne,
> As dayly men may se,
> And to remembraunce call.
>
> (628–33)

The wheel of Fortune thus places at the very bottom those
who, by definition, should stand at the very top:

> Fortune so turneth the ball
> And ruleth so ouer all
> That honoure hath a great fall.
>
> (634–6)

At the other extreme are the heretics, people subject to the
ferment of new ideas imported from Germany and who think that

> . . . the Church hath to mykel
> And they haue to lytell,
>
> (559–60)

bold spirits who venture to discourse on the sacraments, pre-
destination and the hypostasis of Christ; men and women indifferently, who have the effrontery to wrangle over sacred things

> When the good ale sop
> Doth daunce in theyr fore top;
>
> (532–3)

scatterbrained folk who, under the several names of Pelagians,
Wycliffites or Hussites,

> . . . haue a smacke
> Of Luthers sacke.
>
> (542–3)

Finally, at the centre of the triptych, stands Wolsey, perfect example of the worldly prelate. And there we find again, orchestrated in every tone, most of the grievances of which the author makes himself the obliging echo: dissipation of ecclesiastical property; dissolution of the first monasteries; ruin of public finances; easy-going and debauched living; ostentatious luxury; taste for magnificent buildings, costly furniture and Renaissance tapestries full of naked figures,[57] pomp and display; nepotism, absolutism, unconstraint; and, above all, arrogance, the indelible stain of a parvenu who even dares to gaze upon the host at the moment of elevation.[58]

With *Colin Clout* the duel between Skelton and Wolsey enters an acute phase. The Cardinal got wind of the mordant satires that were circulating privately, and he was on his guard. It appears that he actually threatened to imprison the insolent fellow who was publishing slanderous verses at his expense.[59] Skelton too was on the alert, and doubtless took steps to avoid disaster; but contrary to what might have been expected, he did not confine his movements to the Sanctuary. Though he had lodgings there, he did not hesitate to go out and walk around in broad daylight, so as to be able to give an accurate account to those whom it might concern of the low opinion held of Wolsey not only at Westminster, but also at Paul's Cross, among the Austin friars, and in those favourite spots with which the poet had been so long associated, St Thomas of Acon where he had received the sub-diaconate, and St Mary Elsyng where he had been ordained priest.[60]

In *Colin Clout* his method was to sink his personal responsibility in the vague mass of recrimination that was mounting against Wolsey, and to entrench himself, as it were, in the anonymous sanctuary of public opinion. He repeatedly told the Cardinal: 'This is what is said about you on all sides, at the crossroads and in public places. It is now for you to decide whether it is I who calumniate you, or whether it is not you who by your insensate conduct, have succeeded in rousing the people against you.'

Finally, he had recourse to this dilemma:

> And eyther ye be to bad,
> Or els they are mad

Of this to reporte:
But, vnder your supporte,
Tyll my dyenge day
I shall bothe wryte and say,
And ye shall do the same,
Howe they are to blame
You thus to dyffame.

(504–12)

His words were destined to bear fruit later, but they were not immediately understood.

This disproof awaited by Skelton was not forthcoming, a fact which confirmed his conviction of the diabolical nature of the Man in Red.

The accumulation of grievances resulted in a gradual rise of the satire's intensity to heights at which the poet acquires as it were the tone of the ancient Hebrew prophets, to foretell, in the name of natural justice which has never failed, the approaching fall of that proud creature. Recalling the persecution endured by those great men, he reaches a degree of mystical exaltation at which martyrdom itself would hold few terrors. Then a great calm falls upon his soul, and *Colin Clout* ends on a note of serenity which attains to poetry:

The forecastell of my shyp
Shall glyde, and smothely slyp
Out of the wawes wod
Of the stormy flod;
Shote anker, and lye at rode,
And sayle not farre abrode,
Tyll the cost be clere,
And the lode starre appere
My shyp nowe wyll I stere
Towarde the porte salu
Of our Sauyour Jesu,
Suche grace that he vs sende,
To rectyfye and amende
Thynges that are amys,
What that his pleasure is.

Amen!

(1253–67)

In 1522 the situation of the kingdom both at home and abroad appeared to the English to be worsening. At the Conference of Calais, Wolsey, under pretext of mediation, had in fact sided with the Emperor. Relations with France again deteriorated, and in May the second continental war of the reign began. England felt herself doubly menaced.[61] Scotland, faithful to her traditions, attacked England as in 1513. The Regent Albany invaded English territory as far as Carlisle. Lord Dacre—who was now responsible for defence of the Scottish frontier, in place of the Earl of Northumberland—finding himself short of men and materials, had the wisdom to negotiate a month's truce, which undid the enemy's success. But the crisis had revealed alarming weaknesses. The treasury was empty: there remained none of the vast resources so laboriously accumulated by Henry VII; it was necessary to fall back on a succession of unpopular loans, and the City was laid under heavy contribution. A royal commission, covering the entire country, proceeded to a general census of all fortunes, of which a tenth was requisitioned in twelve months. England considered herself the victim of unexampled oppression. Wolsey's popularity which had never stood very high, fell to zero. Skelton felt sustained as never before by the general discontent, and in that year (1522) he wrote the most violent of all his satires, *Why Come ye not to Court?* [62]. This time he made his own, straightforwardly and without evasion, the complaints of Colin Clout.

That satire has not, perhaps, the massive surge of the preceding, nor the subtle riches of *Speke, Parrot*. Under pressure of events the poet returned to his favourite method in times of crisis: the intermittent composition of fragments strung together bit by bit. On the other hand, when it takes fire it achieves an intensity uncommon in this class of writing. Not that it is ever uplifted by the mystical exultation which, at its highest moments, transforms Colin Clout into an inspired prophet, although the poet's method here is manifestly the same: the tireless, inexorable accumulation of complaints, set down with all the details of an inventory. What we have in this case is a new spirit. The poet has lost the last traces of respect for his adversary. Consequently he feels to some extent beyond fear, and therefore he allows himself every kind of recklessness. He is impelled henceforward to observe this werewolf with a critical detachment that throws into relief all the fellow's absurdity. His satire is thus embellished with those ingredients which Claudian reserved for vile creatures such as Eutropius, a eunuch raised to the consulship: slapstick sarcasm, coarse raillery, wisecrack.[63] Those elements abound in *Why Come ye not to Court?*. They are the mark of diatribe brought down to the lowest degree of contempt. *Colin Clout* was a catalogue of grievances. *Why Come ye not to Court?* is a series of satirical sketches intended to show Wolsey's faults and vices at work. It is a prosecutor's brief, a mirror held up to a fool in order to show him the hideous features of his folly.

Why Come ye not to Court? contains in this respect hidden analogies with *Magnificence*. The latter depicted an imaginary kingdom from which the spirit of moderation had been banished. *Why Come ye not to Court?* draws up a disastrous balance-sheet of England in 1522, from which Reason has been exiled. The author no longer needs recourse to the trappings of traditional symbolism: he has only to describe in detail what he sees around him every day. From this point of view the apparent disorder of his composition falls, broadly speaking, into three movements. The first is devoted mainly to an account of the political and military situation—threats of defeat and the dictatorship of Wolsey; the second examines with a magnifying glass, as Hieronymus Bosch might have done, the catastrophic caprices of the Cardinal; the third is more or less an allegorical spectacle, a sort of Grand Finale taking for its theme the reign of Folly under the government of the cardinal-legate Thomas Wolsey, Prince of Darkness.

In fine, nothing restrains the poet, now that he is certain of Wolsey's diabolical nature. Unhesitatingly he accuses him of every possible sin, including perhaps the most serious and most extravagant crime of having employed necromancy to win the King's confidence. The last of his caution has disappeared together with his last scruples. He is indeed no safer now than when he wrote *Colin Clout*; but his conviction enables him to forget the danger to his personal security. It could be said that he has only one idea in his mind: to exorcize the Evil One by the power of laughter, in the grotesque manner of the sculptors of gargoyles.

Why Come ye not to Court? in the spirit of *Colin Clout*, is addressed to the highest temporal and spiritual dignitaries. Skelton missed no opportunity to rouse the authorities against the Cardinal; moreover, he assumes full responsibility for doing so. To those who complain of being trampled underfoot, he answers in the self-same words he had used to his pupil Henry in the far-off days of *Speculum Principis*:

> *Quia difficile est*
> *Satiram non scribere.*

> (1213–14)

He claims the responsibility of his acts as a man who has devoted the best part of his life to service as the English Juvenal.

A sequel to *Why Come ye not to Court?* adds to this ferocious diatribe the final insinuations, the final obscure puns, the final broadside of invective. Meanwhile, however, something quite different was about to interrupt the headlong course of his preoccupations. The storm clouds that had gathered above his head suddenly dispersed before the thunderbolt had time to fall.

CHAPTER VIII

The Garland of Laurel

Apotheosis *in camera* and armistice with Wolsey

SKELTON next uttered Wolsey's name a few months later, but in a very different tone. Meanwhile he was invited by the Countess of Surrey to spend New Year 1522–3 at Sheriff Hutton Castle in Yorkshire. There he wrote one of his greatest poems, *The Garland of Laurel*, which was printed on 3rd October 1523 by Richard Faques in London.

Following so close upon the episode of *Why Come ye not to Court?* that journey to the North seems to have been made just in time to save him from the Cardinal's fury. His peril had become so clear that he could no longer move around freely as in the days of *Colin Clout*. He strongly disliked having to remain in hiding, which, he said, was a cowardly thing to do, the sign of a guilty conscience:

> Nor for to hyde
> You cowardly,
>
> (1567–8)

he wrote in an appendix to *The Garland of Laurel*. Besides, a man who had never ceased to fight tooth and nail on the side of Good, of established Order and Freedom, might well consider his dignity insulted by having to share the privileges of sanctuary with criminals, thieves, murderers, common-law offenders. This stay in Yorkshire, coming at so opportune a moment, gave him a sense of freedom. At Sheriff Hutton he found himself once again on friendly ground, not without bravado, at the very heart of the opposition, but sheltered from the Cardinal's men, despite the authority exercised by Wolsey over the diocese of York. In that kindly home, where he was petted and flattered, life resumed a significance it had lost at Westminster. The hierarchy of values was restored, and John Skelton recognized without demur as the national poet and champion of the aristocracy.

Yorkshire was the cradle of Skelton's family, and Sheriff Hutton, standing proudly amid mighty oaks in the forest of Galtres, overlooking the great Vale of York, could not but stir the poet. Before coming into possession of the Howards, the castle had belonged to the Nevilles of Middleham. Richard of Gloucester had resided there with his young bride Anne, who was attended by a maid-in-waiting also named Skelton.[1] There too, in 1497, Thomas Howard, successor of the Percies as lord-lieutenant of Yorkshire and governor of the Scottish march, had celebrated his marriage with Agnes Tilney. Sheriff Hutton thus epitomized a troubled chapter of English history, dominated by a change of dynasty, by the eclipse of the Percies and by the rise of the Howards to positions of responsibility in the defence of the realm.

The Earl of Surrey, master of the house, was absent on business, and Skelton found himself the focus of a brilliant female society. Friends and relations of the Norfolks, most of them from East Anglia, formed a little court around the Countess of Surrey, anxious that the elderly poet should enjoy all the comfort and kindness that hospitality could confer. Among the guests was *Lady Elizabeth Howard*,[2] third daughter of the old Duke of Norfolk, and her sister-in-law *Mistress Margaret Tilney*,[3] a member of the Brewse family in whose home, it will be remembered (page 76), Christopher Garnesche had long ago served as a kitchen-boy, and where, more recently, Lady Brewse's grandson Thomas had married the orphan of Carrow, Jane Scrope, unwilling heroine of *Phyllyp Sparowe*.[4] Others were *Lady Anne Dacre of the South*,[5] wife of Thomas, Lord Dacre, and daughter of Sir Humphrey Bourchier by Elizabeth Tilney, granddaughter of Lord Berners the writer; *Mistress Margery Wentworth*, daughter of Sir Richard Wentworth, twice sheriff of Norfolk and Suffolk and veteran of the battle of Guinegatte [6]; *Mistress Jane Blennerhasset*,[7] daughter of Sir Thomas Blennerhasset, whom the Duke of Norfolk appointed his executor in the following year; *Mistress Gertrude Statham*,[8] née Anstey, of an ancient family settled near Cambridge and (probably) married to Roger Statham (a couple with whom the poet, faithful without respect of persons to his satirical leanings, would find a bone to pick in the course of his stay [9]); *Mistress Isabel Knight*;

Mistress Margaret Hussey; *Lady Miriel Howard*,[10] 'my little lady', doubtless a child and daughter of the Countess; and lastly *Mistress Isabel Pennell*—'Your mammy and your daddy brought forth a goodly baby'.

As the New Year approached, this pleasant company decided to offer the poet-laureate a crown of laurel worthy of his fame, and we know that the entire household set to work on this masterpiece of female industry, in which silk and gold embroidery vied with pearls and precious stones.

Understandably, Skelton resolved to thank his benefactors with a masterly poem that should be worthy of their kindness and skill. The delicately chiselled rondeaux addressed to each of them are little masterpieces of poetic modelling. But he did much more. In that haven of peace, far from the tumult of London and Westminster, the poet experienced the profound emotions which were intensified by the scenery, confronted as he was at every step with his past. The scenery of Yorkshire took him back to the old days of his friendship with the Percies and Dr Ruckshaw; that brilliant East Anglian society recalled the long years he had spent in Norfolk; nor had the presentation of the Garland failed to revive in his memory the indelible image of the ceremony at Oxford, which had illumined all his life. Finally, the welcome he had received from Lady Surrey's little circle threw into relief the humiliations he had suffered at the Tudor Court. Moreover, having recently led the life of a hunted man, he could not but be acutely conscious of Fortune's caprice. Today that goddess, changeful as an English sky, favoured him, like a ray of sunshine through a storm-cloud, with a private triumph in the very midst of adversity; he could not help seeing in this winter landscape the image of his own winter, but also the promise of everlasting spring. Thus everything led him to turn backward upon himself. He had only to close his eyes in order to behold at a glance the principal stages of his career; and in true medieval fashion he made this dream one of the episodes of his great poem. On the journey from the pavilion of Dame Pallas, seat of Science and Reason (his University), to the wonderful castle of the Queen of Fame (dear to Chaucer as the Temple of Fame), the poet, led by Dame Occupation like Guilleville's pilgrim by Grâce-Dieu, passes through two very different settings. The first is a walled field, haunted by dubious characters and representing the Court; the other is Lady Surrey's home, an enchanted arbour, an oasis of pleasure where eternal summer reigns. Finally, a dramatic detail which assumes peculiar significance in view of the recent crisis, it is a symbolical cannon-shot that suddenly hurls the poet in an eddy of smoke from the first place to the second.

It is impossible, then, to mistake a certain bitterness behind those drolleries and those ingenious allegories which indirectly come back to the inspiration of *The Bowge of Court*.

The poet was in a paradoxical situation: feted at Sheriff Hutton and cold-shouldered in the rest of the kingdom.[11] Thus, his lasting resentment of the Court is equalled only by the indignation he continues to harbour against Wolsey, who had driven him into obscurity and retarded his fame, because in the topsy-turvy world engendered by his tyranny the good were exiled while the wicked had free rein, and calumny triumphed where 'wysdome and sadnesse be set out a sunnyng' (line 201).

On the threshold of old age, therefore, the poet realized to what extent full and entire recognition of his genius had been prevented by those evil forces whose target he had rarely ceased to be. But he remained sure that everything would change if only he were enabled to convince his adversaries, once for all, of the mystical and transcendent character that distinguished the poet-laureate's very nature. He saw himself as a victim of calumny:

> Sith he is slaundred for default of konnyng.

> (140)

Here was matter for some brilliant pleading. The time for invective had gone. With *Why Come ye not to Court?* the old poet had momentarily shot his bolt. Distance had reduced the formidable outline of Wolsey; the big Tom-cat looked much less dangerous from afar. The real problem was no longer the struggle against Wolsey, but the rehabilitation of Skelton. The little ceremony of which he had been the object had seemed to foreshadow his future glory. This was a theme on which he had touched in *Speke, Parrot,* and upon which he could now dwell to his heart's content. In choosing to enlarge the triumph *in camera* at Sheriff Hutton to the proportions of eternity, the poet freed himself at a single stroke from his gilded prison, repaired an error on the part of Fate and at the same time gave striking proof of his good faith. The central theme of *The Garland of Laurel* is thus nothing less than the reception of England's poet-laureate, John Skelton, among the immortals of every age and clime. He also provided a vivid and picturesque account of an initiation ceremony well calculated to please his feminine audience.

The Garland of Laurel is a high-flown fantasy, conceived somewhat after the style of a novel in verse which might have been called *New and droll adventures of Master Skelton, poet-laureate, in which is seen that notwithstanding his disgrace at Court, he is admitted to the Temple of Eternal Fame.*

The poem begins with a stanza of astronomical particulars, comparable to the opening stanza of *The Bowge of Court,* but with this difference, that the earlier warlike Mars gives place here to 'Mars retrogradant', who provides the clue to the new atmosphere. *The Bowge of Court* was a declaration of war; *The Garland of Laurel* proclaims an armistice.

Walking alone in the forest of Galtres, the poet is musing on the instability of man's condition. Lying down against the stump of a huge oak blasted by the winter winds, he eventually falls asleep and, as in *The Bowge of Court,* begins to dream. Under a princely pavilion Dame Pallas, goddess of Wisdom and academic Science, receives a request from the Queen of Fame. The two immortals merrily discuss the 'Skelton case'. What is to be done with him? Since he has already been given the laurel crown, he should long ago have been admitted to the Palace of Fame. Dame Pallas had given the necessary instructions to that effect. But has he in turn done all he should to deserve that honour? Has his literary output been sufficient? Has he not wasted precious time writing satires? Was not Ovid driven into exile, and Juvenal threatened with death, precisely for having written satire? Maybe; but on the other hand, if he had fallen into the aureate style, would he not have been accused of flattery? May not a poet handle parable for his own pleasure?

Finally, there is the long-debated precedent of Aeschines, who lost the case of the Crown against Demosthenes but was not on that account struck from the registers of Fame. A dangerous precedent, thinks Dame Pallas, who reproaches the Queen of Fame for conferring notoriety on people of all conditions and qualities, including thieves and murderers, persons of no account, whereas men of merit, whose virtue consists in the fulfilment of their duty, are ignored.

It is ultimately agreed that if Skelton can prove he has not cultivated idleness, if he can furnish proof of his poetical labours, his case will be considered. Aeolus is forthwith ordered to sound his trumpet 'tyll bothe his eyen stare', in order to see whether Skelton will come and mix with the international throng of poets. Straightway a noisy and impatient crowd hurries together from all sides, heaving and shoving one another. A second blast of the trumpet, more deafening than the first, is needed to restore order and silence. Then is heard a harping so melodious that the great trees of the forest tremble and the majestic oaks descend from the hills to join the dance. The trunk against which the poet is leaning suddenly starts back a hundred feet, and Skelton is thrust as if by magic towards Dame Pallas's tent. There he finds a great concourse of poets of all lands and of every age, dominated by Phoebus himself, still lamenting the fate of Daphne, poor Daphne stricken by the leaden shaft, deprived of love and transformed into a laurel.

Next comes a procession of laureates 'of many diverse nations', among whom Skelton notices at random Theocritus, Quintilian, Hesiod, Homer, Cicero, Sallust, Ovid, Lucan, Statius, Virgil, Juvenal, Livy, Aulus Gellius, Horace, Terence, Plautus, Boethius, Maximian, Boccaccio, Quintus Curtius, Poggio the Florentine, Gaguin the 'brother of France', Plutarch, Petrarch, Lucilius, Valerius Maximus, Vincent of Beauvais, Propertius, Pisander and, a little apart, England's national trio, Gower, Chaucer and Lydgate, who offer to support his candidature. Lydgate is described as 'protonotary' of the Court of Fame.

As is only polite in such circumstances, the candidate is urged by each of his sponsors to join their company, declines twice, but eventually, at their joint insistence, agrees to take his place in the pavilion. Dame Pallas then directs that the poet be conveyed to the Queen of Fame's palace to hear what she has to tell him. The whole crowd of poets is likewise ordered to proceed together to the said palace, a masterpiece of elaborate architecture, bristling with towers and turrets, paved with turquoise and chrysolith, closed with gates of ivory encrusted with lozenges of gold and precious stones. A staircase of a hundred steps leads to a grand colonnade glimmering with cut diamonds and opening in turn into the main hall adorned with columns encrusted with azure sapphires and lit by a clerestory bright with rubies and other sparkling stones. News is busily exchanged. While awaiting the moment of audience—and we all know how slow that business can be—Skelton finds in the person of Dame Occupation, registrar of the tribunal, a welcome mentor with whom to while away the time. She is, incidentally, an old acquaintance who has already done him service in days when the poet had much to endure from men,

> When broken was the mast
> Of worldly trust.

(542-3)

Occupation suggests a walk in the neighbourhood. Shouldering their way through the crowds, avoiding the loafers, they soon reach a field walled with flint, in which are to be seen a thousand gates, new and old. These are the gates of the different nations, among which is that of Anglia, surmounted by a leopard crowned with gold and pearls, in a pose so menacing that he might have been a living creature. From the top of the ramparts the two strollers perceive a disreputable herd of ribalds and good-for-nothings, hypocritical and dissolute folk strangely reminiscent of the courtiers in *The Bowge of Court*.

At that very moment there is a tremendous burst of gunfire that catches everyone within range. Some are lamed, others blinded; and one man, the top of his head blown off by a bullet, continues running with no more brains than a hare. At length, when the clouds begin to clear, the poet is astonished to find himself in an 'arbour' surrounded with sanded pathways, where birds are singing in the greenery. The banks are covered with soft lawns; rose-trees and vines enclose the scene; streams of water clearer than crystal fall from golden pipes into pools alive with roach, barbel and bream, whose silvery scales glitter in the sun. The poet then notices a laurel-tree on top of which sits a phoenix holding branches of olive whose fragrant flowers are 'chief preservative against all infections' and able to relieve pain caused by old wounds. Through this enchanted garden there blows a gentle breeze. Dryads and Maenads, their tresses newly soaked in oil, dance around the laurel led by the goddess Flora, Queen of Summer.

Skelton soon learns that they are in the Countess of Surrey's domain. Entering a postern gate they climb a winding staircase which leads to a 'goodly chamber of estate'. Here sits the Countess surrounded by her ladies-in-waiting busy with some embroidery that cannot fail to warm the poet's heart. They are fashioning a garland intended for the laureate as reward for his loyal services. By way of acknowledgment, he in turn composes a series of charming rondeaux in praise of his hostess and her companions, forgetting no one, not even the youngest of the group, Mistress Isabel Pennell, who is still in her cradle.

Occupation, however, brings this interlude to a sudden end, for Aeolus has once again been ordered to sound his trumpet. The hour of audience has arrived. Gower, Chaucer and Lydgate introduce Skelton to the throne-room, where the public is already assembled. As he passes, all admire the garland worn proudly by the poet from Sheriff Hutton. At length the whispering dies away; a great silence falls upon the room, and the Queen of Fame begins to speak. She invites Skelton to justify his claim to the laureate's title. The poet then, with all humility, waits for Dame Occupation to present a list of his works. He sits down in the place appointed by Calliope, and Occupation proceeds to open the great book containing the titles of his works, a magnificent book, a bibliophile's treasure with its binding of precious materials encrusted with gems, its wrought clasps, its margins illuminated with bars of gold and blue, adorned with grasshoppers and wasps, butterflies and gorgeous peacock feathers, flowers and slimy snails—marvels that 'would have made a man whole that had been right sickly'.

Occupation then solemnly reads out the long list of works

written by the poet-laureate (including the satire *Apollo*, which, because of a last-minute scruple, the author would have liked to suppress, but, as he is given to understand, what is written is written). Everyone is convinced that the poet Skelton is not guilty of idleness. Not only is he absolved from all blame, but the general enthusiasm is tremendous. 'What a triumph!' they shout. Trumpets and clarions blare, and their echo reaches Rome. The starry sky shakes, the ground groans and trembles. The book is closed and Skelton—wakes up, still amazed by the tumult. He rubs his eyes, looks up to heaven and sees two-faced Janus, who is preparing his almanack for the New Year.

Thus, *The Garland of Laurel* consists of a series of romantic episodes linked together by sudden transitions borrowed either from the marvellous apparatus of the medieval world, e.g. the dream, or from brilliant inventions such as the cannon-shot, or from the presence at the poet's side of an allegorical guide such as Dame Occupation, who reminds one rather of Grace-Dieu in Guillaume de Guilleville's poem than of Virgil leading Dante to Inferno.

Here the poet gives free rein to his fancy by placing all sorts of topics and commonplaces at the service of the great crescendo that leads to the triumph of the closing scene.

Notice that the work begins in a manner quite as conventional as does *The Bowge of Court*, and in an identical way with the customary astronomical particulars and a realistic account of the author's situation on the threshold of a medieval dream, which in turn transforms the scene into a marvellous world of allegory. Next, it has recourse to the scholastic dialogue, as in the opening of *Magnificence*, and begins to take fire with a revival of *Speke, Parrot's* satirical allusions and veiled sarcasm. Then, doubtless in order to please its feminine readers, it contains numerous passages in the aureate diction of courtly poetry, describing in the childlike manner of fairy tales wonderful castles and paradisal 'arbours', descriptions that rival the most sugary inventions of Stephen Hawes in *The Pastime of Pleasure*. But—and it is here that Skelton's originality and daring are most apparent—those descriptions match, just as in *The Bowge of Court*, the picture of that sordid environment so strongly reminiscent of the Court. Finally, combining the theme of

Lydgate's *Assembly of the Gods* with that of Chaucer's *Temple of Fame*, it elaborates in a spectacular finale the subject Skelton had most at heart, an interest personal to him above all others, the consecration of his eternal fame by an international court of poets.

Alongside this piece of bravado, the poem abounds in picturesque asides. The poet excels notably in depicting crowds, those turbulent medieval crowds, exchanging news at the fairs, and at the crossroads of a Catholic Europe where the trumpetings of Aeolus echo as far as Rome. He manages to endow those crowds with life and at the same time to isolate curious and sometimes grim little details, such as that individual with the top of his head blown off but continuing to scamper about like one of those grotesque figures in a painting by Hiero-nymus Bosch. Elsewhere, Skelton's art inclines to miniature. One of the most charming features of *The Garland of Laurel* is the way in which the poet has mingled with the real and allegorical characters of his *extravaganza*, as in a tapestry, an entire small world of insects, fish, flowers and birds.

Finally, there is the humour which suffuses the whole with a delightful air of parody, or rather with a youthful spirit of fun. Skelton indulged without restraint in the pleasure of presenting himself along with the noble ladies whom he sought to honour.

There he achieved one of the most curious encounters of the academic and the chivalric spirit in all literature. Skelton crowned by female hands thus rises higher than at any time in his career above the little hunted intellectual of *The Bowge of Court*, whom a gang of slippery courtiers would have liked to throw overboard.

In the contemporary edition of 1523 the poem is followed by an *Envoi* which exalts the advantages of English over the Latin of clerks,[12] and, because he still entertained some distrust of the world, makes some prudent reservations on the ever possible assaults of calumny. A short Latin poem eloquently proclaims the superiority of the laurel over all other trees. Lastly, a small piece of verse, *En Parlement de Paris*,[13] together with translation into Latin and English, repeats, in the three languages familiar to pre-Renaissance England, that 'Justice is dead and Truth asleep', satirical themes which tally on the whole with that undercurrent of rancour and hostility towards the Government which emerges so clearly in the critical passages of *The Garland of Laurel*. This feature was especially topical because, since 18th April 1523, the English Parliament had been repeatedly attacked by the chancellor, Wolsey, who was determined to obtain a loan of £800,000 for the furtherance of his policy.[14]

An uncorroborated story in Hall's Chronicle, referring to May in the same year, would suggest that the poet had not yet ceased to make war upon his enemy. 'In that season the cardinal used his powers as legate to dissolve the Convocation of St Paul, summoned by the archbishop of Canterbury, and required the latter, with all his clergy to attend his Convocation at Westminster, upon which the poet, Master Skelton, wrote:

> Gentle Paul laie down they swearde
> For Peter [of Westminster] hath shauen thy
> beard.' [15]

The day, however, was not far off when Skelton and Wolsey would have occasion to make peace.

In fact, the general situation was altering rapidly, substituting new problems for old. The increasing menace of Lutheran ideas would soon reconcile men as different as Wolsey and Thomas More on the one hand, on the other Skelton and Standish, who had lately disagreed as to the value of Greek and the New Learning. Before that, England, living in fear of an imminent twofold invasion, was to see her anxieties removed by unexpected military successes which would raise the Cardinal's prestige and reconcile him momentarily with the hero of the hour, the Earl of Surrey. Therefore a reconciliation between Skelton and Wolsey, which would have seemed impossible a few months earlier, was furthered by this latest episode in the struggle against the Scots.

After Flodden, Margaret Tudor, sister of Henry VIII, had given birth to a posthumous son of James IV[16]. Then, in order to strengthen her position in that foreign land, she had married a Scotsman, the Earl of Angus; but the Scottish nationalists obtained the appointment of the Duke of Albany as Regent. Now, Albany, second son of James II, had been born in France,

and was partial to the French way of life. The result was a state
of hostility between the Queen and the Regent, which reflected
not only a personal antagonism, but also a rivalry between two
policies. Next, Margaret quarrelled with Angus and was briefly
reconciled with Albany, who, being still in love with France,
left Scotland in 1521. When he returned a few months later, at
the urgent request of François I, it was in order to recruit a
powerful army (80,000 men) with which England would be
attacked in the rear in the case of her deciding to move against
France. Finally, there was no want of underhand intrigue:
Scotland conspired with one of the Pole family, a Yorkist pre-
tender, to dethrone Henry VIII, while the Emperor plotted
with the Constable de Bourbon to dethrone François I.[17] Thus
it was that in September 1522 Lord Dacre, finding himself confronted by greatly superior forces, had the presence of mind to
negotiate, on his own authority, a truce of one month, the
Truce of Solan,[18] which averted the peril of invasion in the nick
of time. When Surrey returned from France, after an inglorious
campaign in Picardy [19] which had been cut short by lack of
funds, he was invited to resume the traditional role of watching
the Border, which his father had fulfilled with such distinction.
Consequently, when the Duke of Albany returned to the charge
in November 1523, he found someone to dispute his passage.

The Regent appeared before Wark Castle on the night
of Saturday–Sunday, 31st October–1st November.[20] Surrey,
warned of the threat by Sir William Lyle, commander of the
garrison, hurriedly alerted the troops in the vicinity, the men of
Northumberland, the company called 'my Lord Cardinal's', the
troops under Lord Dacre and some others. On Monday, at
three o'clock in the afternoon, the Tweed running too strong to
be fordable, Albany sent two thousand Frenchmen by boat
to storm the place. The French forced their way into the outer
courtyard of the fortress, where the besieged with great difficulty held them in check for an hour and a half. Then they
managed to reach the inner courtyard, only to be dislodged by
a violent counter-attack which hurled them back to their
starting point. Meanwhile Albany had got wind of Surrey's
approach with reinforcements, and decided on a hurried with-
drawal. Fear of the wolf had sufficed to make him relax his hold.

'Never has a military leader been seen to raise a siege more shamefully than that coward Albany,' was more or less what Surrey told the King in his report on 3rd November.[21] Next day, he wrote to Cardinal Wolsey confirming that brilliant feat of arms and that easy victory.

Such was the episode which afforded Skelton an opportunity to make his official reappearance with one of those triumphal rhapsodies in the style of the warlike poems written in 1513. After ten years, history was repeating herself in a curious way: England, once again menaced by a Franco-Scottish pincer-movement, was once again delivered by an earl of Surrey, son of the glorious victor of Flodden.[22] The prestige of the Howards shone with added lustre, while behind the scenes credit of those successes went, as it had done at the time of the French campaign, to the foresight and administrative talents of Cardinal Wolsey. And Skelton, suddenly reconciled with the world, broke once again into ferocious raillery against his hereditary enemies, the Scots, and their French allies.[23]

He described with great gusto Albany's flight by night,[24] shut in a kind of litter borne on men's shoulders and with all its curtains drawn. When he compares this expedition against England to the Punic wars, it is in order to declare that those who took part in it had none of the courage which redeemed the enemies of Rome.[25] The poem is nothing but a long, garrulous invective against Albany, Scotland and the Scots, together with a vibrant eulogy of Surrey ('flower of knighthood') and of Henry VIII, model of a magnanimous sovereign, adored by his people. Among other praises, Skelton had a word for the soldiers who had fought under the banner of the Archbishop of York:

> With the noble powre
> Of my lord cardynall.

(59–60)

It was, indeed, the first time since *Why Come ye not to Court?* that Skelton had spoken in such friendly terms of Wolsey, and it was not the last. No one was more ready than he to judge the tree by its fruits. Well, he could only rejoice at the happy turn of military events and in the energetic steps taken every day against the Lutherans. Had not his former pupil received from the Pope the title 'Defender of the Faith?' Skelton, therefore, had cause to rejoice as he watched a return of the good old days of 1512–13, when the closest understanding between the Pope and the King of England had coincided with the period when he himself had stood in highest favour.

Everything seems to suggest that Wolsey, on his side, took advantage of this honeymoon in his relations with Surrey to neutralize an importunate but honest foe. Skelton had certainly not spared the Cardinal, but amid the euphoria engendered by the new understanding, even *Why Come ye not to Court?* could, at a stretch, pass for a sort of 'flytyng', full of exaggerations that were offensive rather than dangerous to the security of the State. Perhaps, in spite of repeated threats, Wolsey had always felt himself restrained by the Sovereign's indulgence towards his old tutor. Wolsey, so prompt to strike hard at the nobles whose political power he wished to reduce, was occasionally prepared to use diplomacy with an individual. He did so in the case of Thomas Bilney some years later.[26] So too, and with greater reason, he dealt with Skelton who had had a long career of loyalty to the Tudors. It is timely to remember here that in *Colin Clout* Skelton had left the door open to an explanation.[27] That explanation was now due. The Cardinal had probably not much difficulty in convincing the aged poet that he was, like himself, a man misunderstood and grossly calumniated, whose one purpose was the happiness of his sovereign, the greatness of England and the safeguard of the Church. On these essential points, then, they were in agreement. And, as earnest of his good will, he whispered in his ear the promise of a grey amice, meaning in ecclesiastical terms a post in the Chapel Royal.[28]

An echo of that interview has come down to us through the *Envoi* that appears at the end of the poem on Albany's flight:

> Go, lytell quayre, apace,
> In moost humble wyse,
> Before his noble grace,
> That caused you to deuise

This lytel enterprise;
And hym moost lowly pray,
In his mynde to comprise
Those wordes his grace dyd saye
Of an ammas gray.
Je foy enterment en sa bone grace.[29]

Wolsey, however, forgot his promise. Skelton found himself
obliged to remind him of it. He appears to have written a poem
in praise of Henry VIII and the Cardinal which has not survived but of which we have *L'Autre Envoi*—following perfectly
on the first—in which Skelton allows us a glimpse of contradictory sentiments, hope and fear, and even a threatening
gesture:

Twene hope and drede
My lyfe I lede
But of my spede
Small sekerness;
Howe be it I rede
Both worde and dede
Should be agrede
In nobleness:
Or els, etc. [30]
'. . . Tu tamen esto Palladis almae
Gloria pollens plena Minervae!'

(207)

History does not say whether Skelton obtained satisfaction,
but allows us to suppose that he did. From this time onward he
seems to have entrenched himself in silence until the day when
we find him at the side of Thomas More, wielding his pen as a
supporter of Cardinal Wolsey in the struggle against the tide of
Lutheran ideas.

CHAPTER IX

Last Years, and the Struggle against the Lutherans

AFTER THE winter of 1523 we hear no more of Skelton for about four years, except for one allusion which is, however, so vague and distorted that it amounts almost to confirmation of the veil of oblivion that seems to cover both himself and his work during that period. The reference occurs in an isolated story, number LI of a collection entitled *A C Mery Tales*—one of the jest-books of Shakespeare [1]—which appeared in London in 1526. The story in question speaks of 'a certain Master Skelton, poet-laureate', as if the author of the poem on the Duke of Albany's flight belonged already to another world. Moreover, it presents not the Skelton of the Court and of the recent conflict with Wolsey, but the rector of Diss, in the remote and faded years of his sojourn in Norfolk. Its exceptional interest lies in the fact of its being the first written document in which the Skelton legend appears during the poet's lifetime.

The editor of this book was none other than John Rastell,[2] brother-in-law of Thomas More, which entitles us to think that the Skelton legend originated in English humanistic circles. This is hardly surprising when we consider the marked taste for comic stories shown by the humanists in general and by More's coterie in particular.

The *Hundred Merry Tales* recall the long tradition of the *Decameron*, Poggio's *Facetiae* and those of Heindrich Bebel. Nearer in time, they reveal similarities to the *Joci ac Sales* [3] by the Alsatian humanist Ottomar Nachtgall or Nachtigall, published in 1524 at Augsburg, which is divided into Centuries and in which Thomas More figures on several occasions.

The humanists, in fact, were in the habit of making their friends or their enemies the heroes of their inventions. In 1525 John Rastell himself had published a first collection of gay stories, *The Merry Jests of Widow Edith*, which featured Thomas More and the solemn John Fisher.

The story concerning Skelton tells how, following a rumpus with the Bishop of Norwich, the rector of Diss tried to regain the prelate's favour by presenting him with a brace of pheasants. Stopped at the gate by a watchful porter, he decides to cross the palace moat on a shaky plank. He falls into the water, climbs out safe and sound, still clutching his pheasants, and appears before the bishop dripping wet, much to the amusement of the bystanders. But the bishop persists in refusing him audience. Then Skelton—and here the story wavers a little—considering how often the bishop has called him a fool, and in order to avoid 'confirmation' under that name, escapes from his embarrassment by means of a wisecrack: 'You'ld certainly accept my pheasants,' he suggests, 'if only you knew their names.' The bishop is curious, and Skelton answers him: 'This one is called Alpha, the first, and this one Omega, the last; in other words, if it pleases your Grace to accept them, be sure that it's the first present I've ever given you, but also, by God, the last.'

The story is amusing and perfectly harmless. It appears to be based on quite probable biographical facts: a temporary disagreement with the Bishop of Norwich, a reputation for eccentricity and a liking for whimsicality and independence of spirit. It is not, for all that, entirely convincing. Allowing for typical exaggerations, there is something false about this wriggling puppet, something that does not ring true with all we know about the poet-laureate's normal behaviour. It may be urged that the story was not devised to caricature Skelton, but rather that Skelton was chosen as a peg on which to hang a story in search of a character. Indeed, we find it again in another form with Scoggin, not Skelton, as its hero.

This time the story concerns a sponging rogue of the episcopal court who loses the favour of his bishop for having remarked one day that the prelate's nose was so long that there was no one whom he could embrace. Told never again to darken the palace door, Scoggin is not discouraged, but arms himself with a long pole with which he intends to cross the moat and so enter by another way. In order to regain the bishop's confidence, he brings him a brace of grouse. The pole snaps and Scoggin tumbles into the water. Eventually he appears before the bishop, dripping wet, at dinner time. 'Didn't I tell you, knave, never to darken my door again?' shouts his lordship. 'Saving your honour,' Scoggin corrects him, 'I've not darkened your door. I crossed your moat, where I was actually baptized by falling into the water; and now you confirm me, calling me knave.' Thereupon the guests roar with laughter and Scoggin is forgiven.[4]

Thus the story appropriated to Skelton becomes much more intelligible if we can agree that on the whole it is nothing but a second-rate rehash of an anecdote much more suitable to the mischievous and sycophantic character of Scoggin.

This interpretation, however, faces a chronological difficulty. The legend of Scoggin does not really take shape in England until about 1565-6, when the publisher-printer Thomas Colwell purchased for 4*d.* the rights in the 'Geystes of Skoggon',[5] although there is mention of the latter as early as 1542 in *The Dietary of Health* by the celebrated Dr Andrew Borde, who is generally supposed to be Scoggin's creator.[6]

What then is this Scoggin, more elusive than a will-o'-the-wisp? Surely, he is a kind of hybrid, born from the confusion of two persons: the gentleman Henry Scogan, object of Chaucer's famous *Envoi*, who really existed and was no court fool, and one John Scoggin, Scoggan or Skoggon, an alleged court fool who never existed, although he was said to have lived under Henry VII. On the other hand, as a legendary figure, he does condense a number of well-known elements of international folklore, borrowed either from the German Ulenspiegel[7] or from the character of Marklof, familiar in France through the rich and ancient tradition of the stories of Marcoul and Solomon.

In other words, we have here a concerted attempt to acclimatize in England certain foreign traditions of a humorous nature by grafting them into vintage characters; a hesitant and clumsy attempt which may be said to have taken a wrong turning when it chose the eccentric but intransigent Skelton, and which afterwards laid hold on the fictitious and more pliant Scoggin.

But the ambiguity thus introduced at the outset between John Skelton and John Scoggin (Skoggon in Colwell), aggravated by a resemblance of names, was destined to produce continual misunderstandings. John Bale mentions both successively in his catalogue of English writers and likens each to Demo-critus.[8] Gabriel Harvey [9] and Ben Jonson [10] coupled the two names, which ended by denoting a pair of inseparable clowns in the Elizabethan Interludes. The confusion reached its utmost with Drayton's remark in the preface to his *Eclogues*: 'The Colin Clout of Skoggan under Henry VII is pretty.' [11]

The fifty-first of the *Hundred Merry Tales*, which originated the Skelton legend, may therefore be fairly suspected of being largely imbued with foreign influence. We find confirmation of this in another aspect of the same story—the typical conflict between priest and bishop.

The sixteenth century derived a new thrill from those tales of the humorous insubordination of recalcitrant priests in their dealings with proud prelates. There is no lack of such stories in Nachtigall's *Joci ac Sales*. But Germany, where class distinctions were sharper than elsewhere, had already stylized a type of dis-obedient priest in the person of *Kalenberger*, a more or less historical person from southern Germany, whose real name is thought to have been Weigand von Theben and who is sup-posed to have lived at the court of Otto, Duke of Austria, at the beginning of the sixteenth century. Appointed parish-priest of Kalenberg, he earned a twofold reputation as an incorrigible jester and a priest of dubious morals who, for example, when ordered by his bishop to engage a forty-year-old housekeeper, preferred to take two of twenty.[12] Now, at the period with which we are concerned, we find in England undeniable infiltrations of German tradition. *The parson of Kalenborowe* [13] appears in a number of English jest books, including a *Tyll Howleglass*, which were published in Holland for the English market by the Antwerp printer Jan Van Doesborgh [14] after 1519–20. There were also two editions of *The Parson of Kalen-borowe*, issued by the English printer R. Copland, which were little more than reprints of the first.[15] Referring to the parish priest of Kalenborowe, Herford remarks: 'His career in England ended at about the time when the stories that were circulating about two heroes of local humorous tradition, who strongly resembled him, crystallized in a collection which kept alive their memory for a hundred years—the student Scoggin and the merry Skelton.'

It is therefore safe to say that there is something of *Kalen-berger* as well as of *Ulenspiegel* in the Skelton of the *Hundred Merry Tales*. Notice, however, that the story makes no allusion whatever to private misconduct. It was not until after Skelton's death—and the fact must be emphasized—that we find exactly the same story, excepting a few details, blown up into a matter of concubinage.

Be that as it may, the fifty-first story of the *Hundred Merry Tales* introduced something quite new into the poet-laureate's reputation. By placing him in a grotesque situation of low comedy it opened the door to a whole series of preposterous anecdotes with Skelton as the hero. It thus prepared the way for those many future embellishments that were to establish for centuries the burlesque figure of the English *Kalenberger*.

In the same year that witnessed publication of the *C Mery Tales* a heresy trial inaugurated a new phase of the struggle against the infiltration of Lutheran ideas.[16] Since the Bull *Exsurge* of June 1520 and Luther's official condemnation by the Pope on 12th May 1521, opposition to the Lutheran menace had taken shape in a mixture of practical measures, symbolical gestures and doctrinal controversy. Eight days after the promulgation of the papal Bull, Cardinal Wolsey organized an *auto da fe* of Lutheran books at Paul's Cross,[17] and John Fisher, Bishop of Rochester and chancellor of Cambridge University, denounced in four points the heretical character of the new teaching. Henry VIII wrote to Duke Ludwig of Bavaria urging him to put down the growing disorder in his territory before it was too late, and he published the famous book against Luther which earned him the title Defender of the Faith.[18] An impassioned controversy started between the two camps, in which, on the English side, Powell, Fisher and Thomas More were destined to win renown.

Meanwhile, the Lutheran ideas found adherents in England, particularly among undergraduates of the two universities. German books were smuggled in by way of the Norfolk coast. From the moment when Tyndale published in exile his English translation of the New Testament (1525), it was apparent that the Reformation would enjoy a great deal of support. On 24th October 1526 Tunstall, Bishop of London, issued an urgent proclamation intended to put the faithful on their guard against the tendentious character of translations deriving from Germany or Holland.

This was followed on 3rd November in the same year by an appeal from Warham, Archbishop of Canterbury. As for Wolsey, he busied himself with the purchase abroad of prohibited books *en bloc*, and ordered a search of the London residences of Hanseatic merchants, who were suspected of favouring the Lutherans. This duty was entrusted to John Islip, Abbot of Westminster, and it led to the arrest of one Hans Ellerdorpe, who appeared before a court in the Abbey chapterhouse, a few yards from Skelton's lodging.

Meanwhile, trouble had broken out at Cambridge, where Dr Barnes had delivered, in a slightly modified form, a sermon by Luther on the epistle for the Fourth Sunday of Advent. Barnes abjured on 11th February 1526, at a solemn ceremony in St Paul's. But the affair had drawn attention to a small group of ardent neophytes who, in the shadow of Cambridge University, were secretly practising the new doctrine, reforming their way of life, visiting the sick and those in prison. They held their meetings at the 'White Horse' inn, which soon became known as 'Little Germany'.

The recognized leader of that group was Thomas Bilney, a frail young man from Norfolk, to whom was attributed the conversion of Barnes and Latimer. He did not profess such extreme views as Luther, and had even obtained from the Bishop of Ely a licence to preach throughout the diocese. But the vigour with which he denounced pilgrimages and worship of the Virgin and the saints brought him to the notice of Wolsey who tried first, in a personal interview, to wring from the young reformer a promise not to spread the doctrines of Luther. In 1527, however, driven by his zeal, Thomas Bilney, assisted by Thomas Arthur, once again attracted the attention of Authority. We find him at Whitsun preaching in the neighbourhood of London, at Newington and Willesden, and also at Ipswich, the Cardinal's home town. Here the two young men were arrested by order of Tunstall. They were brought before an ecclesiastical tribunal which sat, from 27th November to 7th December 1527, alternately in the chapter house at Westminster and at the

London residence of the Bishop of Norwich. Thomas Arthur and Thomas Bilney, having abjured, received absolution and went in procession, barefoot and carrying a faggot, to St Paul's, where they stood to hear the customary sermon.

Skelton played some part in those events, placing his pen at the Cardinal's service in order to fight heresy at the side of Thomas More, in close alliance with his friends John Islip and Prior William Mane, Henry Standish and Richard Nykke, Bishop of Norwich, to whose jurisdiction he was still, in theory, subject.

The affair of the Cambridge students inspired the last of his surviving poems, *A Replycacion agaynst certayne yong scolers abiured of late* . . .[19]

This reply was particularly important in his eyes because the guilty parties were members of his old University, the pavilion of Dame Pallas, the seat of Minerva.

> . . . Tu tamen esto Palladis almae
> Gloria pollens plena Minervae.

> (p. 207)

Worse still, one of them, Thomas Bilney, had received with his scholarship the sum of £10, which, the poet thought, 'might have been better employed other ways'. But 'the tree is known by its fruits', or as is also said, 'the blind eateth many a fly', retrospective sarcasm against the advocates of the New Learning, and all the more pungent in that they could be considered as addressed to Wolsey.[20] But Skelton felt old enough, sufficiently independent and self-assured to fling at the Cardinal a last 'I told you so!' [21]

None the less, his *Replycacion* is dedicated to Wolsey in fulsome and extravagant terms, for in the sphere of conflict with heresy the two ex-enemies were in complete accord. *The Replycacion* is a combative poem, a disorderly jumble of 'Skeltonics' and eccentric prose, heavy with alliteration, 'euphistic', *avant la lettre* and accompanied throughout with lengthy marginal glosses.

It forms a pendant to the *Dialogue against Heresies* written by More on the same subject at Wolsey's request.[22] Later on, either because the poet's active participation in the great campaign of counter-reform undertaken by Wolsey was unknown, or was not understood, Skelton came to be regarded for centuries as a herald of Nonconformity favouring the spread of Protestantism in England, which he most certainly was not.

Indeed, it is quite plain that there was no break, no vacillation even, in Skelton's religious attitude. The *Replycacion* does nothing else than repeat in this respect the warnings he had uttered against the rising tide of heresy in *Ware the Hawk*, before Luther had appeared on the scene. The former work was written some time after the ceremony of abjuration at Paul's Cross on 8th December. The fury with which the author denounces two young people who, after all, had done their penance, might come as a surprise, but for our knowledge of his propensity to trample on his fallen enemies—James IV of Scotland, for example.

The case of Bilney and Arthur, naturally, was of particular importance. The poet was concerned to dismantle the mechanism of heresy working here in immature minds, to confound it with the inexorable logic of reasoned argument, and finally to discourage it by threatening the stake. Because he was above all else a poet, Skelton simply put poetry at the service of religion in the typically clerical spirit of his salutary and comminatory satire-sermons.

After setting the example of his own most humble submission to Cardinal Wolsey and to the prelates of Holy Mother Church, and at the same time addressing, in the style of a classical invocation, a *Eulogium consolationis* to his old University, to which, alas, the two young heretics belong, the poet denounces in his usual strain of ironic contempt the aberration of those striplings who, under pretext of having 'licked a little of the liquorous electuary of lusty learning, in the much studious schoolhouse of scrupulous Philology', set themselves against the great doctors and pretend to solve the highest problems of theology from the pulpit of the 'Three Cranes' tavern in the Vintry. Add to the natural arrogance of youth a thirst for domination and fame 'which begets sedition', and you see how juvenile minds allow themselves to be seduced by error, once 'bitten by the flesh-fly of Lutheran heresy borne on the East wind'.

Then, coming to the heart of the matter, the poet turns to the charges brought against Bilney and Arthur, namely that they had denounced as idolatrous the veneration of statues of the Virgin and the saints, as well as the practice of pilgrimage.

Here, Skelton appeals to the principle of authority based on conciliar decisions (notably that of the seventh oecumenical council held at Nicaea in 787) which had distinguished three degrees of religious worship: *latria*, the supreme worship due to God alone; *dulia*, the veneration due to His servants, the angels and saints; and *hyperdulia*, the special veneration due to the Virgin Mary. Recalling, on the subject of idolatry, St Jerome's work against Jovinian, he draws attention to that fourth-century opponent of Christian asceticism, and thence derives an argument against what he calls the 'insensate sensuality' of the young heretics, while his mention of the Lateran Council probably refers to that of 1215 under Innocent III, whose main object was reform of the universal Church and the extirpation of heresy.

We see Skelton profoundly shocked by the indirect attacks on the Blessed Virgin, to whom he had the greatest devotion. He breathes his indignation in long passages of invective, in a rhythm that becomes more and more urgent as he recalls the principal heresies, enumerated in marginal exclamations, in the style of the vehement apostrophes of *Ware the Hawk*. He mingles Christian heresies, Hebrew vagaries and Muslim unbelief, all confused in the same intolerance of anything that is not strictly orthodox, an attitude strongly reminiscent of the Psalmist's fulmination against the indistinct host of his enemies.

The allusion to the Psalmist is by no means fortuitous. In a second movement, almost as elaborate as the first, but which is in fact merely a postscript to the diatribe against heretics, John Skelton undertakes to answer those evil tongues which—in the interval, no doubt—have denied that the poet is in any way qualified to deal in verse with religious questions. To doubt what he considered in some sort as the priestly mission of a poet, was to touch him on the quick. But he was armed to parry this fundamental objection. He had only, it seems, to remind his opponents of the example of David, king and prophet, poet of poets, equal and even superior to the greatest poets of antiquity,

Greek or Latin. He quotes St Jerome. He gives his references, and then he proceeds to one of the most curious definitions of inspired poetry, a landmark in the history of English literature. He had not waited until the end of his life to formulate the concept of divine inspiration. As early as his first poem, on *The Death of the Earl of Northumberland*, he had spoken of poetic inspiration

> Enbrethed with the blast of influence deyune.

> (v. 157)

It is to his credit, above all, that he rescued laureate poetry from the narrow confines of academic rhetoric in which it languished, and raised it to the level of inspired poetry.[23]

Here he is seen as a true precursor of the Renaissance who mingles without discrimination ancient and medieval concepts, the Greek idea of enthusiasm or 'energy'—

> Howe there is a spyrituall
>   And a misteriall
>   And a mysticall
>   Effecte energiall,
>   As Grekes do it call—

> (365–9)

called in Latin *efficax operatio*, and the Christian idea of the divine breath which speaks by the voice of the Holy Spirit:

> By whose inflammacion
> Of spyrituall instygacion,
> And diuyne inspyracion
> We are kyndled in suche facyon
> With hete of the Holy Gost,
> Which is God of myghtes most,
> That he our penne dothe lede,
> And maketh in vs suche spede,
> That forthwith we must nede
> With penne and ynke procede . . .

> (379–88)

Here we have a capital description and definition of inspiration considered as an imperious expression of the divine presence within us, but one that was not fully adopted by the Renaissance until it had been laicized.

Repeating almost word for word some very ancient reflections of the *Speculum Principis*, he recalls for the last time that in comparison with the enormous crowd of sophists, logicians, philosophers, theologians, doctors, professors and magistrates, poets are extremely rare and therefore infinitely precious. That, he adds, is why the greatest monarchs, the Alexanders and the Caesars, always cherished famous poets . . .

Those are the last surviving words of the poet-laureate John Skelton. They shed a final ray of light on the very sources of his basic optimism, his absolute conviction of the inspired poet's quasi-sacerdotal function, his pride in having been called to attend his Sovereign and in having been complimented by Erasmus as the country's leading poet, and the agonies he must have endured when he found himself far from Court. They illuminate, too, even his most glaring faults, particularly the facility apparent in formless and undisciplined 'Skeltonics', which are not, as might be supposed, the product of carelessness, but much rather the result of an almost mystical submission to the dictates of inspiration, the shorthand, as it were, of inspired poetry.

On 4th May 1528 we find Master Skelton present as a witness at the abjuration of Thomas Bowgas, a fuller of Colchester, in the course of yet another trial, which took place, like earlier ones, in the chapel of Norwich Inn, Bishop Nykke's residence, at Charing Cross.[24] This event is significant from several points of view. It shows a humble artisan affected by the ideas of the Reformation, which, especially since Tyndale's translation, had spread far beyond academic circles. It shows likewise the keen interest taken by Skelton, to his dying day, in the struggle against the new movement. Finally, it suggests once again that, contrary to legend, he remained on friendly terms with his bishop.

Skelton died on 21st June 1529,[25] and was buried before the high altar of St Margaret's, Westminster.[26] His alabaster tombstone was engraved:

IOANNES SKELTONVS VATES PIERIUS HIC SITVS EST.

According to the registers of St Margaret's, 2s. 8d. were spent on the purchase of four candles and 3s. for four torches. The sum of 12d. (out of 6s. 8d. received for the purpose) covered the cost of knell and peals. Lastly a gift of 20d. was paid to the Brotherhood of Our Lady.[27] Skelton died intestate. William Mott, vicar of St Margaret's, was granted administration of his estate.[28]

On 17th July 1529 one Thomas Clark was appointed to the rectorship of Diss, left vacant 'by the natural death of Master John Skelton'.[29]

Such was the peaceful end of John Skelton's belligerent life, in the very year when there began the affair of the Divorce, a prologue to upheavals that would have severely tried his attachment both to the King and to traditional religion.

Thus departed one of the most clamorous of poets, one of the most eccentric, one of the most representative of that early Tudor period when the royal authority was re-established on foundations of a conservative absolutism which admitted the Renaissance but rejected the Reformation.

John Skelton had been largely associated with that task, both as preceptor and as poet of the new regime. Haloed with the prestige of his academic laurels, he had been the first and for long the only poet of distinction to uphold the renown of Tudor England. We know how proud of it he was, but we know also the independence of spirit he affirmed in the fulfilment of his duties at Court.

Proclaiming with such vigour the imprescriptible right of a clerk-poet to serve as the 'priest of Truth', he had met with a certain amount of unpleasantness, but he had preferred to act as firebrand of the opposition rather than stand by and say nothing while the King was imposed upon by a minister whose influence he considered disastrous. And it was quite in his manner to sign the satires against Cardinal Wolsey with his title 'Orator Royal'. That, however, was only one episode in his long career, inspired, we may be sure, by wounded pride that quickly turned to jealousy when the interests of his former pupil were at stake. It remains true that in forty years of service, as Churchyard observes, 'he had seldom been in disgrace'.

Strictly speaking, therefore, he was not himself a rebel, as has so often been suggested. He was much too strongly imbued with the principle of authority for that. But as regards the public good, he entertained views that were not in perfect accord with the anti-feudal doctrine of the early Tudors. Skelton, who came from the entourage of one of the great aristocratic families in the North (probably the Percies of Northumberland), is found to have oscillated continually between his devotion to the King's service and his attachment to the great feudal leaders in the provinces, Percies and Howards, natural defenders of the realm against foreign invasion.

A critic rather than a rebel, John Skelton belonged in fact to a curious and still fairly widespread political type: the recalcitrant conservative, always ready to remind the government of the day that there can be no compromise with Evil. He often appears as a die-hard, lavish of far-fetched advice, chauvinistic, a ferocious enemy of France and Scotland, and hostile generally towards anything new that he considered dangerous to the established order, whether in the sphere of politics, of religion or of education.

One feels that he is anchored to a well-tried cultural system that had lasted for a thousand years, and been codified, too, by three centuries of scholasticism. Thus we find him posing as the scourge of everyone who challenges the established order, delighted, whenever he takes up his pen against an adversary, to show the world that Skelton's foes cannot be other than enemies of Church and State, that the enemies of Church and State must be enemies of Reason and Faith, and that the enemies of Reason and Faith must be either fools or heretics.

This sense of unassailable superiority is certainly one of the secrets of his habitual gaiety. It rests upon a mystical belief in the permanence of the medieval order.

Ironically, the most self-assured of English poets lived just at that stage of English history which was leading unconsciously to the most radical changes. Hence the extraordinary interest of his mordant criticisms, of his righteous indignation which affords us such suggestive and such truthful pictures of contemporary abuses. For the historian can, of course, accuse him of exaggeration, but never of prejudice against the regime of which he was indeed one of the most zealous defenders.

It is in this respect that the very virulence of his satires has managed most easily to create an illusion. The partisan was forgotten, and only his criticism remembered. By a final twist of fate, Skelton was welcomed there and then as a herald of the next generation, that of the Reformers. Hence the misfortunes of his posthumous reputation, which we must now briefly consider.

CHAPTER X

Legend and Reputation

THERE emerged, even in the poet's lifetime, the most divergent opinions which paved the way to future contradictions. The aged Caxton was zealous in his praise on the threshold of his career; Erasmus, from politeness, exalted him to the skies. But Garnesche called him a knave and a fool; and Lily, a friend of Erasmus, categorically denied that he had any poetical talent. One of the most persistent of his adversaries was the poet Alexander Barclay, a Benedictine monk with whom he was at loggerheads at almost every stage of his career, in his relations not only with the King but also with the Howards. Barclay criticized Skelton several times in his translation of the *Nef des Fous* and in his *Eglogues*. He appears even to have composed a separate work (now lost) entitled *Contra Skeltonum*.[1] He scorned his title as laureate, and described his muse as 'stinking Thaïs'. He was the first, with his stern comments on *Phyllyp Sparowe*, to draw the twofold picture of a Skelton shamelessly making fun of the funeral service and scattering the seeds of vice,[2] a picture that would later prove valuable to the advocates of the Reformation.

Meanwhile Henry Bradshaw, a churchman who lived remote from such polemics, linked the two rivals, Skelton and Barclay, in a single eulogy of English poetry and the Virgin Mary:

> It were a pleasaunt werke for the monke of Bury
> For Chaucer or Skelton / fathers of eloquens
> Or for religious Barkeley to shewe theyr diligens.[3]

It is undeniable that by his satirical flashes, by the comic touches with which his work is strewn, and by his images which passed from mouth to mouth (that for example, of Wolsey in hell threatening to usurp Lucifer's throne, in *Why Come ye not to Court?*), John Skelton earned himself the reputation of a jolly poet, while his epic controversies with the powers that be won him the sympathy always accorded to the underdog. Even so, the legend to which he gave birth appears to have been fashioned at a time when he was more or less forgotten and to have included elements that hardly tallied with his character or his public conduct. We have seen the embryo of that legend, about three years before his death, in the fifty-first of the *Hundred Merry Tales*, published by John Rastell in 1526, a legend which established the poet-laureate as a figure of low comedy.[4] We have pointed out the consequent gulf between the known model and that slippery customer, and we have noted the stamp of humanist fancy in the somewhat incoherent endeavour to acclimatize in England a humorous tradition combining the characteristics of the German *Ulenspiegel* and *Kalenberger*.

A new Skelton had been born. Thenceforward the poet's reputation was merged in this literary patchwork figure. The legend of Skelton prospered rapidly, and, laced with new elements, it acquired once for all its essential features and served as his passport to posterity.

Immediately after his death, we find among the papers of no less a person than Thomas Cromwell a collection entitled *The Jests of Skelton*,[5] a specimen of comic literature which in Hazlitt's view, judging by the status of its owner, suggests an author favourable to the Reformation.

We notice also, between 1530 and 1535, the appearance of a collection of witticisms, Protestant in tone, entitled *Tales and Quicke Answers* and published by the printer Thomas Berthelet, in which Skelton occurs—rather to his disadvantage—in a single and rather trivial anecdote.[6]

In 1542, after the final break with Rome, Henry VIII issued a decree whose purpose was to ban all such old writings as were too manifestly Catholic, 'in order to promote true religion'.[7] Thanks, however, to the critical tendency of his work, to the censures of *Colin Clout*, and probably also to the tincture of Protestantism that already coloured his legend, Skelton, along with Chaucer, was to be one of the few authors of the old regime to pass through that official barrier. The great diatribe *Vox populi, Vox dei*,[8] written in Skeltonics and ascribed to him in the following year (1543), confirmed his transfer to the Protestant camp.

The same period saw a deliberate re-issue of some of his works that appeared most favourable to the new ideas: *Colin Clout* and *Why Come ye not to Court?*, considered as anti-episcopal diatribes, and *Phyllyp Sparowe*, a parody of the Office of the Dead. This generation was passionately in favour of a married clergy, and numerous treatises on the subject appeared.[9] It is at about this time that we first hear mention of the famous concubine whom Skelton was supposed to have kept hidden in the rectory at Diss, before recognizing her as his lawful wife on his deathbed. John Bale, an ardent Protestant propagandist, gave the story considerable prominence in the manuscript article which he devoted to Skelton in 1548 [10] and which recurs in extended form in the definitive edition of 1557–9.[11]

Thus, ten years later (1558), on publication of the *Merie Tales, Newly Imprinted and made by Master Skelton Poet Laureate*,[12] it is not surprising to meet once more the fifty-first of the *Hundred Merry Tales*, the story of the two pheasants, elaborated with a new reference to the concubine mentioned by Bale.

Alexander Dyce properly described this collection of gay stories as 'that tissue of extravagant figments put together for the amusement of the vulgar'.[13] It was due to the exertions of the printer Thomas Colwell, who in the same year published also *The Gestes of Skoggon*.[14] The cycle closed once again with the inevitable combination of Skelton and Skoggon. The *Merie Tales* of Skelton (no. vii) added to his legend the existence of an illegitimate son, but Skelton had to await the inventive imagination of Thomas Fuller before he was debited with the paternity of 'many children'.[15]

The legend of Skelton, thus consolidated, fatally obscured the natural development of the poet's own reputation and that of his work. It is a subject over which confusion has long reigned, and for the sake of clarity we must here distinguish three series of phenomena which often overlap: the poet's fame and its decline; the second life of the comic character and his successive incarnations; the underground persistence of his work and its remarkable influence.

Once the first flame of the Reformation had died down, Skelton's star rapidly declined. Paradoxically, the vigour of his satire had helped to sustain a cause which during his lifetime he had strenuously opposed. But as the satire ceased to be relevant, it was his reputation as an entertainer that prevailed. In 1568 Thomas Marshe did him the honour of a general edition, prefaced with a warm eulogy by the poet Churchyard.[16] But the work, laden with many apocryphal writings, bore the stamp rather of humorous literature. On 20th December 1578 young Edmund Spenser, who borrowed from it the name of his own poem *Colin Clout*, sent his friend Gabriel Harvey at Cambridge the *Merie Tales* of Skelton, together with the *Gestes* of Scoggin, Howleglass (the English Ulenspiegel) and Lazarillo.[17] Again, the maturing literary art refined the vocabulary and worked against the sovereignty of rhyme. About 1580 Puttenham, the La Harpe of Elizabethan literature, spoke disdainfully of Skelton as a 'Buffoon', a sneer that silenced at a stroke the admiration he had hitherto enjoyed.[18] Skelton had suddenly grown old, outmoded. He disappeared from the poetic scene. No one dreamed of republishing him. Nor did the considered judgment of William Webbe, in his *Discourse of English Poetrie* [19] (1586), alter the situation. Skelton was out of fashion.

Other forces, however, were also at work, such as the current of puritanism unleashed by the Reformation. Somewhat later, about 1590, we find Arthur Dent, in *The Plaine Man's Pathway to Heaven* (one of the recognized sources of *Pilgrim's Progress*), condemning *Elynour Rummyng*, which he considered, among many other examples of humorous literature, as a work of the Devil.

'. . . And I shall tell you my opinion of them,' says Philagathus; 'I do thus think that they were devised by the Devil, seen and allowed by the Pope, printed in Hell, bound up by Hobgoblin and first published and dispersed in Rome, Italy and Spain.' [20]

Thus, in the sunset of the sixteenth century, John Skelton found himself twice condemned, on the literary and on the moral plane. Francis Meres, in *Palladis Tamia*,[21] repeats

Puttenham's censures. William Vaughan, in *The Golden Grove*, denounces poetry in general: 'The lascivious rimes of our English poets doe discredite the commonwealth and are the chiefe occasions of corruption and the sources of lecherie. Therefore Poetrie is blameworthie' [22]; a condemnation that heralds the solemn excommunication pronounced against poets in his next book, *The Golden Fleece* (1626), in which Skelton among others, the laureate Skelton, by a cruel turn of events, is officially banished, with his crony Scoggin, from the Court of Fame! [23]

However, he was not completely dead. As a comic figure, on the contrary, Skelton had taken a new lease of life. It was in 1597 that Anthony Munday introduced him to the theatre. In a play entitled *The Downfall of Robert Earl of Huntington*,[24] he acts the part of Friar Tuck, Robin Hood's jolly companion. More exactly, he appears under his own name in a sort of Prologue or general Recital intended to precede a performance before the Sovereign. Then, having explained the meaning of these preparatory remarks, he announces that he is going to play Friar Tuck. He speaks quite naturally in 'Skeltonics', displaying an intemperate flow of language that has to be checked. In accordance with his old reputation as a satirical poet, he devotes himself to the satire of contemporary manners. The dramatist, moreover, does not conceal his sympathy for his model, and on the stage Skelton becomes again 'Good Skelton'.

Wherever Skelton is, we may be sure that Scoggin is not far off, and in fact Henslowe's Journal (1600) mentions a play (now lost) by Richard Hathwaye and William Rankins, entitled *Scogan and Skelton*.[25] At about the same date we hear an unexpected but highly significant defence of our poet from the mouth of Sir John Oldcastle's manservant, a spokesman of popular opinion:

'For I have there English bookes, my Lord, that I'll not part with for your Bishoppricke, Bevis of Hampton, Owleglasse, The Friar and the Boy, Ellen of Rumming (sic); Robin Hood and other such godly stories, which if ye burne, by this flesh, I'll make ye drink their ashes in St Marget's ale.'[26]

Here we clearly see the fork-roads of Skelton's reputation. Rejected by the high priests of official poetry, he is stoutly defended by the 'people'.

In 1619 Drayton repeated his defence of Skelton and also the defence of popular, *rhymed* poetry. It was an answer to Puttenham. He went so far even as to write a *Skeltoniad*,[27] the belated homage of a courageous man.

In 1626 Ben Jonson conceived the idea of bringing to life that inseparable pair of marionettes, Skelton and Scoggin. In *The Fortunate Isles and their Union*, a masque written for the court of Charles I, we can see the two cronies 'in habits as they lived'. Ben Jonson as poet-laureate, wishing to remind this prince of his duty as a patron, resolved to call up the shade of his predecessor, the 'Virgil' of the age,

> . . . and he was paid for it
> Regarded and rewarded, which few poets
> Are now-a-days . . .[28]

Skelton was introduced in this case to support an argument. The anti-masque presents Howleglass, Elinour Rumming, Mary Ambree, Long Meg of Westminster—all the best society of humorous literature—along with 'Skipping Skelton and Moral Skogun, that pair of crafty clerks'.

The case of Ben Jonson is both curious and revealing. It affords the typical example of a great poet who in one play, *The Fortunate Iles*, accepts unhesitatingly the legend of Skelton as a figure of low comedy, but in another, *Cynthia's Revels*, shows a thorough knowledge of the poet-laureate's work, particularly of *Magnificence*. In *Cynthia's Revels* Ben Jonson imitates Skelton in the smallest details. Just as in *Magnificence* we see the court vices managing to secure the dismissal of Measure, so in *Cynthia's Revels* we see the courtiers plotting to bring about the disgrace of Crites, the queen's far-sighted counsellor. The four villains of Ben Jonson's play are drawn from Skelton's four vices, even to the alliteration of their names. Skelton gives us Cloaked Collusion, Crafty Conveyance, Counterfeit Countenance and Courtly Abusion; Ben Jonson's rogues are Amorphus (the deformed), Anaides (the impudent), Asotus (the prodigal) and

Hedon (the voluptuous). Among his female characters, Moria is the Greek equivalent of Folly, Phantastes of Fancy. Finally, the courtiers and their companions appear before Queen Cynthia under the names of the virtues opposite to the vices which in fact they represent, just as the four vices of *Magnificence* assume names descriptive of their faults.[29]

Nor is that an isolated example. While the poet's reputation, distorted and vilified by the puerilities of his legend, continued to animate the behaviour of a puppet, the real poet Skelton was protected by the perpetuation of his works. That influence was exerted upon a number of Renaissance dramatists and poets in England and Scotland, chiefly through three of his major works: *Magnificence*, *Phyllyp Sparowe* and *Elynour Rummyng*. The political morality play *Magnificence* was imitated even during the author's life, by plays written likewise against Wolsey, but at a time when Skelton had already made his peace with the Cardinal. They are *The Godly Queene Hester*,[30] crammed with verbal reminiscences, but in very poor style; and a lost play, *Lord Governance and Lady Public Weal*, performed at Gray's Inn at Christmas 1526, for which its author, John Roo, was imprisoned by Wolsey.[31]

In Scotland, Sir David Lyndsay's great morality *Ane Satyre of the three estaits*,[32] played for the first time on 6th January 1540, shows, at least in its first part, striking similarities to Skelton's. The fall of Rex Humanitas, led astray by his evil counsellors under the influence of Dame Sensuality, the rise of Flattery, Falsehood and Deceit in the disguise of virtues, the banishment of Good Counsel, the imprisonment of Truth and Chastity, and the ultimate defeat of the forces of evil on the arrival of Divine Correction, recall the essential features of *Magnificence*.

Similarly, although in the very different political climate of Mary Tudor's accession, the play entitled *Respublica*[33] (1553) presents the sufferings of Widow Republic and her servant People at the hands of a gang of avaricious and unsrcupulous counsellors who, under the preceding reigns, despoiled the Church and squandered the revenues of the Crown until Nemesis—in the person of the new monarch, heiress of sound principles—intervenes to unmask the guilty and make them disgorge their ill-gotten wealth.

Phyllyp Sparowe, which had so disgusted Barclay but which Coleridge later described as 'exquisite', was much enjoyed by the English Renaissance and imitated by some of its best poets.[34] William Cartwright was inspired partly by Catullus and partly by Skelton. But it was from Skelton that he borrowed the essentials of his narrative, including such striking details as that of the sparrow moistening his beak on the lips of his mistress:

> Tell me not of Joy: there's none
> Now my little Sparrow's gone.
>> He, just as you
>> Would toye and wooe,
> He would chirp and flatter me,
> He would hang the wing awhile,
> Till at length he saw me smile,
> Lord how sullen he would be!
> He would catch a Crumb, and then
>> Sporting let it go agen,
>> He from my lip
>> Would moysture sip,
> He would from my Trencher feed,
> Then would hop and then would run,
> And cry Phillip when h'had done.
> O whose heart can choose but bleed? [35]

Gascoigne pays tribute to Phyllyp Sparowe in verses that skip, though slightly mechanical:

> Of all the byrdes that I doe Know,
> Phillip my Sparrow hath no peare:
> For sit she high, or lye she lowe,
> Be shee farre off, or be shee neare,
> There is no byrde so fayre, so fine,
> Nor yet so fresh as this of myne.[36]

Sir Philip Sidney [37] twice found inspiration in Skelton's poem. In *Arcadia* there is a pastoral scene where the two shepherds

Klaius and Straphon notice a girl playing, like Jane Scrope, with her pet bird:

> They saw a maid who thitherward did runne,
> To catch hir sparrow which from hir did swerve,
> As she a black-silke cap on him begunne
> To sett, for foile of hir milke-white to serve,
> She chirping ran, he peeping flew away
> Till hard by them both he and she did stay . . .

Again:

> How rosy moist'ned lips about his beake
> Moving, she seem'd at once to kisse, and speake.

As in Skelton's poem, the gentle sparrow finds refuge between his mistress's breasts:

> Betwixt them two the peeper tooke his nest.

This detail is repeated and developed with great delicacy in the Sonnet devoted by Sidney to *Phyllyp Sparowe*, whom he addresses affectionately thus:

> Good brother Phillip, I have forborne you long,
> I was content you should in favour creepe,
> While craftely you seemed your Cut to keepe,
> As though that faire soft hand did you great wrong:
> I beare with envy, yet I heare your song,
> When in hir necke you did love ditties peepe,
> Ney (more foole I) oft suffred you to sleepe,
> In lillies nest where loves selfe lies along.[38]

With Richard Brome, finally, we have a conscious imitation both in form, in sentiment and in humour. Like Jane Scrope, Constance, the heroine of his poem *The Northern Lass*, adores her sparrow so much that she would not exchange it for Juno's bird, nor for Venus's dove, nor even for Philip of Spain's wealth . . .

> A bonny, bonny Bird I had,
> A Bird that was my Marrow:
> A Bird whose pastime made me glad,
> And Philip 'twas my Sparrow.

A pretty Play-pere: Chirp it would,
And hop, and fly to fist.
Keep cut, as 'twere a usurer's Gold,
And bill me when I list.
Philip, Philip, Philip it cryes,
But he is fled and my joy dyes.
But were my Philip com'd again
I would not change my Love,
For Juno's Bird with gaudy train,
Nor yet for Venus Dove,
Nay, would my Philip come again,
I would not change my state
For his great Namesake's wealth of Spain,
To be another's Mate.[39]

As MacPeek has rightly observed, 'the tradition of Philip Sparow is one with that of Lesbia's bird, so much so that in England for many years the story of Catullus's sparrow is that of Skelton's'. On the threshold of the Renaissance the poet-laureate had unknowingly succeeded in substituting his own model for that of the Ancients.

But while the book of *Phyllyp Sparowe* remains, in spite of all, the choice of connoisseurs, *Elynour Rummyng* is acknowledged as the poetic creation that was to earn him the loudest applause. *The Tunnyng of Elynour Rummyng* holds a distinguished place in lighthearted and facetious literature. The unforgettable inn-keeper of Leatherhead may perhaps be recognized as the source of a long line of jades and viragos whose names echo in the dim regions of written and oral tradition. 'Even Mother Bunch,' wrote Hazlitt, 'is nothing more than Elinour Rummyng revived with certain additions and melodramatic embellishments'.[40] Elynour Rummyng, Widow Edyth, Meg of Westminster, Mother Bunch and Mother Watkyn all bear a family likeness. There, as elsewhere, Skelton gave a vital impulse to a tradition which thereafter needed only to flower.

Apart from anonymous literature, we also find something of Elynour Rummyng in John Cleveland's *Old Gill*, 'born, like Venus, of an old half filled jug of barley-broth!'[41]

There are, to be sure, numerous affinities between John

Skelton and John Cleveland. Both were north-countrymen, former students at Cambridge, supporters of the Catholic monarchy, satirical writers with a caustic wit, authors of patriotic verses against the Scots, enemies of dictatorship (Skelton of Wolsey's, Cleveland of Cromwell's), equally attached to the poetic laurels (Cleveland's pseudonym was Helicon Dew) and equally proud of having been awarded the title *Orator Regius*. The coincidence seems all the more remarkable when we consider that in Cleveland's day Skelton was beginning to be pretty well forgotten.

'Touching your Poet-Laureat Skelton,' wrote James Howell, 'I found him at last (as I told you before) sulking in Duck-Lane, pitifully tatter'd and torn; and as the times are, I do not think it worth the labour and cost to put him in better cloathes, for the genius of the Age is quite another thing.' [42] So Abraham Cowley could ask without awakening an echo: 'Who now reads Skelton?' [43]

For several decades Skelton remained unknown to the general public. He lived only in dusty articles by antiquarians busy transmitting from one generation to another the remnant of confused and contradictory notions that had survived oblivion.

His slow recovery may be held to have started with the biographical notice published by Fuller [44] in 1662, followed in 1691 by Anthony à Wood's bibliographical notice of his works. [45] In 1736 there appeared the first general edition of his poems [46] since that of Thomas Marche (1568).

Men soon began to speak of him again and to discuss the particulars of his life. Fuller had declared him a native of Cumberland. Blomefield, on the authority of an erroneous document, claimed him for Norfolk. [47]

The credit of having rediscovered his poetic talent belongs, perhaps, to a woman, Mrs Elizabeth Cooper, who in 1741 wrote in *The Muses' Library* a warm commendation of *The Bowge of Court:*

'His Bowge of Court is, in my opinion, a Poem of great Merit: it abounds with Wit, and Imagination, and argues him well vers'd in Human Nature, and the Manners of that insinuating Place. The Allegorical Characters are finely describ'd, and as well sustain'd; the Fabrick of the

whole, I believe, entirely his own, and not improbably,
may have the Honour to be a Hint, even to the
inimitable Spencer (sic), but as his poems have been
lately reprinted, I shall only annex the Prologue and
submit this conjecture to the Correction of better
Judges . . .'[48]

Here at last was someone who had read Skelton! But just as
it might have been thought that his popularity was about to
revive, Pope hurled an annihilating epithet ('Beastly
Skelton') [49] which was to deter generations of readers.

The first comprehensive study of Skelton, by Thomas
Warton,[50] appeared in 1778; but its judgments draw too hard-
and-fast a line between praise and disapproval. Warton, himself a poet and a strongly romantic lover of 'poetic diction',
stood at the very antipodes of Skeltonian vigour.[51] He had
nevertheless inaugurated the great movement of research,
which, in England as in France, set out in the name of roman-
ticism to return to the ancient sources of the nation's poetry.

Parallel with the literary movement, a reprint of the *Merry
Tales* in 1807 prolonged the poet-laureate's legendary existence.

The publication, in 1810, of his principal works in Chalmers'
collection, 'a cemetery of English poetry',[52] added nothing to
contemporary knowledge of the author, though it modified
Warton's view in the light of Mrs Cooper's eulogy. In 1819
there appeared in America the first transatlantic edition, based
on Chalmers. In 1831 Robert Southey [53] devoted to Skelton a
study that was to form a landmark in the rediscovery of the
poet. He concluded with these words: 'The power, the strange-
ness, the volubility of his language, the intrepidity of his satires
and the perfect originality of his manner, render Skelton one of
the most extraordinary poets of any age or country.' Southey
was followed by Elizabeth Barrett,[54] who did not hesitate to defy
the stream of Victorian convention in order to declare her
sympathy with a much maligned poet.

'Skelton "floats double, swan and shadow" as poet
laureate of the University of Oxford, and "royal orator"
of Henry VII. He presents a strange specimen of a court-

poet, and if, as Erasmus says "Britannicarum literarum lumen", at the same time,—the light is a pitchy torch-light, wild and rough. Yet we do not despise Skelton: despise him? It were easier to hate. The man is very strong; he triumphs, foams, is rabid, in the sense of strength; he mesmerizes our souls with the sense of strength—it is as easy to despise a wild beast in a forest, as John Skelton, poet laureate. He is as like a wild beast as a poet-laureate can be. In his wonderful dominion over language, he tears it, as with teeth and paws, ravenously, savagely, devastating rather than creating, dominant rather for liberty than for dignity. It is the very sans-culottism of eloquence; the oratory of a Silenus drunk with anger only. Mark him as the satyr of poets! fear him as the Juvenal of satyrs! And watch him with rugged, rapid, picturesque savageness, his "breathless rhymes" to use the fit phrase of the satirist Hall, or—

> His rhymes all ragged,
> Tattered and jagged

to use his own—climbing the high trees of Delphi and pelting from thence his victim underneath, whether priest or cardinal with rough rinded apples. And then ask, would he write otherwise than so? The answer is this opening to his poem of the Bouge of Court and the im-pression, inevitable, of the serious sense of beauty and harmony to which it gives evidence. But our last word of Skelton must be, that we do not doubt his influence for good upon our language. He was a writer singularly fitted for heating out the knots of the cordage, and strain-ing the lengths to extension: a rough worker and rough work. Strong, rough Skelton!'

In France, Philarète Chasles likewise did pioneer work by linking the study of Skelton to the revival of sensuality under the Renaissance (1842).[55] The following year, there appeared in London the first critical edition, by Alexander Dyce. John Skelton, poet-laureate, had resumed his place in the Temple of Fame.

CHAPTER XI

Past and Present

JOHN SKELTON'S poetry turns upon the here and now. In this respect he shared the opinion of his master Juvenal: he saw no reason why he should follow so many others in dwelling on the past.[1] He was not a man, like Lydgate for example, to devote some thirty thousand lines to retelling the story of Thebes or the Trojan War. His work was in no way retrospective; still less was it anticipatory like More's *Utopia*, that extraordinary intellectual fantasy which, on the morrow of the great geographical discoveries, sketched the relative nature of a world and, above all, of a civilization regarded hitherto as absolute.

Skelton's interest was limited to the present because he considered poetry from the sole viewpoint of action. His poems are acts. And in the privileged position to which his laurels had raised him he intended to shoulder his responsibilities. Thus he comments on the present not with the detachment of a chronicler, but rather with the prejudice of a militant, with the bravado of a champion who sees everything in terms of himself. He treats events of national importance with the familiarity of a private quarrel (witness his ridicule of James IV of Scotland) and, conversely, endows the various episodes of his private life with the importance of national events (witness the little ceremony of the garland at Sherrif Hutton Castle magnified to the proportions of an apotheosis).

And so, like a tightrope dancer, Skelton deploys all his talents on the wire of actuality. There he exhibits his culture, which he relates to the present by way of allusion to the past; his moral passions, which give life to his satirical work; and lastly that high-flown fancy which, freeing itself both from moral and from poetical restraint, has entitled him to be called the *enfant terrible* of early Tudor poetry.

Consequently, the geographical and onomastic elements of

his occasional poetry are part of a fundamental realism: actual events, real persons whose names are to be found in contemporary documents—Jane Scrope of Carrow, Christopher Garnesche, squire of Henry VIII, Lady Margaret's treasurer Bedel, and even Elinour Rummyng whose family has left traces in the history of Leatherhead.[2] The spur of danger was needed before Skelton would employ pseudonyms to disguise the victims of his satires.

Every place-name, too, lies within the field of his personal experience, the eastern half of England—the most active and most prosperous until the eve of the industrial revolution—comprising Yorkshire, East Anglia, Westminster, the City, the environs of London and Kent.

When the poet extends his gaze to the rest of the kingdom, he draws its main diagonal lines or familiar routes in such characteristic phrases as: 'from Wainfleet to Wales', 'from Wales to Winchelsea', 'from Winchelsea to Rye', 'from Wentbridge to Hull', 'from Tyne to Trent', 'from Carlisle to Kent', 'from Croydon to Kent', 'from Stroud to Kent'.

In the background of this laureate poetry, we often find royal residences (Eltham, Greenwich, Tottenham, Woodstock Park); the magnificent houses belonging to Wolsey (York Place, Hampton Court, St Albans); feudal strongholds and manors, principally on the Scottish border (Norham, Alnwick, Bamborough, Wark, Topcliffe, Sherriff Hutton); the ports of England's youthful maritime strength (Plymouth, Portsmouth and Dartmouth; the Cinque Ports, key to the defensive system against France; Tilbury and its ferry; Orwell, Harwich and Calais); many religious houses (the Observants at Greenwich, the Austin Friars in Broad Street, the Franciscans of Baldwell-beside-Bury, the Bonshommes of Ashridge); several churches (St Mary Spital, St Thomas of Acon, St Stephen's, Westminster); holy places such as St Mary of Crome, near Greenwich; crossroads (Paul's Cross and the Cross in Cheap); a few inns (the 'Running Horse' at Leatherhead, the 'three Cranes' in the Vintry); a few places of ill repute mentioned in the satires (Half Street, the Stews, 'the Cardinal's Hat'); prisons and gibbets (Little Ease, the Fleet, Tyburn, Tower Hill); and right out in the country, on the Cambridge road, the sinister crossroads of Baldock where the highwayman Jack o' Legs had been hanged.[3]

Behind all this we discover a strongly agricultural civilization with its flourishing woollen and linen industries. Thus there is talk of Cotswold sheep, Leominster, Kendal and Kirby wool, Lincoln green, Bristol red; abroad, he mentions the tapestries of Arras, the linen of Caen and the shirts of Rennes.

As for foreign topography itself, interest centres upon a limited circle of towns and countries which occur frequently in the chronicles of that time: Limerick in Ireland; Edinburgh and St John's Town (i.e. Perth, the ancient capital); the Orkneys, northern limit of that world; and a whole fistful of Scottish names which Skelton jangles time and again by way of ridicule—Dundee, Dunbar, Locrian, Lothian, etc. On the Continent we have a few names that were topical at the time of Henry VIII's French wars: Thérouanne and Tournai, Montreuil where the fleet assembled in 1522, Guisnes, Pontoise, Bordeaux, Lorraine, Flanders and Burgundy, Aix-la-Chapelle, Bohemia, Rome and the Castle of St Angelo, Lombardy, Pouille and the 'Scarpary' Mountains in Tuscany, Navarre, Portugal, Spain, St James of Compostella, 'the Tagus golden waved' (an expression rather mythological than geographical), Granada and the Straits of Morocco. Beyond lay not indeed the unknown (the translator of Diodorus Siculus was not ignorant of the Mediterranean lands), but regions which the poet knew, so to speak, at second hand, as the realm of the Infidels who were at that time exerting pressure on Christendom, and as the locality of countries made familiar by ancient classical writers.

As with all medieval poets, book learning played a leading role even in the field of Skelton's poetry of the here-and-now. It was a matter of fashion as well as of science. A rhetorician lacked good taste if he failed to ennoble his subject by references to Antiquity. The Earl of Northumberland must be as benign as Aeneas and valiant as Hector; Henry VIII was youthful as Alexis, wise as Adrastus and handsome as Adonis, while his mother, the devout Lady Margaret, was likened to Tanaquil, Penelope, Maecenas, Esther and Abigail. Chaucer, Gower and Lydgate had done the same a hundred years ago;

so had all the poets and orators of their age who drank from the common cup of facile erudition which can still be described as medieval because it reflects a world seen only through the 'thick glass' of Latin literature inspired by Christianity, and because it continues to speak of Gentiles or Pagans and not yet of the classics.

Once we admit the superficial aspect of such erudition, which often had only a remote connection with an author's true sources, it is curious to find in Skelton's work that the panorama evoked by such a parade of names corresponds exactly to a general history of the world from the Fall to his own times. That picture does not distinguish between History, Legend and Mythology. It embraces the three great divisions customary in the Middle Ages: the history of the Jews, the history of the Gentiles and the history of the Christians. The whole past is projected, as it were, on to the plane of actuality. It is what might be called the third dimension of Skelton's universe.

For the sake of convenience we shall consider the Hebrew cycle, the mythological cycle, the Greek and Oriental cycle, the Latin and Medieval cycle.

The Hebrew cycle, by the abundance of its allusions, reminds us how well acquainted was that age with the scenes and figures of the Old Testament, which were constantly made familiar by pulpit eloquence, statuary, stained glass, book-illustration, the stage and the street performances organized by the Guilds on great religious festivals. The pre-Mosaic period was represented by Cain and Abel; Noah and his sons; the sons of Shem, Aram and Assur; the Tower of Babel; Melchisedech, the king-priest of Salem; Abraham and his concubine Agar; Isaac and Rebecca, his nephew Lot; Rachel, Job, Hus and Sodom. But it was the Mosaic period that mainly attracted the poet, because of the comparisons it so frequently suggested between the kingdom of Israel, fighting for its existence against faithless counsellors at home and hostile tribes on its frontiers, and the young Tudor dynasty under Henry VIII dominated by Wolsey and surrounded by enemies. Most often mentioned are Moses and Aaron, the Golden Calf, the Ark of the Lord, Dathan and Abiram, Jethro, Joshua, Balaam and Balak, along with Israel's many neighbouring tribes, Midianites, Ismaëlites,

Edomites, Gabaonites, Ammonites, Amalekites and Ammor-
heans. Outstanding in the period of the Judges are the names
of Gideon and Jerobosheth, Samson and Delilah, Samuel, Saul,
the Pythoness, Ure, Nabal, Abigail and, above all, David, the
great central figure of Skeltonian inspiration. In the prophetic
period are Solomon, Absalom and Achitophel, Jezabel the
Phoenician, Isaiah and Jeremiah. In the sacerdotal period,
from the Babylonian Captivity to the revolt of the Macchabees:
Zorobabel, Mordecai, Esther, Ahasuerus and Vashti, Asmodeus
the jealous demon and Macchabeus. In the period of the
Scribes, from the Hasamonean dynasty to the destruction of
Jerusalem by Titus: Aristobulus the murderer, and the
Sadducees, partisans of the sage Sadok and conservatives after
the poet's own heart, to whom Ezechiel, in his description of the
theocratic ideal, assigns the priestly functions.

With the Graeco-Latin mythological cycle we have another
inexhaustible reservoir of comparisons: the masters of Olympus
and of astronomy, the inhabitants of the infernal regions, the
divinities of earth, air and water, the Muses and Helicon, all
occupy a prominent place in the laureate's verse. Then there
are slightly monstrous figures, derived mainly from the *Metamorphoses*: Macareus and Canace, incestuous children of
Aeolus; Pyramus and Thisbe; Ixion in torment; Acontius and
Cydippe; Laodamia; Lycaon, the wolf of Libya; Thracian
Tereus; the Fates, the Eumenides and a whole fantastic fauna
of chimeras, gorgons, medusas, manticores, centaurs, hippo-
centaurs, onocentaurs, recalling Pliny's *Natural History* and the
medieval bestiaries, useful sources for the invective of a satirical
poet. The most common mythological figures are undoubtedly
Phoebus, Mars, Minerva and Calliope; the most infrequent,
Maia, daughter of Atlas, Hyperion, Harpocrates (an infant
Egyptian god associated by the Greeks with Silence) and
Jupiter Feretrius (Jupiter of Trophies), symbol of Henry VIII,
to whom Skelton makes an eloquent appeal in the *Speculum*.
Certain divinities occur under both their Greek and their Latin
names: Pallas and Minerva, Bacchus and Dionysus, Phoebus
and Apollo, Sol and Titan, Hecate and Luna. We notice, on the
other hand, the absence of Hermes alongside Mercury, who
was not revived in his hellenic form until a later date. Likewise,

in connection with Helicon, there is no mention of Pegasus, whose rebirth had only recently occurred in Italy.

The Greek and Oriental cycle, known indirectly through Latin and medieval sources, is closely related to mythology by the importance of its legendary elements which dominate the whole of pre-homeric story. We know how popular during the Middle Ages were the Theban legend, the exploits of Heracles and Jason, the adventure of the Argonauts, and the epic of Troy which recurs in Skelton as a feeble echo of the common-places dear to his direct and indirect forerunners Chaucer, Gower, Lydgate, Raoul le Fèvre, Benoît de Ste More and Guido Colonna. Thus he alludes to twilight myths associated with the beginnings of Greek history: Deucalion, Cadmus, Linus, Thracian Orpheus, Amphion, Actaeon and the dog Melanchetes, while history proper, in unbroken succession from the eighth century B.C. to the second A.D., is covered by allusions to Homer, Hesiod, Pisander, Pherecydes, Arion, Alcaeus, Sappho, the tyrant Phalaris, Anacreon, Croesus, Simonides, Pindar, Sophocles, Zeuxis, Plato, Socrates and Aristippus, Zeno and the Stoics, Hippocrates, Philistus, Alexis, Xenophon, Aeschines and Demosthenes, Aristotle, Philip, Alexander and Abdalonimus, Diogenes, Apelles, Philemon, Pyrrhus, Euphorion, Theocritus, Dioscorides, Plutarch, Ptolemy of Alexandria, Galen and Philostratus. The list is eclectic. It includes poets, dramatists, orators and historians, painters and sculptors, statesmen, philosophers and physicians; names celebrated in the Middle Ages, such as Aristotle and Alexander, Hippocrates, Dioscorides and Galen, others whose vogue spread during the Renaissance, such as the author of the *Parallel Lives*, and many whose erudition was purely formal, those whom Jane Scrope found too 'diffuse', such as Arion, none of whose works has survived.

Skelton's reference to Philostratus's *Life of Apollonius of Tyana* opens a window on the Orient of Alexander, King Phraortes, and the gymnosophists. Acestes, Sardanapalus, Cyrus and Timaretus, Darius, Attalus I, Antiochus, Olibrius, the executioner of St Margaret. The gibbet of Bagdad, the Tower of Babylon, the Meander, river of swans, the Tigris and Euphrates, Persia and Media complete the summary of Asia Minor.

Tartary marks one of the extremities of Skelton's world. *Ultra Sauromatas*, beyond the land of the Sauromatae (the phrase is from Juvenal), seems to suggest an unknown region north of the Black Sea and an allusion to the kingdom of the dead.

Like Greek history, Latin history is covered from its remotest origins with references to Evander, king of Arcadia; Egeria, who inspired Numa; Tanaquil, wife of Tarquin the Elder; Tarquin the Proud, last king of Rome; Porsenna, king of 'Tarky'; Lucretia, idol of the Middle Ages; Quinctius, better known as Cincinnatus.

The name of Marcellus recalls the conquest of Syracuse in 212 B.C., just as the Punic Wars are evoked by allusions to Carthage, Hamilcar, Hannibal, Hasdrubal, Claudius Pulcher, Cato and the great Scipio, one of the models of Henry VIII. The Republic is represented by Cicero, Brutus, Caesar, Pompey; the Empire by Agrippina the Elder (wife of Germanicus), Nero, Galba, Vespasian, Titus, Domitian, Trajan, Caracalla, Gordian, Diocletian, Constantine, Julian the Apostate and Theodosius. There is also mention of Alaric, king of the 'Gothians', and of the Gallic chieftain Frollo of Franko. But it is above all in the domain of literature that the poet-laureate of Oxford and Cambridge finds himself in good company, amid that long, unbroken line of ancient and, later, Christian Latin authors with whom he feels at one, though showing a preference for the satirists. He mentions Ennius, Attilius, Plautus, Terence, Lucilius, Cicero, 'prince of eloquence', Sallust, Catullus, Pollio, Virgil, Horace, Propertius, Livy, Ovid, Valerius Maximus, Pliny, Persius, Josephus, Lucan, Martial, Quintilian, Juvenal, Statius, 'Dame' Sulpicia, Quintus Curtius, Terentianus Maurus, Aulus Gellius, Porphyry, Macrobius, Boethius, the grammarians Priscian and Donatus, Maximian, Vincent of Beauvais and Alexandre de Villedieu; the representatives of the Italian Quattrocento and architects of the Renaissance, Petrarch, Boccaccio, Poggio the Florentine, valued mainly for their Latin works; and that second generation of erudite latinists, those 'ancient humanists', medieval by training and Catholic by conviction, among whom Skelton ranks, men such as Gaguin, Sébastien Brant (whom he does not name, but knew well) and the Mantuan.

On the strictly Christian level, his work contains two distinct categories of names, which declare his orthodoxy. On the one hand, the great saints of the medieval Church to whom he pays homage: Jerome, Augustine, Cuthbert, Dunstan, Bernard, Francis, Thomas; on the other, the principal heresies, which he vehemently condemns: Jovinianism, Nestorianism, Arianism, Pelagianism, Hussites, Wyclifites, Lollards and Lutherans. He shows none of the interest of a Colet or an Erasmus in early patristic literature. His chief bedside books were the Vulgate and the Psalms, as appears by numerous quotations.

Integrated with medieval science, the Arabian scholars Albumazar, Avicenna and Hali afford an opportune reminder that Skelton's world still belongs to the Ptolemaic system of the *Almagest*. More than half a century was to pass before the labours of Copernicus overthrew the traditional ideas. Skelton knows the astrolabe, the volvelle, the quadrant and the tirikis. But his works are searched in vain for echoes of the great voyages of exploration such as are found in Rastell or Thomas More. Skelton belongs to a society for which the great event of 1492 was not the discovery of America but the Spanish victory over the Moors at Granada.

A considerable place is occupied, in his medieval vision, by the legends of vernacular literatures, English and French, linked by the ties between the Anglo-Norman and the Celtic community. Side by side with the matter of Sion, Troy and Rome are the matter of France and that of Britanny, the cycle of Charlemagne and that of Arthur. They are represented by Charlemagne, Oliver, Durandal, Bayard, Montalban, Paris and Vienna, the Forest of Ardenne, the four sons of Aymon, Ferumbras, Malchus the Morion and the episode of the bridge of Mautrible, Galafre, Termagant and Sir Oliphant; King Arthur and his wife Guinevere—'. . . dame Gaynour, his quene, Was somewhat wanton, I wene . . .' (*Ph. Sp.* v. 636–7)— Sir Lancelot; Tristam, Gawain, King Mark, the beautiful Iseult, Sir Kay, foster-brother of Arthur, Priamus, enemy of Gawain, Sir Lybius, Guy of Warwick, and lastly Friar Tuck, the only representative of the Robin Hood story in Skelton's surviving works. Nor, finally, would this survey be complete without at least a general notice of the multitude of virtues and vices that crowd upon his stage and march through his poetry, as so many echoes of that allegorical 'mythology' which the Middle Ages had set over against the pagan divinities of Antiquity. It is, incidentally, a domain in which, as we have seen, the author was not content passively to accept tradition, but one in which he proved his creative mind, notably in the personification of Court vices, his nearest enemies.

Such, briefly sketched, is the learned background to Skelton's world. It forms a coherent aggregate remarkable both for its breadth and for its unity. What surprises us is not that the poet bore within himself the knowledge possessed by his contemporaries, but that he was able to fit so vast an evocation of universal history into the framework of topical poetry. That was a *tour de force* performed without apparent effort, a phenomenon not uncommon in that age and which highlights the importance of the allusive method, the method *par excellence* of communities used to the tonality of a single culture. It similarly highlights the essential unity of Skelton's world, which is explained not only by the egocentricity of a poet who tended to relate everything to himself, but also by the unity of a Christian and medieval civilization which tended likewise to relate everything to itself, including Antiquity.

In this respect there is no major difference between Skelton and his immediate predecessors, Gower, Chaucer and Lydgate. After an interval of one hundred years, the poetry of Skelton represents a principle of continuity on the road of the Renaissance, which is found also, to a greater or less extent, in the writings of his colleagues Barclay and Stephen Hawes. That unfailing solidarity with the past is what perhaps best distinguishes them from the rising generation, that of the humanists in open revolt against the medieval tradition, in the field whether of scholasticism, of Latin, of pedagogy or of religion.

CHAPTER XII

Satire and Poetry

JOHN SKELTON, a product of the medieval University, was essentially a cleric-poet, endowed with the formalism of an extensive rather than profound culture, but also cultivating a typically independent attitude toward the temporal power, and even toward the Crown, an attitude which he associated with the role of moral activity considered as the privilege of the poet—of the inspired poet—within the framework of Christian society.[1]

Hence the predominance of moral tendencies that were directly manifested in many didactic works (now unfortunately lost) and indirectly, with perhaps more vigour, in the domain of satire.

Skelton's satire, in fact, is nothing else but the aggressive expression of his orthodoxy in moral and political matters. In accordance with an approved medieval formula, he made satire a branch of didactic literature. He was the author both of dogmatic treatises such as *The Book how we should flee sin* and of satires intended in his own words, 'uyce to reuyle/And synne to exyle' (*Col. Cl.* v. 11–12).

He spent his time lashing his contemporaries whenever their malice or their back-sliding seemed to imperil the community, 'the commune weal'. He was guided, then, less by an ideal of individual moral perfection than by a vigilant anxiety for the public welfare. Considering the position he occupied in relation to his sovereign, it is not difficult to understand the importance he attached to the part he was called upon to play. Skelton wrote satire with the outlook of a scholastic theologian. Behind every one of his satires it is possible to discern an armature of logical and somewhat harsh reasoning, according to which, since the prevailing orthodoxy was founded upon the great medieval synthesis of Aristotelian Thomism—the alliance of reason and faith—the enemies of England's king, of the

Universal Church and of the poet-laureate Skelton must inevitably, by definition, be either fools or heretics.

Such in essence is Skeltonian satire: personal, topical, corrective, it denounces one by one the enemies of Skelton, of the English monarchy and of the established religion. It is akin to ecclesiastical censures and to the chastisement administered in school. It is quick to wield the birch and to fulminate anathema. When it is inspired by the lofty sentiment of duty, it can be bold to the point of rashness: at such times it subordinates every other consideration of rank or person to the general interest. But it can also be quarrelsome, captious, and about as polite as a gamekeeper to a poacher, with something cruel and gloating in its denunciation which reminds one of the procedures of medieval justice. It delights to pillory the enemies of the public welfare, leading the chorus of jeers and gibes.

Whether they concern the throne, the altar or the poet-laureate, the majority of his satires may be said to turn upon a crime of *lèse majesté* or contempt of authority: the revolt of the Commons against the Earl of Northumberland, representative of the King's authority in Yorkshire in 1489; the threat to which the poet-laureate was subjected by a gang of scoundrels (*The Bowge of Court*); the crazy presumption of a Court musician towards the 'sacred person' of the poet-laureate (*Against a Comely Coystrowne*); the impertinence of one of the King's chamberlains to His Majesty's one-time tutor (*Against Garnesche*); the sacrilegious conduct of a country curate who had brought his hawks and hounds into the church at Diss (*Ware the Hawk*); the sordid impiety of two parishioners (*Epitaphs of John Clarke and Adam Uddersall*); the anticlericalism of Lady Margaret's comptroller (*Against Bedel*); the impious aggression of James IV of Scotland against Henry VIII in 1513, despite treaties signed, ties of blood and the threat of papal excommunication (*Against the Scottes; Ballade of a Scottish King*); Albany's aggression in 1523; the heresy of two Cambridge students (*A Replycacion*); and finally the upstart Wolsey's pretension to eclipse the royal splendour and authority, to supplant the Archbishop of Canterbury, to crush the power of the nobles and silence the poet-laureate.

The satire can be direct and personal when addressing the

guilty face to face, or oblique and allegorical when artistic conventions or reasons of security (the two often combine) persuade the poet to have recourse to abstractions, to hide the audacity of certain utterances beneath the veils of allegory, or to attack vices rather than men.

Whereas Skelton's direct satire is always fundamentally anecdotal, the satire of vices, particularly of Court vices, forms a *leit-motif* which is found, like a golden thread, from end to end of his poetical work. We meet it first in the poem *On the Death of the Earl of Northumberland*, among the advice lavished by the poet upon the young orphan who was receiving his education at Court:

> All flayteryng faytors abhor and from the cast;
> Of foule detraction God kepe the from the blast.
> Let double delyng in the haue no place.
> And be not lyght of credence in no case.
>
> (172–5)

Again, in the evening of his life, his last lines were those of a moralist preparing to leave the world below, realizing that the problem of evil is eternal:

> For be ye wele assured,
> That *frenzy* nor *ielousy*
> Nor *heresy* wyll neuer dye.
>
> (*Rep.*, 406–8)

Those three lines sum up the battles he had fought on three fronts, according as his enemies constituted a threat to himself as laureate (jealousy), to the management of the State (frenzy) or to the safety of the Church (heresy).

Skeltonian satire seldom took a specific form. Instead a satirical *spirit* finds its way into widely differing kinds of poetry: elegy, serious epitaph, burlesque epitaph, morality, flytyng, cradle-song (e.g. *Lullay, lullay, like a child*) and descriptive pieces such as *Elynour Rymmyng* and *The Garland of Laurel*. Finally, a number of poems addressed to women, though not strictly speaking satirical, break into reproaches or fire steely darts. Thus his entire work assumes the tinge of satire. More-

over, the spirit of satire, whether associated with allegory as in
The Bowge of Court or with esoteric language as in *Speke,
Parrot*, is controlled in such a way as to become an instrument of
high virtuosity. In its pure state it concentrates with a single
impulse upon a single subject. Satire in that case winds and
unwinds like a powerful spring. It becomes a well-constructed
and effective weapon of chastisement, whose every word
wounds like a projectile and whose every movement fulfils its
particular function; description serving to denounce the fault,
syllogistic argument to reveal its guilt, diatribe to flay the
culprit, and the comic element to ridicule him.

Skelton's satires combine the outspokenness of clerical
intransigence with the ruggedness of ancient Latin satire and
the Hebrew spirit of the Old Testament. Indeed, a well-
known feature of medieval life was the alliance of satire with
homily [2]:

> This worke deuysed is
> For such as do amys;
> And specyally to controule
> Such as haue cure of soule . . .

> (124)

From pulpit-eloquence it borrows its general movement
and the art of heading its paragraphs with most effective
exclamations: *Observate! Considerate! Deliberate! Vigilate! Deplorate! Divinate! Reformate! Pensitate!* The satire *Against
Venomous Tongues* develops quotations from Scripture; while
A Replycacion, entering into the spirit of controversy and
dialogue with heresy, goes back to the sources, enumerates
precedents in the shape of conciliar decisions and the *distinguos*
of the schoolmen.

The homily, in turn, did not disdain to borrow certain of its
methods from poetry. One priest addressed his congregation in
this versified exordium:

> Herkneth alle goode men
> And stylle sitteth a-dun,
> And ich wil tellen
> A lutel sooth sermun.[3]

'A little sooth sermon.' Might not one describe *Colin Clout* as the very type of the 'sooth sermon'? Was it not this kind of bitter drug, this elixir of truth, that Skelton sought to administer to his contemporaries? The frankness of medieval preachers was proverbial. The darkest picture of the Church is not invariably drawn by her detractors. One need only refer to homiletic literature or to those satires which, 'though often harsh and mordant, were so far from being inspired by irreligion or even by a general hostility towards the clergy (though traces of that sentiment occur here and there), that many of them were written by clergymen who desired most earnestly that she should be worthy of the power and veneration they wished she might enjoy'.[4] Such were those 'States of the World', a widespread type of satiric poetry which passed in review all classes of society, noting their vices and defects and not seldom written by churchmen.[5] Such, in England, were the treatises of William of Rymyngton, professor of theology and chancellor of Oxford University; they were intended to refute the errors of Wycliff and contain fierce denunciations of the vices that defiled the ecclesiastical body. Such, again, were the famous Latin sermons of Thomas Brunton, Bishop of Rochester, a former Benedictine monk of Norwich and another enemy of Wycliffe; they criticized the state of affairs at a time when Alice Perrers dominated the throne, and denounced the weakness of men in high places who maintained a guilty silence for fear of displeasing the Sovereign—*Tacent domini temporales, qui timent offensam regis . . . Tacent confessores . . . tacent predicatores . . .*—and quoting the Psalmist: *Omnes declinaverunt, simul inutiles facti sunt; non est qui facit bonum, non est usque ad unum* (Ps. liii).[6] So also Skelton, in very similar circumstances and in the same state of mind, regretting that no one follows him in his campaign against Wolsey, quotes the Psalmist: *Quis consurget mecum adversus malignantes? Aut quis stabit mecum adversus operantes iniquitatem? Nemo, Domine* (Ps. xciv).

The cleric who could show such independence of spirit was led quite naturally to play the part of an intercessor, capable of pleading in the name of the laity, of making known to the Sovereign the grievances of his subjects, of presenting the voice of the people as the voice of God—*Vox populi, Vox Dei*. As *Piers Plowman* says,

> . . . for lewed men ne coude
> iangle ne iugle, that justifie hem shulde
> But suffren and serven.[7]

Those words are echoed by Colin Clout, except for the fact that Colin Clout is not, like Piers Plowman, the symbolical spokesman of the Commons, but of public opinion generally.[8]

The outspokenness of medieval preachers did not exclude humour. On the contrary, it welcomed humour as an ally, sometimes embellishing it with mimicry and little tableaux.[9] That is the spirit which suffuses the preachers' manuals, such as *Summa Predicantium* by the learned Dominican Bromyard, and which inspires such collections of anecdotes as the *Gesta Romanorum*. We find it prominent in Skelton too. His satires abound in delightful grimaces and whirligigs. *Why Come ye not to Court?* is the most typical piece in this respect. It is full of drollery. The supposition, for example, that if Wolsey went to hell he would usurp Lucifer's throne, is a model of its kind:

> God saue his noble grace,
> And graunt him a place
> Endlesse to dwell
> With the deuyll of hell!
> For, and he were there,
> We nede neuer feere
> Of the fendys blake:
> For I vntertake
> He wolde so brag and crake,
> That he wolde than make
> The deuyls to quake,
> To shudder and to shake,
> Lyke a fyer drake,
> And with a cole rake
> Brose them on a brake,
> And bynde them to a stake,

And set hell on fyer,
At his owne desyer
He is suche a grym syer,
And suche a potestolate,
and Suche a potestate,
That he wolde breke the braynes
Of Lucyfer in his chaynes,
And rule them echone
In Lucyfers trone.

(*Wcyn?* 966–90)

This studied drollery, which has its roots in the extensive
jocular literature of the period, blends in turn with the comic
side of old Latin satire. One must bear in mind Skelton's great,
though not apparent, familiarity with the Latin satirists,
Lucilius, Persius, Horace, Martial, Juvenal, Claudian. *Why
Come ye not to Court?*, for example, seems to follow the pattern
of Claudian's satire against Eutropius, the eunuch who
became consul; it is a medley of devastating satirical strokes
and amusing sallies, revealing the poet's contempt for his
victim.

Finally, like the Latin satirists, Skelton cultivates a kind of
'civic' spirit, a thoroughly Roman puritanism applied to
public affairs and manifested in a jealous care of State revenues,
a very English tendency to control the use of public money.[10]
Add to that a regret at the passing of old ways and the commendation of ancient virtues. This twofold characteristic might
have been more conspicuous in the laureate's work but for the
Tudor dynasty's antipathy towards the troubled period of the
Wars of the Roses and Skelton's own marked preference for the
reign of Henry VIII over that of his predecessor.[11] Skelton
nevertheless is clearly *laudator temporis acti*. In the *Epitaph for the
Tomb of Lady Margaret*, written in 1516, he could not refrain
from slipping in a half-spoken but fiercely satirical passage
contrasting the sound morality that prevailed in that pious
lady's time with the 'goatlike' randiness introduced by the
Renaissance. He likewise frowned upon the Renaissance
tapestries, full of nude figures, which adorned Wolsey's rooms
at Hampton Court, a refinement of luxury that he was not

alone in considering as unworthy of a prelate's house. One of the most original aspects of *Speke, Parrot* is the fact of its sharing with the old Latin satires that moral outlook that had been fostered in contemporary England as in Juvenal's Rome by the diffusion of Greek, the language *par excellence* of an effeminate civilization,[12] an outlook which combines here, in Skelton's work, with a peculiarly Anglo-Saxon repudiation of the new fashions lately arrived from France ('the new jet'). Skelton's unpolished language is thus a mark of sturdiness and good health. It is to some extent at one with the crudity of school textbooks in that age.[13] It makes no bones about the use of a vocabulary that is raw, familiar and even trivial, but at the same time racy and wonderfully energetic. One might say of him, as has been said of Juvenal, that in defending virtue he caused modesty to blush. But he excuses himself:

The whyte apperyth the better for the black.

(*G. of L.* 1236)

Still, we must not exaggerate the importance of his *gauloiseries*. As Dyce correctly says: '. . . though expressions of decided grossness occur in his writings, *they are comparatively few*'.[14] It is quite certain that he never went as far as his Latin models in this field. While he adopted something of Lucilius's civic spirit, something of Persius's obscurity, something of Martial's epigrammatic sarcasm, something of Claudian's drollery and contempt, it was to Juvenal that he was principally indebted, with whom he had the closest affinity, and to whom he constantly appealed in his own defence.[15]

Together with the medieval and the Latin influence is that of the Old Testament. Skelton had been reared on the Psalms of David, and some of the Hebrew spirit pervades his satires, whether he is venting his wrath against intolerable evil, voicing that mystical intransigence in whose name he seeks to exile sin and extirpate heresy, expressing the bitterness he feels at finding himself persecuted by the wicked, speaking the sibylline language to which he has recourse in *Speke, Parrot*, or unleashing the prophetic ardour of *Colin Clout* to call down the weight of divine retribution upon the heads of sinners, Skelton is a just man in whom, at certain moments, satiric vehemence attains to the stern belligerence of the biblical prophets.

But such moments are rare indeed. Mostly, even when the danger is at its height as in *Why Come ye not to Court?*, Skelton prefers to stay at a more human level, to make laughter his ally. He fulfils his duty as a satirist with a jovial, as it were Rabelaisian warmth, with a gaiety worthy of Merry England. He belongs to an age in which melancholy was considered as opprobrious. One of his most ferocious thrusts at Wolsey is the declaration that he had a 'sad eye'.

Two great streams of satire have reached us from the Middle Ages. One is mocking scornful, goliardic, rebellious, anticlerical. It is a spirit of opposition to the established order, to conformity, to whatever bullies the individual. Though addressed to persons, it is directed in fact against authority and institutions. The other is equally critical of all that is amiss, and employs the language of raillery but in a very different spirit. It takes individuals to task, but it respects institutions. It is not anticlerical. It is corrective and coercive. It is an auxiliary of the established order.

Skelton was long regarded as belonging to the first stream— and more than one feature in his works, can be misleading—his impish fantasy, his sense of parody, his criticism of the church, his bold opposition to Cardinal Wolsey. But we should not be deceived by the paradox of appearances. Skelton has left us sufficient proof that he belonged to the second stream, which put satire in the service of orthodoxy.

Skelton put forth all the resources of his imagination and his art in defence of a political and religious order to which he felt himself attached by innumerable ties and which he viewed from the standpoint of eternity. In doing so, he mingled the comic and the satirical elements with a thoroughly medieval freedom and a wholly Nordic vigour. He is, in England, 'the last of the medieval satirists as he is the greatest'.[16]

At the same time, Skelton has the faults of his brilliant gifts: the impetuosity of his satires is offset by the disorder of a literary form that has not yet found its true path; he himself helped to diminish the prestige of his moral authority by the violence of his prejudices, by the facility of his invective or by the unwonted eccentricities of his dialectic.

There remains a poet who always manages to go beyond mere censorship of morals, a poet of contradictory urges who wrote 'Eyther for delyte/Or else for despyte',[17] who brushed aside traditional categories with the utmost freedom, who experimented with rhythms and juggled with commonplaces. It may be that the true rebel in Skelton is not the man but the poet.

He had indeed no great reason to feel much respect for the poetical tradition he had inherited, considering the abysmal decadence in which he found English poetry. As he makes Gower say in *The Garland of Laurel*, after one hundred years of sterile imitation of the triumvirate Gower-Chaucer-Lydgate, he was the first to set about restoring the fortunes of the national poetry 'that welny was loste when that we were gone' (406).

He had been encouraged principally by his lofty idea of poetic inspiration, which enabled him to lift laureate poetry above academic rhetoric and courtly dithyrambs. Summoned to Court as official poet, he transformed himself into a satirist. By virtue of his median situation as cleric-poet, he claimed the right to draw freely sometimes from the courtly and chivalric tradition, sometimes from the popular and jocular, but never allowing himself to be absorbed completely by one or the other. Thus *The Bowge of Court* opens with a dream of the purest courtly inspiration, a mere excuse to introduce a satire of the Court. Again, *The Garland of Laurel* appears at first sight to have been composed in honour of some great lady, but eventually becomes a personal apotheosis; while the 'cradle-song' *Lullay, lullay, like a child* is nothing of the sort, except in its refrain, and belongs rather to popular doggerel.

The real continuator of the courtly and chivalric tradition was not Skelton but his younger contemporary Stephen Hawes, a former page at Court, whose *Pastime of Pleasure* heralded the *Faerie Queen*. The real continuator of didactic poetry was not Skelton but his rival Alexander Barclay, studious translator of Sébastien Brant and the *Eclogues* of Virgil, forerunners, in their respect for form, of the great tradition of English pastoralism.

John Skelton, on the contrary, disregarded the forms in favour of a personal poetry that obeys no rules other than his own whim. Courthope deplored his having 'broken the instrument of poetry'. 'We find hardly a trace of the chivalric sentiment or of the refined art of composition, introduced by Chaucer'.[18] True, but one may ask whether that lack of constraint had not also a salutary effect on an anaemic and stereotyped poetry, and whether it is not indeed to Skelton's credit that he rose above the conformism of his age by proclaiming with uncommon forthrightness the intrinsic merits of inspiration.

By doing just that he rendered signal service to English poetry as well as following a difficult road on which he was not always clear as to which turning he should take. Skelton is at once a poet who conceived a high idea of inspiration and who, in order more faithfully to obey its dictates, forged that frail instrument known as 'Skeltonics'. Hence the possibility of charging him with an internal contradiction between the lofty demands of inspiration and the mediocre triviality of his means of expression. In that respect Skelton suffered all the mortifications of a precursor who was profoundly aware of the metrical inadequacy of the poetry of his time and made praise-worthy experiments, but who was inevitably outstripped by the greater successes of the next generation which would endow the English Renaissance with its permanent instruments of expression. Skelton thus found himself divided between the use of *rime royale*, decorative but unsuitable for satire, and the employment of 'Skeltonics', ingenious but unsuited to great poetry, between the clavichord and the flageolet.

The surprising fact is that he played like an expert on such second-rate instruments. A virtuoso of difficulty, he found in the needs of esoteric poetry the very virtues of constraint, and wrote *Speke, Parrot*. A virtuoso of facility, he composed about twelve hundred lines on the death of a bird, *Phyllyp Sparowe*.

Skelton, therefore, was constantly torn by the contradictory requirements of freedom and discipline, and it can be said that, despite his prowess, he never fully solved the dilemma. His work reveals profound dualities not only between one poem and another, but even within the motley, disparate construction of a single poem. Actually, he troubled himself very little about composition. He often allowed his works to grow haphazardly as inspiration might from time to time dictate, excepting his morality play *Magnificence* which stands curiously like a well proportioned temple in a field of rough-hewn stones.

He remains the most gifted poet of his generation, notwithstanding a deceptive appearance of monotony, he displays a disconcerting variety of touch.

Grave and meditative, he could write in the ardour of an almost romantic reverie, inspired both by Ecclesiastes and by the vagaries of the English climate:

> In place alone then musynge in my thought
> How all thynge passyth as doth the somer flower,
> On euery half my reasons forthe I sought,
> How oftyn fortune varyeth in an howre,
> Now clere wether, forthwith a stormy showre.

> (*G. of L.* 8–12)

A poetic observer of nature, he described the instant when the moon veils herself behind a black cloud (*G. of L.* 644–7); the lark soaring on a summer's day (*G. of L.* 533–6); or the spongy undergrowth of the forest of Galtres in autumn (*G. of L.*, 22–3). A painter of animals in almost oriental detail, he draws with unforgettable charm the portrait of a tame sparrow (*Ph. Sp.*) or of a drawing-room parrot (*Sp., P.*).

His magic rivals that of Stephen Hawes in describing the enchanted palace of his dreams (*G. of L.*) or the fresh springs alive with bream and tench. He employs the consummate skill of a Flemish painter in depicting a group of gentlewomen busy at their needlework (*G. of L.*), or the illuminations of a medieval manuscript 'that would have restored a sick man to health' (*G. of L.* 1162). He excelled no less in describing the movements of a crowd, the jostling on the arrival of a ship (*B. of C.*) and the remarks exchanged amid all the noise and bustle. He could reproduce the spirited dialogue of ordinary folk, spiced with oaths and picturesque comments. With the expert eye of a caricaturist, he could spot at a glance the salient feature that brings a portrait to life. Wolsey, for instance, with a bandaged eye:

> So fell and so irous
> So dull of malencoly
> With a flap afore his eye;

(*Wcyn.*, 1164–6)

the lanky, bow-legs of Garnesche:

> Your wynde schakyn shankkes, your long lothy legges
> Crokyd as a camoke, and as a kowe calfles;

(*Garn.* I, 29–30)

the fresh beauty of Jane Scrope or the repulsive ugliness of Elynour Rummyng.

On the threshold of the sixteenth century, his literary work appears as a striking affirmation of the English language in the tradition of Chaucer. At a moment when the Tudor dynasty was devoting itself to the task of national revival, Skelton's confidence in his native tongue was all the more significant in that the songster of the new reign was as yet an isolated figure in a crowd of poets, orators and Court secretaries from France and Italy. He appointed himself champion of the vernacular, but with a mixture of audacity and modesty that betrays the difficulty of an undertaking opposed by the prestige of better-established tongues.

The old Franco-Latin-English trilingualism of the Norman period, which had for so long stunted the growth of the indigenous language, had been dead for scarcely a hundred years. It survived here and there in secondary form, fostered notably by the cosmopolitanism of the Court, and we catch a faint echo of it even in Skelton's work.

But Skelton's instinct led him to become a keen advocate of English. 'Latin is good for clerks,' he exclaims, and he plunged enthusiastically into the waters of everyday speech. It was in this vernacular English that he sought to convey his message to the general public and secretly to compete with the Ancients. It

was not until the next generation and the progress of instruction
that a poet, addressing the world at large, could parade his
imitations. Skelton, in this respect, belonged only to the Pre-
renaissance.

Meanwhile, he understood clearly how ungrateful was his
task. He lamented the rusticity of English in his day.

> Our naturall tong is rude,
> And hard to be enneude
> With pullysshed termes lusty;
> Our language is so rusty,
> So cankered, and so full,
> Of frowardes and so dull
> That if I wolde apply
> To wryte ornatly,
> I wot not where to fynd
> Termes to serue my mynde.

(Ph. Sp., 774–83)

A half-century before the French Pléiade, Skelton strove to
'adorn' the English language. But his attempt was neither so
systematic nor so varied as that of his successors across the
Channel. And just as his satiric streak eventually won the day,
it finished also by relegating to second place all that did not
spring directly from action.

The result is a body of work which, from the linguistic standpoint, represents the characteristics of a very extensive vocabulary in which the learned terminology of the schools rubs
shoulders with polite phraseology and, particularly, a crowded
throng of energetic and picturesque words springing from the
common people.

Words of Norman or French origin are extremely numerous.
This was to be expected in a disciple of Chaucer, at a time when
the English language was still impregnated with Franco-
Norman influence. Only a detailed study would reveal the
extent to which early sixteenth-century English contained
Franco-Norman words in a form still close to their origins.
Hardly less important, however, than the vocabulary of
Franco-Norman origin is that of Saxon, Germanic or Scan-

dinavian origin. It goes far to prove that, although Skelton inherited from Chaucer a strongly French-imbued language, he gave it a definite swing in the opposite direction, with a wealth of terms belonging more typically to the North Country.

Finally, because of his satirical and familiar turn of mind, Skelton's poetry makes frequent use of popular wisdom. It is a treasure-house of axioms and proverbs that are, in themselves, a living commentary on contemporary life. Yet, in the domain of comparisons, metaphors and images, with a few rare exceptions, we discover how uncomplicated were the poet's mental processes. Skelton was not a man to think, like Shakespeare, in terms of complex and flamboyant imagery. He is satisfied with generally succinct comparisons, introduced quite simply, nine times out of ten, with the words 'like' or 'as', used indifferently. There is, however, one domain in which he excels, that of animal comparisons. One can speak of him as employing a regular animal symbolism which works, moreover, in both directions. Humans are likened to brute beasts and thereby mercilessly caricatured in their attitudes, their gestures, their eccentricities, their faults. Conversely, beasts are viewed as if they were human, in accordance with the old tradition of the bestiaries, the *Roman de Renard* and the *Parlement of Foules*. The most fully developed example of this latter kind occurs in *Phyllyp Sparowe*, where the author evokes no fewer than seventy-seven animals, the majority birds, to which he assigns a human part in the burial of the famous sparrow.

By turns ludicrous and playful, indignant and fierce, insinuating and brutal, now sickened by the world's injustice to himself, and now thrilled with joy at the downfall of his enemies, he poured into his verse the frenzied ardour of an essentially combative temperament. Lyrical and yet superficial, sage and childish, scholarly and fanatical—such was the inimitable John Skelton, poet-laureate, tutor to his king and *enfant terrible* of his age. He was at home in many different fields of poetry, using the courtly brand to criticize the Court, and *rimes royales* to vilify members of the Royal Household. He was daring in his choice of subjects, flying in the face of convention. Though a courtier-poet, he applied to his Sovereign's Court the image of the Ship of Fools; though a country priest, he embroidered poetical variations on the theme of the funeral service; though a poet, he boldly celebrated his own apotheosis. He was a master of parody and the mock-heroic, notably in *Phyllyp Sparowe*, with the virtuosity of an academic mind whose modesty and subtlety were not always understood by the public at large. He practised the virtuosity of the great rhetoricians trained in the methods of medieval amplification. He treated rhythm with the freedom of an innovator, rhyme with the liberty of a humorist. He gave free rein to a dazzling and inexhaustible fluency of words, writing thousands of lines on the most tenuous subjects. Finally, even in an hour of peril, he always gave proof of irrepressible heartiness and good cheer, which make him incontrovertibly the merriest poet of Merry England.

We must be careful, on the other hand, not to think of him as a mere figure of fun. Nothing could be more unlike the real John Skelton than those salacious caricatures popularized by the jocular distortions of his legend. It has been proved beyond contradiction that such legend, which began in his lifetime, was the work of facetious humanists who held up to scorn one of their most trenchant foes. The truth is that in Skelton the entertainer and the warrior are one and the same. We have here two complementary facets of a single person who taxed his ingenuity to treat the medieval literary tradition he had inherited not as a model of inspiration, but as an arsenal for the defence of an established order which he identified in his mind with the permanence of Christian civilization. That order, restored to its pristine strength by the first Tudor, he would have to defend, under Henry VIII, when its back was to the wall, at the very moment when the Reformation was beginning to seep in and prepare in secret for the great transfiguration scene of the Renaissance.

While, as a traditional Catholic, he systematically opposed the novelties of his later years, he spent himself without reserve fighting tooth and nail against the absolutism of Wolsey. During that brief episode he brilliantly identified his own cause with that of freedom. The incredible daring, the astonishing bravado with which he resisted the encroachments of personal dictatorship suffice to rank him among the most talented of pamphleteers.

Separated from his predecessors by the literary void that enfolds the Wars of the Roses, from his contemporaries by his unshakeable attitude of independence in the very bosom of the Court, from his successors by doctrinal differences that mark the historical dividing line between the old Catholic England, to which he belonged heart and soul, and the Protestant and modern England whose approach he withstood, how could sturdy Skelton be other than an isolated figure?

If then, by some special benevolence of Destiny, reserved exclusively for poets, that lonely rebel manages to find a place in tradition, it cannot be any other than one diametrically opposed to conformism. There he is in good company, among the undoubted champions of free speech. His work, so gay and full of boisterous energy, has its appointed place in the garden of colloquial poetry, although his manifold talent overflows on every side the limits of any category within which one seeks to confine it. Poet, pamphleteer and prophet, John Skelton, the least conventional of all poets-laureate, takes his place at last not on the stool of a docile courtier offered him by Fate, but at table with the most rugged minds of English literature, Langland, Cleveland, Browning, Carlyle, Samuel Butler and even Byron—the Byron of *Don Juan*. He has been recognized as a master by a whole line of recent poets, from Robert Graves to T. S. Eliot. He is indeed quaintly in tune with modern times inasmuch as he finally preferred vigour to beauty.

NOTES ON THE TEXT

APPENDIX

BIBLIOGRAPHY

INDEX

NOTES ON THE TEXT

Introduction *Page xv*

1. Robert Southey, *Select Works from the British Poets from Chaucer to Jonson*, London, 1831.
2. E. Browning, 'The Book of the Poets', *Athenaeum*, 2 July 1842.
3. Samuel Taylor Coleridge; Commentary on *King John* I. i.
4. Dyce, i, pp. *viii–xi*.
5. J. B. Mullinger, *History of the University of Cambridge*, Cambridge, 1873.
6. *Athenaeum*, 2 May 1881. John Ashton (ed.), *A Ballade of the Scottysshe Kyng*, 1882; reprinted in *A Century of Ballads*, Boston, 1888.
7. Ernest Law, *The History of Hampton Court Palace*, London, 1885.
8. Henry Bradley, 'Two Puzzles in Skelton', *The Academy*, 1 August 1896.
9. H. Krumpholz, *John Skelton und sein Morality Play 'Magnificence'*, Prossnitz, 1881.
10. G. Schöneberg, *Die Sprache John Skeltons in seinen kleineren Werken*, Marburg Dissertation, 1888.
11. Ewald Flügel, *Neuenglisches Lesebuch*, Halle, 1895.
12. A. Koelbing, *Zur Charakteristik John Skeltons*, Berlin, 1904.
13. B. A. Thümmel, *Studien über John Skelton*, Leipzig, 1905.
14. Fr. Brie, 'Skelton-Studien', *En. Stn.* XXXVII, 1907.
15. John Berdan, *Early Tudor Poetry*, New York, 1920.
16. Robert L. Ramsay, *Magnificence: a Morality*, London, 1908.
17. R. L. Dunbabin, 'I. Skelton's birth-place'.—'II. Skelton's relation to humanism', *M.L.R.* vol. 12, 1917.
18. M. R. James, *A Descriptive Catalogue of the Manuscripts in the Library of Corpus Christi College*, Cambridge, 1912. Cf. Nelson, pp. 245–6.
19. Westlake, 'Skelton in Westminster', *T.L.S.* 27 November 1921.
20. W. H. Williams, *Selections from the Poetical Works of John Skelton*, London, Ibister (Tasmania), 1902.
21. Richard Hughes, *John Skelton: Poems*, London, 1924.
22. Leslie J. Lloyd, 'John Skelton, a forgotten poet', *E.N. RW.*, 1925.
23. Robert Graves (ed.), *The Augustan Book of English Poetry*, No. 12 (modernized).

24. E. P. Hammond, *English Verse between Chaucer and Surrey*, Duke University Press, 1927.
25. *Elynour Rummynge*. Illustrations by Pearl Binder, Fanfrolico Press, London, 1927.
26. *Elynour Rummynge*. Illustrations by Clair Jones, San Francisco, 1931.
27. Edmund Blunden, 'John Skelton', *T.L.S.*, 20 June 1929.
28. Humbert Wolfe, *Notes on English Verse Satire*, 1929.
29. F. M. Salter, 'Skelton's *Speculum Principis*', *Speculum.—A Journal of Medieval Studies*, Cambridge (Mass.), IX.
30. H. L. R. Edwards and William Nelson, 'The dating of Skelton's later poems', *P.M.L.A.—VI*, 1938, LIII.
31. R. Vaughan Williams, *Five Tudor Portraits, a Choral Suite founded on Poems by John Skelton (laureate), 1460–1529*, Oxford, 1935. Cf. Martin Cooper, *Modern English Musicians*, 1933
32. Cf. Renwick and Orton, *The beginning of English Literature to Skelton*, 2 vols., 1939; Vera L. Rubel, *Poetic Diction in English Renaissance from Skelton through Spenser*, New York, 1941.
33. Ph. Chasles, 'La Renaissance sensuelle: Luther, Rabelais, Skelton, Folengo', *Revue des Deux-Mondes*, 1 March 1842.
34. J. J. Jusserand, *Histoire littéraire du peuple anglais*, vol. i, Paris, 1896.
35. H. Taine, *Histoire de la littérature anglaise*, tome i, 1891 edition, pp. 218–19.
36. E. Legouis and L. Cazamian, *History of English Literature*, 1965, pp. 162–4.

CHAPTER I

Epoch, Origins and Beginnings *Page 1*

1. William Caxton, *The Boke of the Eneydos compyled by Vyrgyle*, ed. Culley and Furnivall, E.E.T.S. (E.S.) No. 57, 1890, pp. 3–4.
2. *See infra*, p. 14.
3. Gladys Temperley, *Henry VII*, London, 1914, pp. 404–5.
4. The new design was by Pietro Torregiano, disciple of Donatello and rival of Michelangelo, a man of proud and irascible temperament. He lived in the precincts of Westminster. His contract, which named the sum of £1500 for the royal tomb, was signed on 22nd October 1512. *See* Brayley and Neale, *History and Antiquities of the Abbey Church of Westminster*; Stanley: *Memorials of Westminster Abbey*; *D.N.B.*
5. This theory derives from the unproved statements of Thomas Fuller, *History of the Worthies of England*, London, 1662.
6. J. P. Collier, *The Household Book of John, Duke of Norfolk*, 1884. Cf. R. L. Ramsay's edition of *Magnificence*, 1908.
7. *See*, for example, Dyce, i, pp. lii and xxvi. Harry Levin, 'Skelton and Oxford', *T.L.S.* 9 May 1936, and H. E. Salter's reply, *T.L.S.* 16 May 1936.
8. *See* M. Pollet, 'Skelton et le Yorkshire', *Etudes Anglaises*, February 1952.
9. H. L. R. Edwards, 'John Skelton: a genealogical study', *R.E.S.* XI, 1934.
10. Lewis, *Topographical dictionary of England and Wales.*
11. J. Nicholson and R. Burns, *The History and Antiquities of the Counties of Westmoreland and Cumberland*, 1777, ii, p. 384.
12. A. H. Smith, *The Place-Names of the North Riding of Yorkshire*, English Place-Name Society, Cambridge, 1928, vol. v., pp. 16–17; *The Place-Names of the East Riding of Yorkshire and York*, p. 255; Ekwall, *The Oxford Dictionary of English Place-Names*, Oxford, 1936.
13. E. B. De Fonblanque, *Annals of the House of Percy*, 1887, vol. i, pp. 329–30.
14. William Ruckshaw, doctor of theology, was the son of a pharmacist at York. He studied at Peterhouse, Cambridge, and started his career as a priest in Percy's household. Curate of

Topcliffe in 1472, rector of Lowthorpe in 1473, he was appointed *succentor canonicorum* at York Minster on 18th August 1480. On 27th October 1498 he accepted from Archbishop Rotherham a stall in the Chapel of the Holy Sepulchre at York. We have his Will, dated 10th October 1504, whereby he bequeathed his books to the Master of the Gilbertine priory at Sempringham. *Reg. Test. Capit. Ebor.* I. 337 b, published in *Testamenta Eboracensia*, No. XCIV, Book III, pp. 248–50.

15. *Index of Wills in the York Registry, 1389 to 1514.* The Yorkshire Archaeological and Topographical Association Records, VI, 1888–9, p. 151, 21 July 1448: *Thomas Skelton, Topcliff*, vol. ii, fol. 175.

16. 'From Bamborow (Bamborough) to Bothombar (Bootham Bar)'. *WCYN*, v. 136. Dyce ii, 31.

17. *MAG.* v., 1075–6.

18. De Fonblanque, *op. cit.*

19. 'Of paiauntis that were played in Joyows Garde (G. of L., V. 1383). Cf. *The Morte Arthur*: S(o) whan he was howseyld and enelyd and had al that a Crysten man ought to have, he prayed the Bysshop that his felowes myght bere his body to Joyous Garde. (Somme men say it was Anwyk, and somme men say it was Bamborow).' *The Works of Sir Thomas Malory*, ed. E. Vinaver, Oxford, 1947, vol. iii, p. 1257.

20. Sir N. H. Nicolas, *The Controversy between Sir Richard Scrope and Sir Robert Grosvenor in the Court of Chivalry. A.D. 1385–1390*, London, 1832, vol. ii, pp. 60–1; T. Blore, *The History and Antiquities of the County of Rutland*, Stamford, 1811, vol. ii, part I page 5. We have his Will: *Test. Ebor.*, op. cit., vol. iii, pp. 297–9.

21. Eleanor, née Washbourne, married as her second husband Sir John Wyndham. Cf. Sir N. H. Nicolas, *Testamenta Vetusta*, London, 1826, vol. i.

22. The *Lamentations* conform closely with the Sarum rites. But the *Commendations*, addressed more personally to Jane Scrope, are in almost exact accordance with the rite of York. Cf. *Horae Eboracenses, the prymer of hours of the blessed Virgin Mary, according to the use of the illustrious church of York with other devotions as they were used by the layfolks in the northern province in the XVth and XVIth centuries.* Surtees Society, vol. cxxxii, 1920; *Manuale et processionale ad usum insignis ecclesiae Eboracensis*, Surtees Society, vol. lxiii, 1875. Cf. *The Athenaeum*, 1903, p. 154.

23. Francis Grose, Thomas Astle and other eminent antiquaries, *The Antiquarian Repertory: a miscellaneous assemblage of Topography, History, Biography, Customs and Manners*, 4 vols., London, vol. i, 1807, pp. 55 and 59. Cf. M. Pollet, 'Skelton et le Yorkshire', *ET. AN.* February 1952, pp. 11–16.

24. MS. E. 101, fol. 414–16. P.R.O. Edwards, p. 288.

25. J. A. Venn, *Alumni Cantabrigienses*, Cambridge, 1926, vol. iii, p. 495 B.

26. Grace Book A, p. 134. Cf. Nelson, p. 61.

27. *Al. Cantab.*, op. cit.; *D.N.B.* He was son of William Blythe of Norton, Derbyshire, by a sister of Thomas Rotherham, archbishop of York. Educated at Cambridge. Two facts deserve notice: (i) He was appointed archdeacon of Richmond, in Lady Margaret's immediate neighbourhood, on 8th October 1485; (ii) near Richmond, in the valley overlooked by the castle, is the village of Skelton Hall.

28. W. Nelson, p. 62.

29. T. Warton, *History of English Poetry*, 1879 edition, pp. 401 ff.; W. Hamilton, *The Poets-Laureate of England, being a history of the office of Poet-Laureate*, 1879; E. K. Broadus, *The Laureateship*, Oxford, 1921; C. E. Mallet, *History of the University of Oxford*, 1924, vol. i, p. 182; Edwards, pp. 34–6.

30. Nelson, p. 49.

31. *See* especially *A Lawde and Prayse made for our Souereigne Lord the Kyng*, Dyce i, p. ii, and photographs of the MS. in the present volume.

32. MS. 357. Library of Corpus Christi College, Cambridge.

33. Generally attributed to Poggio the Florentine, who is accused by John Bale and his successors of having taken it from an Englishman, John Free. W. F. Schirmer (*Der Englische Frühhumanismus*, Leipzig, 1931, p. 123) leaves the question open. Cf. H. L. R. Edwards, *The humanism of John Skelton, with special reference to his translation of Diodorus Siculus*, Ph. D. Dissertation No. 944, 1938 (MS.), Cambridge University Library.

34. Fol. 231, quoted by Nelson, p. 64.

35. We find the French poet Henri Baude (*c.* 1430–1490) using the phrase 'Bien m'en souvient' in a *Supplique au Roy faicte en Rondeau*, which provides an interesting sidelight on our poet's motto:

'Souviengne-vous, ce dit Baude, de moy.
Bien m'en souvient, ce luy respond le roy.
Mais de quoy sert sans effect souvenir?
Autant vauldroit promettre et riens tenir.'

M. J. Quicherat, *Les Vers de Me Henri Baude, poète du quinzième siècle, recueillis et publiés avec les actes qui concernent sa vie*. Collection: le trésor des pièces rares ou inédites, 1856, pp. 35–6. Among other features common to the two poets we may note a morality which dealt gently with the sovereign and attacked his courtiers, and for which Henri Baude was for a short while in disgrace.

CHAPTER II

A Cleric-poet at the Court of Henry VII *Page 13*

1. H. F. Westlake, Westminster Abbey, London, 1923.
2. *D.N.B.*; Nelson, pp. 4–39.
3. J. Gairdner; *Chronicles and Memorials*, chap. X, pp. 133–53 and 307–27.
4. Wilhelm Busch, *England under the Tudors* (translated from the German), vol. i, 1895; Bacon: *The Reign of Henry VII*, pp. 502–4; Polydore Vergil: *Hist.*, p. 735; Hall: *Chronicle*, p. 443; Campbell: *Materials*, vol. ii, pp. 443–4, 447; *Plumpton Corresp.*, p. 61; *Paston Letters*, vol. iii, pp. 359–61; *Gentleman's Magazine*, N.S. XXXVI, 1851, pp. 463–8.
5. *Rev. Pruss. Script.* vol. iv, p. 774.
6. De Fonblanque, *op. cit.*; G. Brenan: *History of the House of Percy*, ed. Lindsay, 1902; Grose: *op. cit.* iv. *The Northumberland Household book*, pp. 342 ff.
7. *De Northumbrum comitis nece*, Chronicals and Memorials, vol. 8, pp. 48–9.
8. For his royal ancestors, see De Fonblanque, *op. cit.*
9. Known through *The Garland of Laurel*: 'Prince Arturis Creacyon', 1178. On this occasion the Earl of Northumberland's son was installed as knight of the Order of the Bath. De Fonblanque, *op. cit.* p. 311.
10. Louis Thuasne, *Roberti Gaguini epistolae et orationes*, Bibliothèque littéraire de la Renaissance, Paris, 2 vols., 1903; H. L. R. Edwards: 'Robert Gaguin and the English Poets, 1489–1490,' *M.L.R.*, vol. 29, 1934. *See also* Alcide Bonneau: *L'Immaculée Conception de la Vierge Marie*, poème de Robert Gaguin, docteur en Sorbonne, général des Mathurins. Paris, 1885.
11. *Recueil des Poésies Françoises des quinzième et seizième siècles*, ed. A. de Montaiglon, t. vii, pp. 275 ff.
12. *G. of L.*, 1187
13. F. M. Salter, 'Skelton's *Speculum Principis*', *Speculum, a journal of Mediaeval Studies*, Cambridge (Mass.), vol. ix, 1934.
14. *Grace Book B . . ., of the University of Cambridge*, ed. Mary Bateson, Cambridge, 1903, p. 54.

15. *Ibid.*
16. W. Busch, *op. cit.*
17. 'Item die Mercurii pro Jantaculo cum Magistro Skelton *quia* fuit cum episcopo Sarum.' Grace Book B., *op cit..* i, p. 92.
18. *Ibid*, pp. 148–9.
19. W. Busch, *op. cit.*
20. *G. of L.*, 1182.
21. e.g. The Book of Honourous Estate; the Book how men should flee sin; Royal Demeanance; The Book to speak well or be still; The Book to learn you to die; Good Advisement (on the inspired character of poetry); etc. Cf. *G. of L.*, 1172 ff.
22. Cf. MS. Fayrfax, B.M. Add. 5465, which contains musical works by Cornish with words by Skelton.
23. *Romania*, vol. XVI, pp. 387–8.
24. Dyce (p. xcii) attributes them to Pynson. Edward Hodnett, on the strength of the illustrations, credits them to Rastell, who did in fact use Pynson's blocks. Cf. *English Woodcuts, 1480–1535*, pp. 56–7.
25. It contains:

(1) *My darlyng dere, my daysy floure*, imitated from Lydgate's *Ballad on an ale-seller*. Cf. M'Cracken, *Minor Poems*, vol. ii, pp. 429–30. The author recounts briefly, in the ironic rhythm of a cradle song, the misfortune of a drunkard who falls for a public-house tart and wakes with a hangover to find himself abandoned—and relieved of his purse—while the girl is already far away in the arms of another.

(2) *The auncient acquaintance, madam, between us twayne* rebukes an imprudent woman who makes too light of her favours at the risk of grieving her husband 'that ryght jentyll knyght'.

(3) *Knolege, acquayntance, resort, fauour with grace* is more a kind of litany of love, in aureate style, which laments the absence of the fair *Kateryn* whose name is revealed in an acrostic, after the manner of rhetoricians.

(4) The bilingual piece *Cuncta licet cecidisse putas. Though ye suppose* may refer to the heroine of (2) above. It is one more warning, at a later date when, despite appearances, all danger is not past; its intriguing details do not reveal their secrets.

(5) Lastly, the two stanzas of *Go, pytyous hart, rasyd with dedly wo*, express with genuinely Petrarchian conceits the hopeless torment of a lover who finds himself obliged by the cruel irony of fortune to silence his great love. The poem was written 'at

the instance of a noble lady'. It too alludes to circumstances completely unknown to us.

26. Skeltonics, Skeltonic doggerel, half lines, half-line couplets, rhymed hemistichs, tumbling verse, short verse, 'rhythm peale-meale', sprung rhythm, linekins, saturnian verse, Skeltoniads, Skeltonical verse, Skeltonese. Sidney Lee emphasized the possibility of French influences. See *The French Renaissance in England. An account of the literary relations of England and France in the Sixteenth Century*, Oxford, 1910, pp. 103–7. Brie invokes the sequence-hymns; Berdan, the Latin rhythms; Lloyd the goliardic verse; Nelson the *tiradenreim* and the *homoioteleuton* or *similiter desinens* of the *reim-prosas*. Attention has also been drawn to the Norman *laisses*, comparable with the *laisses* of the French chansons de gestes, the medley, the *frottola* and macaronic verse. *See also* Pyle, 'The origin of the Skeltonics', *N. & Q.* CLXXI, 1936.

27. Episcopal Register *Hill* 1489–1505, diocese of London Dyce XX–XXI.

28. 'Item for offring at master Skelton masse XX S.' MS. E 101. P.R.O. (11–16 Nov. 1498).

29. 'Apostolus: Non habemus hic civitatem manentem, sed futuram perquaerimus.' Dyce, i. p. 410.

30. *See* 'Reforms in the Royal Household', *Tudor Studies presented by the board of studies in history in the University of London to Albert Frederick Pollard, being the work of twelve of his colleagues and pupils*, edited by R. W. Seton Watson, London 1924, pp. 231–256. At the beginning of Henry VII's reign numerous individuals moved in orbit around the King, performing ill-defined duties to which were attached advantages in kind, through the workings of a sort of 'truck system'. The traditional allowance provided for each one was called Bouge or Bouche of Court. It consisted of bread, wine, tallow and fuel, and must have been fairly large to enable the recipient to provide in turn for his own domestics.

31. This picture, which might be considered exaggerated, is exactly similar to a description of the dissolute life of courtiers from the pen of Erasmus: 'These fine fellows of the Court sleep until midday. They breakfast. Dinner follows soon afterwards, to be succeeded by play, charlatans, buffoons, *filles de joie* and inspired punning. It is fair to enjoy it at least once. Supper comes and the night is spent drinking. Thus do they put boredom to flight and thus the hours, the days, the months, the

centuries flow away. As for myself, their pomp sometimes makes me lift up my heart.' Quoted by Champfleury, *Erasme*, p. 299.

32. *Catal. (Primus) Lucubrationum*, prefixed to vol. i of *Erasmi Opera*, 1703.

33. 'Iam puer Henricus genitoris nomine lactus
    Monstrante fonteis vate Skeltono sacros
    '. . . Et domi haberes Skelton, unum Britannicarum literarum lumen ac decus, qui studia possit non solum accendere, sed etiam consummare.' B.M. MS. Egerton 1651. One wonders whether the concluding phrase of this much-quoted sentence was tinged with irony, in the humanist manner characteristic of Erasmus.

34. 'For the cliffes of Scaloppe they rore wellaway
    And the Sandes of Cefas begyn to waste and fade.'
    (*S.P.* 282–3), where *Cefas*, an Aramaic word, is synonymous with Peter, i.e. Saint-Pierre de Calais, and *Scaloppe* with Ecaille or Escalles, another village near Calais. Cf. Nelson, p. 169.

35. Grace Book B., pp. 148–9.

36. B.M. Add. 26. 787, ed. F. M. Salter, *Speculum*, op. cit.

37. Here is an example containing some advice as to the behaviour of the future King Henry VIII. 'Ante omnia gulam abhominare. Sobrietatem et temperanciam cole. Crapulam proscribe. Luxuriam detestare. Prostibulum scortorum fuge. Noli nuptias temerare. Virgines noli deflorare. Coniugem tibi dilige quam unice semper dilige. Non sis immemor beneficii. Facile non credas omni spiritui. Alteram partem audito. Affabilis esto. Adulatores prosequere odio. Acquiesce sano consilio. Non sis parcus. Sis cum ratione munificus, largus, benignus et dapsilis.'

38. 'Amplectere poetas . . . quia multi mulliones sed pauci Polliones.'

39. *Poems of William Dunbar*, ed. W. M. Mackenzie, 1932, p. 107.

40. Nelson, p. 75.

CHAPTER III

The Rector of Diss   *Page 42*

1. Norwich Consistory Court. Reg. Nix (1504–7), fol. 112, Nelson, p. 81.
2. J. D. Mackie, *The Early Tudors, 1485–1558*, Oxford, 1952.
3. Edwards, p. 78.
4. D.N.B.
5. Diss was about half way between Thetford, cradle of the Howards, and Framlingham, their usual residence.
6. It is curious to find that the various people likely at that date to take an interest in Skelton's future were all in touch with Lady Margaret when Margaret Tudor went to Scotland for her marriage with James IV. *Prince Henry* escorted his sister as far as the estate of his grandmother *Lady Margaret*, at Colly-weston near Northampton, where his place was taken by *Thomas Howard*, Earl of Surrey. The Bishop of Norwich, Richard Nix, was also of the party. De Fonblanque, op. cit., p. 3.
7. Grace Book 1504–5, ed. Searles 1908, p. 37. 'Item conceditur Johanni Skelton poete laureato quod possit stare eodem gradu hic quo stetit oxoniis et quod possit uti habitu sibi concesso a principe'.
8. Dyce, i, p. xxix.
9. His Will was proved on 14th April 1506. Norwich Consistory Court Reg. Nix, 1504–7, fol. 460–1. Blomefield, i, p. 27, Nelson, p. 103 (n. 4) H. L. R. Edwards, 'Skelton at Diss', *T.L.S.*, 22 May 1937.
10. In malitia vir insignis.
    Duplex corde et bilinguis (v. 13. 14).
11. Cf. *G. of L.* 1247–1253:
    'Of one Adame all a knaue, late dede and gone,—
    Dormiat in pace, lyke a dormows!—
    He wrate an Epitaph for his graue stone,
    With wordes deuoute and sentence agerdows,
    For he was euer ageynst Goddis hows,

All his delight was to braule and to barke
Ageynst Holy chyrche, the preste, and the clarke'
  See the *Choral Suite* composed by Vaughan Williams (*op. cit.*) on these strange lucubrations.

12. Dyce, i, p. 174.
13. Dyce, i, pp. 155–66.
14.   Sicculo lutueris est colo buraara
     Nixphedras uisarum caniuter tuntantes
     Raterplas Natabrian umsudus itnugenus
     18. 10. 2. 19. 4. 13. 3. 3. 1. teualet.
  Omitting superfluous letters, the syllables are inverted. The figures correspond to the letters of the alphabet taken in normal order, i and j being identical and the vowels being numbered from 1 to 5. This gives
  Sic velut est arabu(m)
  Phenix avis unica tantu(m)
  Terra Britana suum genuit
  SKELTONIDA Vate(m).
  H. Bradley, 'Two Puzzles in Skelton', *The Academy*, 1 August 1896, p. 83A.
15. 'Libertas veneranda piis concessa poetis
  Dicendi est quaecunque placent, quaecunque juvabunt.'
  Dyce i, p. 167.
16. A. Jessop, *Visitations of the Diocese of Norwich, 1492–1532* Camden Soc.
17. *Testamenta Eboracensia*, vol. iii, pp. 297–9.
18. *D.N.B.*
19. *Testamenta Vetusta*, vol. i, pp. 470–1 ; Edwards, pp. 293–5.
20. Martial d'Auvergne, *Les Vigiles de la Mort du Roy Charles VII* (*à neuf psaumes et neuf leçons: contenant la chronique et les faits advenus durant la vie dudit Roy*), Paris, 1493, 1505, 1528.
21. Cf. 'Who cannot weep come learne of me', in R. L. Greene, *The Early English Carols*, Oxford, 1935, No. 161, and Carleton Brown, *Religious lyrics of the XVth Century*, Oxford, 1939, No. 9, pp. 17–18.
22. Lines 210–36.
23. Ph. Chasles, 'La Renaissance sensuelle: Luther, Rabelais, Skelton, Folengo', *La Revue des Deux-Mondes*, 1 May 1842.
24. '*Sic juvat interdum rigidos recreare labores*' (line 1265).
25. 'Wherefore shoulde I be blamed,
  That I Jane haue named,
  And famously proclaimed' (1255–7).

26. *The Ship of Fools*, ed. 1874, vol. ii. *A Brefe addicion of the syngularyte of some newe Folys*, p. 331.

27. Dyce, xxxvi.

28. Cf. John Bale, *Index Britanniae Scriptorum*, s.d., ed. Lane Poole, 1902, pp. 252–3; Id., *Scriptorum Illustrium maioris Brytannie . . . Catalogus*, Basel, 1557–9, pp. 651–2.

29. *Consistory Court Act Book*, Norwich Cathedral, 1509–10. Cf. Nelson, pp. 113–14, Appx. p. 401.

30. *Institution Boox XVI*, 1511: Norwich Cathedral, fol. 50.

31. *A Lawde and Prayse made for our Souereigne Lord the King*.

32. *Skelton's Speculum Principis*, ed. F. M. Salter, SPEC., vol. IX, 1934, p. 37.

33. Edwards, p. 129 and p. 272 (n. 9).

34. Pardon Roll, 1509–10. C.67/57/2. M.31 P.R.O. In the same list we find the name of his friend, the Earl of Northumberland, upon whom Henry VIII had inflicted a colossal fine of £10,000 for some obscure affair concerning the abduction of a ward. De Fonblanque, *op. cit.* Perhaps the poet had been obliged to sue for pardon on account of his independence of thought and language as regards the Tudors. It is possible to see a veiled expression of his rancour in a Latin quotation in *Phyllyp Sparowe* (line 1215): *Principes persecuti sunt me gratis*.

35. Published by Wynkyn de Worde in 1509.

36. *Westminster Abbey Muniments*, ee.325, fol. 17 v. (Saturday, 5 July 1511):

Item ij playce	vij d	
Item ij copull soliz	vj	d this day at dyner wt your
Item ij Congger snekes	xiij	d Maisterchp the soffrecan and
Item a syd saltffishe	ij	d Skeltun the poet wt othere
Item ij dishes buter	ij	d

37. Anthony à Wood notes a collection of *Poetical Fancies and Satyres*, published at London in October 1512. *Athenae Oxonienses*, vol. i, p. 52 (ed. Bliss). Cf. Dyce, p. xcix.

38. *See infra*, p. 112.

39. 'And among the evidence of Mr. Thomas Coggeshall I find the house in the tenure of Master Skelton, laureat'. Blomefield, *op. cit.*, vol. i, p. 30 (M.2).

40. *See supra*, p. 41.

41. *Tribuat michi Iuppiter Feretrius ne teram tempus apud Eurotam.* SPEC., p. 37.

42. 'Skeltonis Laureatus, didascalus quondam Regius, etc., tacitas

secum in soliloquio ceu vir totus obliuioni datus aut tanquam mortuus a corde . . .

Proh deum atque hominum fidem, unde hoc mihi quod ego seorsum ab aliis tanto tamque singulari sim fato! Cui nec regalis munificentia nec fortune benignitas adhuc opulentius dignatur aspirare. O Celum, O Maria, cui imputabo illud? Ah, imponam ne illud diis iratis forsan mihi. Insaniam tantam non committam. Sed ne imponam ego tanto tamque munifico regi remisse largitatis notabilem labem? Auertat hoc deus optimus, maximus amplissime largitatis sue, quique dat omnibus affluenter.' *SPEC.* p. 37.

43. CAL. ST. P. (Venetian), 1867, vol. 2, 1509–19, No. 64. Cf. H. A. L. Fisher, *The History of England*, 1906, vol. v, p. 162.

44. Cic. *De Officiis*, I, ii.

45. Some commentators have seen here a personal reference to Wolsey. They have interpreted 'Tolle Ismaelem' as 'Get rid of Wolsey'. This seems to me a somewhat premature forecast of Wolsey's dictatorship. The Cardinal, indeed, was beginning to be powerful, but was concerned chiefly to make himself useful in an enterprise fully supported by Skelton, the military campaign against France. At this date, therefore, there were no real grounds of conflict between Skelton and the King's Almoner. Cf. F. M. Salter, *SPEC.* loc. cit., p. 292; H. L. R. Edwards, 'The Dating of Skelton's Later Poems', *P.M.L.A.*, vol. LIII, June 1938, p. 603.

46. Published from the 14th cent. MS. in the King's Library, by Louis Paris, Paris, 1838, in —8°. Cf. Dyce vol. i, p. 147. The MS. presented by Skelton to Henry VIII is now at Corpus Christi College, Cambridge (MS. 432). Cf. illustrations in Nelson, pp. 116 and 174; text in H. L. R. Edwards, *P.M.L.A.* loc. cit., pp. 601–3.

47. *Fragmenta Antiqua.* B.M. C.18. e.2 (70).

48. Published by Pynson, in —4°, n.d. The work (now lost) evidently referred to this episode about which many books were written both by supporters and by opponents of Julius II's policy. It is mentioned in Andrew Maunsell's *Catalogue*, London, 1595, p. 7ᴮ.

CHAPTER IV

Orator Royal   *Page 65*

1. Histoire de l'Académie des Inscriptions (Mémoires de Littérature), vol. x, p. 522. Dyce, vol. i, p. 15.

2. Cf. infra p. 107. H. L. R. Edwards ('The dating of Skelton's Later Poems', *P.M.L.A.*, vol. liii, 1938, pp. 601–2) relied upon the approximate date 1515–16 suggested by Ramsay for *Against Venomous Tongues*. It is true that the title *orator regius* occurs for the first time with the *Epitaph* composed by Skelton for the tomb of Henry VII, 30th November 1512. But that work, the MS. of which has unfortunately disappeared, contains also a passage on the battle of Flodden (evidently interpolated after 9th September 1513), which invalidates its chronological testimony.

3. Dyce, vol. i, pp. 179–80.

4. *Ibid.*, lines 13–19

5. In order to justify, by the same reasoning, the date 1512, H. L. R. Edwards was led to invoke the landing at Passage, in the Gulf of Gascony, of English troops commanded by the Marquess of Dorset. But that landing represents nothing more than a secondary preventative operation, a year earlier than the actual declaration of war, and was intended in case of need to help the Spaniards conquer Navarre and Guyenne; an abortive campaign if ever there was one. In the following October the troops, reduced to inactivity, decided of their own accord to return home. Shortly afterwards, moreover, Ferdinand negotiated with France.

6. Dyce, vol. i. pp. 197–8.

7. Cf. Ernest Law, *England's First Great War Minister: How Wolsey made a New Army and Navy and organized the English Expedition to Artois and Flanders in 1513* . . . , London, 1916, pp. 179–84.

8. Cf. supra, pp. 83–4.

9. Cf. CAL. S.P. (*Spanish*), vol. ii, H. VIII, 1509–25, No. 97.

10. Treaty of mutual assistance, 22 May 1512.

11. Treaty of Blois, 7 September 1512, whereby Louis XII promised Jean d'Albret to help him regain his kingdom. Cf. Paul

Boissonnade, *Histoire de la réunion de la Navarre et de la Castille, 1479–1521*, Paris, 1893.

12. James IV was in principle allied with England by a treaty of perpetual peace signed under Henry VII and renewed on the accession of Henry VIII. But he accused the latter:

(1) of having caused the death of the Scottish corsair and national hero Andrew Barton;

(2) of having left unpunished the murder of Sir Robert Ker by the bastard Heron;

(3) of having failed to deliver all the jewels which Henry VII had bequeathed to Margaret, Queen of Scotland, his wife. However, he made numerous sincere efforts to preserve the peace, which earned him the blessing of Pope Julius II on 1 July 1512. As further proof of his good will, he adhered not to the schismatic Council of Pisa, but to the Lateran Council summoned by the Pope.

13. Cf. L.P. H. VIII (Venetian), vol. ii, No. 211, p. 86. Letter from the Venetian Ambassador, Andrea Badoer, to the State of Venice, 8th Jan. 1513: 'The King inclines to war. His Council rejects it. The Queen desires it.'

14. In a message addressed in the spring of 1513 to Percy, Earl of Northumberland, requiring his services, Henry VIII states: '. . . wee, according to our dutie to God and to his Chyrche, and at the instant requests and desyres of the Popes holiness and other Christian Princes, our confederates and alyes, have, for the defence of the said chyrche, being by our enemy the Kyng of France, oppressed, *and the extinction of detestable scism,* raised by certain powers (peruers) cardinals and mayntayned by the same, entend actuall warre agaynst him . . .' B.M. Add. MS. 5758. F. 165. Cf. De Fonblanque, *op. cit.,* p. 335.

15. Erasmus was bitterly opposed to the policy of Julius II. Cf. *The Praise of Folly,* the *Julius Exclusus,* etc. When war broke out he was kept informed of operations by Ammonio and even allowed himself to be slightly affected by the prevailing enthusiasm. John Colet, on the other hand, made it a matter of conscience. Cf. his famous sermon before Convocation in St Paul's, 6th February 1512, followed by the sermon on the Victory of Christ, delivered in presence of the King on Good Friday, 27th March 1513. Meanwhile, across the Channel, opposition to the policy of Julius II unleashed a spate of literature, of which the following are a few examples: *Le traité de la Différence des Schismes et des Conciles* by Jean Lemaire

de Belges; *L'invective contre la guerre papale,* by Guillaume Crétin; *L'Epître Elégiaque pour l'Eglise militante,* by Jean d'Autun; *Déploration de l'Eglise militante,* by Jean Bouchet; *Chasse du Cerf des Cerfs* (Servus Servorum); *Jeu du Prince des Sots,* by Pierre Gringore.

16. The 'Middle Ward' or 'King's Ward' numbered 14,032 men, of whom 9,466 were soldiers. Cf. E. Law, *op. cit.* pp. 180–1: 'Passing from the purely military components of the King's Ward, there were many semi-civilian officials accompanying the King, representative of, and in some cases, the whole staff of the Royal Household. *They were most of them in white and green* ... Among many such were the 'Grooms and Pages of the Privy Chamber','The Clerk of the Council', the 'Gentlemen-Ushers and Servers', even the King's Latin Secretary, Andrea Ammonius—with his four assistants— . . . also the King's luter or 'lutanist', Peter de Brescia (Carmelianus) . . . and even the 'King's minstrels and players' to the number of ten— *all in the royal uniform or livery of 'white and green'.* The 'Priests and Singers of the King's Chapel' who numbered 115 wore, of course, only their clerical garb, with perhaps *a white and green baldrick.*

17. Harl. MS. 787, fol. 58. Harl. MS. 2252, fol. 42–3. Rymer, *Foedera,* vol. xiii, pp. 282–3. —Hall, *Chronicle,* pp. 547–8. —Nelson, pp. 129–33.

18. The battle of Guinegatte (modern Enguinegatte), called derisively 'Battle of the Spurs'. Cf. Guillaume Crétin's poem. *Oeuvres Poétiques,* ed. Kathleen Chesney, Paris, 1932, No. XLII, pp. 203–10.

Bayard, who refused to flee and was taken prisoner, found an old acquaintance in the Emperor Maximilian; he had relieved him at the siege of Padua during an earlier campaign. Cf. M. L. Cimber and F. Danjou, *Archives de l'histoire de France depuis Louis XI jusqu'à Louis XVIII.* Paris, 1835, tome II, p. 142 ff. Thus the Emperor proposed to pay his ransom. As a young prince, Maximilian had already won a battle in the same place, 7th August 1479, celebrated by Jean Molinet. Cf. *Recueil de chants historiques français,* ed. Leroux de Lincy, Paris 1841, pp. 389–99.

19. Dyce, vol. i, p. 191
    Henricus rutilans, Octavus noster in armis
    Tirwinnae gentis moenia stravit humi. (3–4)

20. Cf. Nelson, pp. 125–7.

21. *Ibid.*, p. 129, n. 46.
22. Dyce, vol. i, p. 190.
23. This *Te Deum* was obtained thanks to the insistence with the Holy See of the Archbishop of York, Christopher Bainbridge (Cardinal of St Praxedis), who urged the bulls of excommunication he had obtained from Julius II. He played an unspectacular but effective part behind the scenes of the current war. He had been one of that batch of cardinals created by Julius II at Ravenna on 10th March 1511/12, in order to check the schismatic cardinals of the Council of Pisa. Of violent and irascible temper, but deeply attached to Henry VIII, he died at Rome in 1514, poisoned in mysterious circumstances. Wolsey succeeded him as Archbishop of York. Cf. Baronius, *Annales Ecclesiastici*, tome 31, 1513–6, p. 27 (1754 edition).
24. Hall, *Chronicle*, p. 564.
25. *A Ballade of the Scottysshe Kynge*, ed. John Ashton, London, 1882.
26. Baronius, *op. cit.*, tome 31, p. 26.
27. Not Pynson, as Nelson states, p. 227 (n.).
28. *L.P. H. VIII*, vol. i, Part 2, No. 2391, p. 1060. The king's gauntlet and plaid arrived on 20th. *Ibid*, No. 2268. Meanwhile it had been rumoured in France and Italy that the Scots were victorious. *L.P. H. VIII* (*Venetian*), Nos. 306 and 307. An echo of those rumours in Skelton's *Against the Scottes* (1–11) provides additional proof that Skelton was in France and not in England at the time of those events.
29. *Skelton Laureate against the Scottes*, Dyce, vol. i, pp. 182–8.
30. *Hist. lit. du peuple anglais*, Paris, 1904, vol. ii, p. 115.
31. It was ended officially by the agreement of Corbie, 6th November 1513. The King of France retracted on 17th December, disavowed the Council of Pisa and adhered to the Lateran Council. The event was celebrated with a *Te Deum*. The prelates made their submission on 15th May 1514, and the Pope absolved them from ecclesiastical censures.
32. William Roscoe, *The Life and Pontificate of Leo the Tenth*, London, 1842, letter of 5th October 1513, pp. 59–60: 'Terminate as soon as you can your differences with your present enemies and apply yourself to humble the pride and subdue the ferocity of the Turks'. Cf. Fisher, *Political History of England*, vol. v, p. 189.
33. On 15–16 September 1513 Cardinal Bainbridge asked Leo X to confirm the sentence of excommunication pronounced upon

James IV, but he met with a firm refusal. *L.P. H. VIII* (*Venetian*), No. 314.

34. Letter from Leo X to Henry VIII, 29th November 1513. *L.P. H. VIII*, Vol. i, Part 2, 1513–1514, No. 2469. Latin text in Rymer, *Foedera*, tome xiii, p. 385.

35. *The Eclogues of Alexander Barclay*, ed. Beatrice White, E.E.T.S.— O.S. clxxv, 1928, p. 165.

36. Dyce, vol. i, pp. 188–9.

37. The same idea is expressed in the Bull *Exigit contumaciam* (18 February 1513) excommunicating the King of Navarre: The duty of the supreme head is to punish 'audacious obstinacy and the senseless temerity of the guilty, especially where they hold sovereign authority'. This Bull, drafted with exceptional violence, is supposed to have been extorted by Ferdinand of Aragon from Julius II on his death-bed. Cf. Paul Boissonnade, *op. cit.*, pp. 354–5.

38. Dyce, vol. i, pp. 116–31.

39. Cf. Helen Stearns, 'John Skelton and Christopher Garnesche', *M.L.N.* xliii, 1928, pp. 518–23. According to H. L. R. Edwards (p. 151), in the summer of 1514 (cf. Dyce, III, 113–114) before the departure of Garnesche on a mission to Louis XII, 29th August 1514.

40. D.N.B.; Edwards, pp. 146–9; Nelson pp. 144–7. In 1515 he carried out another mission to Margaret of Scotland. In 1520 he was at Calais, preparing the Field of the Cloth of Gold. In 1526 he held a position as military administrator at Calais. A secondary duty was to supply the King with fruit, artichokes and other fresh vegetables.

41. A typical example at that date was *The Flytyng of Dunbar and Kennedy*, by the great Scottish poet William Dunbar, edited by W. M. Mackenzie, Edinburgh, 1932, pp. 5–20. The flytyng was related to the *tensons*, *jeux partis*, *estours*, *estrifs*, Provencal *sirventes*, Scandinavian *loki sennars*, etc. Something of the kind may be seen in the famous disputes of Prince Hal and Falstaff (Henry IV, Part I). Cf. in France the quarrel between Marot and Sagon; in Italy, that between Luigi Pulci and Matteo Franco. Cf. also Horace, Sat. I, 51–69, where the clowns Sarmentas and Cicirrhus rant at one another for the amusement of an audience on the journey to Brundisium.

42. Page 121, line 32.

43. Lady Brewse, of Hasketon Hall, Suffolk, whose grandson Thomas married Jane Scrope, heroine of *Phyllyp Sparowe*. Cf.

N. H. Nicolas, *The Scrope and Grosvenor controversy*, vol. i, p. 60. Edwards, p. 145.

44. W. Nelson points out (pp. 144–5) that Barclay had ridiculed (*Ecl. I, c.* 1513), under the name Godfrey Gourmand, a gluttonous, servile and quarrelsome courtier who, according to him, had both roused Barclay's exuberance and served Stephen Hawes as a model. A groom named Wynant Godfrey, a member of the Royal Household, was present at the obsequies of Henry VII. *L.P. H. VIII*, vol. i, Part 1, 1509–1513, No. 20, p. 14. He served as a gunner at the Tower of London, 1509–10, for a wage of 6d. a day. *Ibid.*, Grants, 289 (40), 632 (67).

45. Cf. *T.L.S.*, 15th November 1934.

46. Emile Picot and Paul Lacombe, *Querelle de Marot et Sagon*, Société Rouennaise des Bibliophiles, Rouen, 1920; cf. introduction by Georges Dubosc.

47. *Vilitissimus* (sic) *Scotus Dundas allegat caudas contra Angligenas.* Dyce, vol. i, pp. 192–4. The same jibes recur in the writings of many versifiers of the period. Guillaume Crétin speaks of 'Angloys Couez' . . . *Oeuvres poétiques*, ed. Kathleen Chesney, Paris, 1932, No. xlii, p. 208, line 160.

CHAPTER V

Magnificence *Page 80*

1. Cf. *Tudor Studies*, edited by R. W. Seton Watson; *Tudor Reforms in the Royal Household*, edited by A. P. Newton, pp. 231–6.
2. *Constitutiones Eboracensis provinciae.*
3. He was accused particularly of supplying the Swiss with enormous sums for their war against the French at Milan. Cf. R. L. Ramsay, *Magnificence, a moral play* (E.E.T.S.), London, 1–908, pp. cix, cx, cxxiv.
4. G. Brenan, vol. i, p. 152: 'And although the new archbishop spent most of his time in London, yet he exercised great influence north of the Humber, and must have proved a most distasteful neighbour to the Percies.'
5. *L.P. H. VIII*, 1515–6, vol. ii, part 1, No. 1959.
6. *L.P. H. VIII, ibid.*, No. 2018.
7. Dyce, vol. i, pp. 132–6.
8. Cf. George Cavendish, *Life of Wolsey*, pp. 149–50, a description of Wolsey's retinue in 1527. 'And all his yeomen, with noblemen's and gentlemen's servants, following him in French tawny livery coats having embroidered upon the backs and breasts of the said coats, these letters: T. and C. under the Cardinal's hat.' Quoted by Edwards, p. 165.
9. 'Recepit se scripturum opus sanctum, laudabile, acceptabile, memorabileque, et nimis honorificandum.'
10. G. Brenan, vol. i, pp. 152–4: Letter from Shrewsbury to Thomas Allen, 30th April 1516: 'I am sorry to hear that my Lord of Northumberland is committed to the Fleet, but hope the King will shortly be good Lorde to him, and that earl will take no displeasure, as it might hurt himself.' A week later Allen replied: 'The King's grace sat in the Star Chamber, and there was examined the Earl of Northumberland, and so commanded to the Fleet; and there remains as yet.' On 16th May, Sir Richard Sacheverell wrote to Shrewsbury: 'No news, but that my Lord of Northumberland came out of the Fleet on Saturday, and was with the King on Wednesday in his Privy Chamber.' (Talbot Papers I, 40. MS. A f 31, College of Arms. Lodge I, ii.) The pretext for imprisoning Percy was a

dispute over wardship, considerable sources of revenue at that time. Wolsey claimed that certain of his wards belonged by right to the sovereign.

11. 'And after took as a great benefit at the Cardinal's hands that he might be delivered out of his danger.' Holinshed, vol. iii, p. 645, quoted by Brenan, p. 152.

12. Cf. T. W. Baldwin, *Shakespeare's Five-Act Structure. Shakespeare's early plays on the background of Renaissance theories of five-act structures from 1470*, Urbana, 1947.

13. Found attached to the anonymous treatise *Ménager de Paris* (1392–4), edited by the Société des Bibliophiles français in 1846. Cf.: *Le Livre du Chastel de Labour*, by Jean Bruyant. *A description of an illuminated Manuscript of the fifteenth century belonging to T. A. B. Widener, Philadelphia, with a short account and synopsis of the poem* (privately printed), 1909.

14. Cf. *The Castell of Labour, translated from the French of Pierre Gringore* by Alexander Barclay, edited with the French text of 1901 by A. W. Pollard for the Roxburgh Club, Edinburgh, 1905. The first English translation (anonymous) was published by Antoine Vérard (*c.* 1503) at Paris, for the English market. It was issued in England by Pynson, *c.* 1505, then by Wynkyn de Worde in 1506 and *c.* 1510.

15. His motto was *Raison par Tout*. But it is not the critical reason of the *Roman de la Rose*; it is the mystic reason of St Thomas, Reason in accord with Faith. Cf. Skelton: 'Al thyng ys contryvyd by mannys Reason' (*Magn.*, 1).

16. Dyce, vol. i, pp. 195–6.

17. John Weever, *Ancient Funeral Monuments*, London, 1615, p. 476: 'This glorious rich tomb is compassed about with verses, plumed by that Poet Laureate . . . John Skelton.' Quoted by Nelson, p. 119.

18. *Periturae parcere chartae* (Sat. I, 18). The beginning of the first Satire attacks the banality of contemporary poetry. Juvenal there remembers the preceding generation, that of Domitian, as Skelton does that of twenty years earlier.

CHAPTER VI

Elynour Rummyng *Page 104*

1. Dyce, vol. i, pp. 95–115.
2. Cf. *Elynour Rummyng:*

>   Her lothely lere
>   Is nothinge clere,
>   But ugly of chere
>   Droupy and drowsy,
>   Scuruy and lowsy.   (12–16, p. 95)

> *Against Garnesche:*
>   Your skyn scabbyd and scuruy,
>   Tawny, tannyd and shyruy,
>   . . . .
>   Men say ye wyll wax lowsy,
>   Drunkyn, drowpy, drowsy   (131–6, pp. 123–4)

> *Against Dundas*:
>   Skabbed, scuruy and lowsy   (50–1, p. 194)

3. Edwards, p. 122.
4. *L.P. H. VIII*, 1517–8, vol. 2, part 2, No. 3. 204. Giustinian, in a letter to the Doge of Venice (5 May), records the attack on the French and Flemish quarters, as well as a raid on the house of the French secretary Meautis, which was looted. The Duke of Norfolk was entrusted with the restoration of order. *Ibid.*, No. 3.218 (9 May) mentions the end of the riots and the arrival at Richmond of the Portuguese ambassador. His interview with the King had been arranged to take place on the following day.
5. Qy 'dwels'? Dyce, p. 98, note 4.
6. Thomas Wright, *Songs and Carols, now first printed from a Manuscript of the Fifteenth Century*, Percy Soc. vol. xxiii, London, 1847, No. lxxiv, pp. 91–5. (Cf. Appendix II.)
7. Dyce, p. 115.

CHAPTER VII

Freelance *Page 113*

1. H. F. Westlake, 'Skelton in Westminster', *T.L.S.*, 27 October 1921. A lease discovered in the Westminster archives (*Abbey Muniments*, Reg. Book II, f. 146), between the monastic authorities and one Alice Newebury, mentions a lodging '*in quoquidem tenemento Johannes Skelton laureatus modo inhabitat*'. Cf. Westlake, *Westminster Abbey: The church, convent, cathedral and college of St Peter, Westminster*, London, 1923, vol. ii, p. 426.

2. The Great Belfry was a tower of strong masonry in which Edward III had placed three bells which were rung at the coronations and obsequies of English sovereigns. It was said that 'their peal soured every drink in the city'. M. E. C. Walcott, *Westminster: Memorials of the City, Saint Peter's College, The Parish Churches, Palaces, Streets and Worthies*, Westminster, 1849, p. 82.

3. *In Bedel, quondam Belial incarnatum, devotum Epitaphium.* Dyce, vol. i, p. 175. Cf. translation by H. L. R. Edwards, p. 157.

4. Identified by H. L. R. Edwards. Cf. Nelson, p. 119, n. 16. Bedell died in 1518. His will was proved at Canterbury on 11th July in that year. Cf. further biographical information in Edwards, pp. 155–7.

5. Dyce, vol. i, pp. xvi–xix. The dedication is acrosticized. The initial letters of the hexameters give: 'QVE VVHITINTONUS CANIT AD LAVD (AE)S TIBI SCHELTON ANGLORUM VATVM GLORIA SVME LIB(AE)NS'.

6. *Opusculum Roberti Whittintoni in florentissima oxoniensi achademia laureati.* Cf. Dyce, p. xix, n.l.

7. *D.N.B.*

8. Cf. Foster Watson, *The English Grammar Schools to 1660: Their Curriculum and Practice*, Cambridge, 1908, pp. 237–8.

9. Beatrice White (ed.), *The Vulgaria of John Stanbridge and the Vulgaria of Robert Whittinton*, E.E.T.S., OS. No. 187, London, 1932.

10. M. R. James (ed.), *Vulgaria* by William Horman, reprinted with an introduction, Oxford, 1931. W. Horman, vice-provost of

Eton, was likewise the author of some thirty works, mainly pedagogic.

11. *See* note 9.

12. William Lily, *Antibossicon*, R. Pynson, 1521. Sig. A.8. Cf. Nelson, p. 149, n. 4.

13. William Lily, at the age of fifty-two, cut a dash as a 'new man', a humanist. He made the pilgrimage to Jerusalem, stayed with the Knights of St John at Rhodes, and on his return studied Greek under Pomponius Laeta. Pupil of William Grocyn and an accomplished hellenist, he had translated in collaboration with Thomas More a collection of Greek poems published in 1518 under the title *Progymnasmata*. For St Paul's School he compiled a Latin grammar, which, revised by Erasmus, continued in use for centuries. Cf. F. Watson, *op. cit.*, pp. 243–59.

14. Skelton was author of a *New Grammar in English*. Cf. *G. of L.*, Dyce, vol. i, p. 409, v. 1182.

15. Cf. S. R. Maitland, *A List of some of the early printed books in the Archiepiscopal library at Lambeth*, London, 1843, pp. 415, 419. No. 408 describes an *Antibossicon* by William Lily, and No. 409 one by William Horman; both were published by Pynson in 1521. (Bossus, 'bear', was the pen-name adopted by Whittinton, who called himself after the Billingsgate fountain, in the shape of a bear, erected by Dick Whittington the celebrated mayor of London). Nelson (pp. 150–2) adds to the list: an epigram by Lily's pupil John Constable, 'In bossum Liliomastigem', in *Ioannis Constablii Londiniensis et artium professoris epigrammata*, published by Pynson in 1520; Whittinton's pamphlet *Autolycon in defensionem Roberti Whittintoni in florentissima oxoniensi Achademia Laureati/contra quendam Zoilum suae grammaticae oblatrantem sub lyci prosopopeia*, published by Wynken de Worde, 5 January 1521; and *The Maryage of London Stone and Fayre Pussel, the Bosse of Bylyngesgate*, an anonymous pamphlet published, without date, by Wynken de Worde and reprinted by W. C. Hazlitt in *Early Popular Poetry of England*, London, 1866, vol. iii, pp. 161–3.

16. Cf. John Colet's historic condemnation of bad Latin in the statutes of St Paul's School, published 18th June 1518, in which he protests against 'all barbary all corruption all laten adulterate which ignorant blynde folis brought into this world and with the same hath distayned and poysenyd the olde laten spech and the varay Romayne tong which in the tyme

of Tully and Salust and Virgill and Terence was usid, whiche also seint Jerome and seint Ambrose and seint Austen and many hooly doctors lernyd in theyr tymes. I say that ffylthynesse and all such abusyon which the later blynde worlde brought in which more ratheyr may be callid blotterature thenne litterature I utterly abbanysh and exclude oute of this scole . . .' J. H. Lupton, *A Life of John Colet*, D.D., London, 1909, pp. 279–80. Cf. M. Pollet, *Le Latin, langue vivante d'antan* (Les Langues Modernes, No. 4), 1938, pp. 394–404.

17. *Op. cit.*, pp. 127–8.
18. *Op. cit.*, p. 122.
19. Cf. supra, 102.
20. John Bale, *Index*, pp. 252–3.
21. Dyce, vol. i, p. xxxviii; Weever, Fun. Monum; ed. 1631, p. 498; Stowe, *Collections*, Harl. MS. 540, fol. 57. English translation by Thomas Fuller, *Worthies (Norfolk)* ed. 1662, p. 257.

> With face so bold and teeth so sharp,
> Of viper's venome, why dost carp?
> Why are my verses by these weigh'd
> In a false scale? May Truth be said?
> Whilst thou to get the more esteem
> A learned Poet fain wouldst seem,
> Skelton, thou art, let all men know it,
> Neither learned nor a Poet.

22. Roberto Weiss, *Humanism in England during the fifteenth Century*, Oxford, 1941.
23. Frederic Seebohm, *The Oxford Reformers of 1498: being a history of the fellow-work of John Colet, Erasmus and Thomas More . . .*, London, 1867.
24. Sir John E. Sandys, *A History of Classical Scholarship*, vol. ii, chapter 15, 'England from *c.* 1370 to *c.* 1600', pp. 230–2.
25. *L.P. H. VIII*, 1519, Part I, nos. 262, 408, 471, 476, 554. Cf. Erasmus, *Apologia Erasmi ad E. Leeum*, Antwerp, 1520; *Epistolae alicot eruditorum*, 1520; J. Gertrophius, *Recriminatio . . . adversus . . . E. Leeum qui ausus est primus Erasmum . . . luto aspergere*, 1520.
26. *L.P. H. VIII*, 1519, Part I, No. 507. Cf. John Jortin, *Life of Erasmus*, vol. iii, p. 365.
27. *D.N.B.*
28. Marcel Bataillon, *Erasme et l'Espagne*, Paris, 1936, p. 105.
29. Cf. Supra, p. 21.
30. Dyce, vol. ii, p. 8, vv. 158–9.

31. *Ibid.*, vv. 146 ff.
32. The notion of a dead language was apparently foreign to him.
33.   For *aurea lingua Graeca* ought to be magnyfyed,
      Yf it were cond perfytely, and after the rate,
      As *lingua Latina,* in scole matter occupyed,
      But our Grekis theyr Greke so well haue applyed,
    That they cannot say in Greke, rydynge by the way,
      Now, hosteler, fetche my hors a botell of hay!
                                 (*Sp.*, *P.*, 146–52)

34. *Plauti* in his comedies a chyld shall now reherse,
    And medyll with Quintylyan in his Declamacyons,
    That Pety Caton can scantly construe a verse,
    With *Aveto in Graeco,* and suche solempne salutacyons,
    Can skantly the tensis of his coniugacyons;
    Settyng theyr myndys so moche of eloquens,
    That of theyr scole maters lost is the hole sentens.
                                   (181–7)

35. Retoricyons and oratours in freshe humanyte,
    Support Parrot, I pray you, with your suffrage ornate,
    Of confuse tantum auoydynge the chekmate.
                                   (199–201)

36. Brenan, vol. i, pp. 156–7.
37. The Venetian ambassador Giustinian reported in 1516 that he
    was 'on intimate terms with the Cardinal'. Rawdon Brown,
    Four Years at the Court of Henry VIII, 1854.
38. On one occasion, when the Cardinal pretended to want to
    rinse his fingers in a bowl that Buckingham had just been
    holding for the King, Buckingham purposely upset the water
    on the Cardinal's feet.
39. *L.P. H. VIII,* 1520, vol. iii, Part I, No. 259. Letters from Sir
    Nicholas Vaux to Cardinal Wolsey, 10 April 1520.
40. J. S. Brewer, *History of the Reign of Henry VIII,* vol. i, pp. 375–404.
41. Thowghe he pampyr not hys paunche with the grete seall:
    We have longyd and lokyd long tyme for that,
    Whyche cawsythe pore suters haue many a hongry mele:
                               (*Sp. P.,* 310–12)

42. Now Parrott, my swete byrde, speke owte yet ons agayne,
    Sette asyde all sophysms, and speke now trew and playne.
                                   (440–1)

43. Cf. Edwards, pp. 182–4.
44. J. Stecher, *Œuvres de Jean Lemaire de Belges,* Louvain, 1882, 1891,
    vol. iii, pp. 3–16. The poem was read throughout Europe.

Anne of Brittany learnt it by heart. Cf. Henri Guy, *L'Ecole des Rhétoriqueurs*, Paris, 1910, p. 184; P.-H. Spaak, *Jean Lemaire de Belges. Sa vie, son œuvre et ses meilleures pages*, 1926. The analogy with Skelton's poem was noted by Sidney Lee, *French Renaissance in England*, London, 1910, pp. 101–7, and by Edwards, p. 184 and p. 279 n. 5.

45. P. S. Allen, *Erasmi Epistolae*, vol. iii, 1517–19, Oxford, 1913. Letter no. 761 to Antoine de Bergen, abbot of Saint-Bertin, 14th January 1518: 'Instituitur hic Collegium trilingue ex legato Buslisi. Sed obstrepunt nonnulli, qui, quod sunt, bilingues esse malunt; iam vetuli psitaci (*sic*) quibus mutandae linguae spe non sit.' Cf. John Jortin, *Life of Erasmus*, vol. i, p. 102. Ep. 355: 'They are vexed,' says Erasmus, 'that three tongues should be in request, and they had rather be, what they are, *double tongued*: and, indeed, there is no teaching a new language to such old parrots.'

46. For a literal commentary, *see* Nelson, pp. 165–84. Alternate articles by H. L. R. Edwards and W. Nelson in *P.M.L.A.*, vol. iii, June 1938: 'The dating of Skelton's Later Poems', pp. 604–8; 611–14; 615–19. Edwards, pp. 183–90; A. R. Heiserman, *Skelton and Satire*, University of Chicago Press, 1961, pp. 126–65.

47. Lines 216–29.

48. Cf. J. de Morawski, *Pamphile et Galatée par Jehan Bras-de-Fer de Dammartin-en-Goële, poème français inédit du XIV siècle, précédé de recherches sur le Pamphilus latin*, Paris, 1917. The Latin Pamphilus, attributed to Ovid, was widely read in the Middle Ages. Its history is linked with that of Richard de Fournival's famous poem *De Vetula*, likewise attributed to Ovid. It was known in England, France, Provence, Italy, Holland, Germany, Norway and Spain. It occurs in the *Battle of the Seven Arts*, among the opponents of Grammar, for it had been read and commented upon in the schools, except at Oxford where it was banned together with the *Ars Amatoria*. ('Necque Ovidium de Arte amandi, nec Pamphilum de amore, nec ejusdem farinae scriptorem quem vis alium, corrumpendis utique puerulorum moribus idoneum, in scholas suas admittere.'—A. a Wood, *Antiquit. Univ. Oxon.*, col. 3b and col. 4b.)

Jean Prot published an edition with commentary, in Paris, in 1449. It is quoted in Chaucer's *Tale of Melibeus* (Skeat, vol. ivB, 1746–8 and 1751) and in Gower's *Mirour de l'Omme*,

Pamphilius, 271–2). It survived mainly in England, where it probably originated (p. 20). On Ovid in the Middle Ages, *see* E. K. Rand, *Ovid and his influence*, London, 1926.

49. Edwards, p. 193, pp. 279–80, n. 20. Cf. Rimbault, *A Little Book of Songs and Ballads*, 1851, p. 71.

50. *Met.*, v. 750 ff.

51. Dyce, vol. ii, p. 65. Cf:

This Naman Sirus,
So fell and so irous,
So full of malencoly:
With a flap afore his eye,
Men wene that he is pocky,
Or els his surgions they lye.

(*WCYN.*, 1163–8)

It is difficult to establish for certain that Wolsey suffered in 1521 from the eye trouble described in *Why Come ye not to Court?* It is known, however, that he had already suffered from various illnesses: '*Whereby, for lack of sleep, I have been inquieted with sundry diseases*' (*L.P. H. VIII*, vol. iii, Part II, no. 1502, 24 August 1521).

'*Thowz my diseases . . . veray paynful and dangerous . . .*' (*Ibid.*, no. 1735, 2 November 1521).

Cf. H. L. R. Edwards, *P.M.L.A.*, *loc. cit.*, p. 616. Edwards glimpsed the allusion to Polyphemus, but made no mention of it in his work *Skelton*. Note that Galatea's ritornello is undated and there is nothing to disprove it having been written in 1522. The passage occurs in Harl. MS. 2252, fol. 133, but does not appear in the first editions.

52. Known, like the whole conclusion, only from Harl. MS. 2252.

53. The reference is to *Thomas* Clerk, Pace's confidential agent, and not to *John* Clerk, resident ambassador to the Holy See. Cf. Edwards, p. 197.

54. A kind of satirical poem familiar during the Middle Ages, which reviews and criticizes all classes of society. The oldest of such works is perhaps the *Livre des Manières* by Etienne de Fougères, bishop of Rennes (*c.* 1170), who spares nothing and no one.

Cf. Gaston Paris, *La littérature française au Moyen Age*, Paris, 1909, p. 169. The 'State of the World' with which we are here concerned is in many respects similar to *A general Satyre*, attributed by some to William Dunbar and by others to Sir James Inglis. Cf. W. M. Mackenzie, *Poems of William Dunbar*,

London, 1932, p. 151. The same rhythm is found in *The Manner of the World Nowadasy*, published (without date) for the first time by W. Copland and attributed to Skelton by Dyce (vol. i, p. 148) who then denies its authenticity in his notes (vol. ii, p. 199) and claims it to be a mere *rifacimento* of another anonymous poem in Sloane MS. 747, fol. 88.

55. Dyce, vol. i, pp. 311–60. For the date, *see* Nelson, pp. 188–90.

56. Nelson, p. 150.

57. Lines 942 ff. Ernest Law (*A Short History of Hampton Court*, London, 1906, p. 28) recognized this passage as an accurate description of some tapestries at Hampton Court.

58. How may this come to passe,
That a man shall here a masse,
And not so hardy on his hede,
To loke on God in forme of brede.

(1023–6)

59. Lines 1167–74.

60. Lines 1184–90.

61. On 14th June 1522 a proclamation called up all men in the age-group 16–60 because of a possible French invasion. In the following August a similar call-up was proclaimed owing to the threat of a Scottish invasion. *Tudor and Stuart Proclamations, 1485–1714*, Oxford, 1910, vol. i, nos. 83 and 84.

62. Dyce, vol. ii, pp. 28–66.

63. See Claudian, *Invectives contre Eutrope*, ed. Fargues, Paris, 1933.

CHAPTER VIII

The Garland of Laurel *Page 135*

1. *See* Maurice Pollet, 'Skelton et le Yorkshire', *ET. AN.* II, 1952.
2. Dyce, vol. ii, p. 321.
3. Edwards, pp. 234–6, 284 and 302.
4. Edwards (*Ibid.*) thinks that the *Apology of Phyllype Sparowe*, inserted in *The Garland* (vv. 1261–1375), was written at the same time as the latter, in 1523, in order to justify himself in the eyes of Margaret Tilney, a relation of Jane Scrope. And he goes so far as to see in Elynour Rummyng a caricature of Jane grown old (p. 123). Regretfully, we cannot agree with him. It is known that this answer to Jane's coldness contains also a reply to Barclay's attacks in 1509 and the *Apology of Phyllyp Sparowe* was written at the same period (1508–9).
5. Dyce, vol. ii, p. 323.
6. Dyce, *Ibid.*, p. 322; *D.N.B.*
7. Dyce, *Ibid.*, p. 323; Sir H. Nicolas, *Testamenta Vetusta*, vol. ii, p. 604.
8. Edwards, pp. 236–8 and 302. Edwards imagines that because Gertrude Statham was a native of Cambridgeshire she had been an 'old flame' of the poet, an entirely gratuitous hypothesis.
9. The 'chastisement' inflicted on Roger Statham for his impudence recalls that suffered by the curate of *Ware the Hawk*. It is a Latin satire, followed by a coded message revealing the offender's name ROGERUS STATHUM. *See* Henry Bradley, 'Two Puzzles in Skelton', *Academy*, 1 August 1896.
10. Dyce. p. 321.
11. The poet compares his lot to that of many ancient poets who were exiled or threatened with death for their courage and outspokenness. *See* vv. 92 ff.
12. Here perhaps there is a pun referring to the tutor of young Surrey (son of the countess, the future poet) whose name was Clerk.
13. The French poem recalls the manner of Henri Baude, author of a moral *dict* on the upholding of Justice, and of short epigrammatic verses which prove him to have frequented legal circles. He was also author of a morality which bears some resemblance to *Magnificence*. In it he likened the King to a

'life-giving spring whence the realm hoped to derive its fertility, but he deplored the presence in that pure water of herbs and roots which hindered its flow, of rubbish and mud which disturbed it and also made room for too much profitable angling'. It was performed on the Table de Marbre in the Great Hall of the Palace on the accession of Charles VIII. But the courtiers regarded it as an attack on themselves, and the author was sent to the Châtelet. See M.-J. Quicherat, *Les vers de maître Henri Baude, poète du XVe siècle, recueillis et publiés avec les actes qui concernent sa vie*, Paris, 1856, Introd. and pp. 35–6.

14. *D.N.B.*

15. Hall, *Chronicle*, ed. 1809, p. 651.

16. Mandell Creighton, *Cardinal Wolsey*, pp. 66–70.

17. *L.P. H. VIII*, vol. iii, nos. 995, 2,340, 2,446, 2,707, 2,755, 3,244, 3,447.

18. Or of Soleme Chapel, 11 September 1522. *Ibid.* nos. 2,532, 2,536, 2,537. Dacre's decision, which amounted to an act of military disobedience, was considered as 'a happy fault', '*felix culpa*'.

19. This was a combination of English and imperial troops which attempted to invade France at that date. The Spaniards tried to retake Fontarabie, while Surrey pillaged Morlaix and some other ports before going to join the Imperials for an attack on Picardy. After razing a few villages he vainly besieged the fortress of Hesdin for six weeks and then struck camp. See 'Invective contre les Angloys, les Flamands et les Espagnols', in A. de Montaiglon and D. de Rothschild, *Recueil de Poésies Françoises des XVe et XVIe siècles*, Paris, 1878, tome xiii, pp. 289–99.

20. *L.P. H. VIII*, vol. iii, no. 3,506.

21. *Ibid.*, no. 3,509.

22. Surrey complained of the young idlers at Court who should have been in the army at the front. In order to cheer him up, Wolsey in person had to remind him of the great deeds done by himself and by his father, the Duke of Norfolk, in 1513. *Ibid.*, pp. cccliii–ccclv and nos. 3,405–21. On his side, Albany encouraged his troops on the eve of battle by reminding them that they had a defeat to avenge. *Ibid.*, p. ccclvii and no. 3,441.

23. Here is an historian's comment on Skelton's poem: 'Skelton's verses are of no value, except as expressing the sort of feeling with which Englishmen in general hailed the ignominious defeat of one who had been so long identified with the

enemies of their country . . . (He) incorporated in its doggerel all the popular prejudices against Albany and the Scots which the statesmen of the time, though fully aware of their falsehood, never scrupled to employ in a more serious style whenever it suited their purpose. In fact, Skelton's verses are no more than the popular refrain of arguments gravely set forth in royal speeches and ministerial manifestoes, whenever Scotland or the Duke of Albany formed the subject of remonstrance. Here is to be found the calumny, so industriously repeated by Dacre and Surrey, that the patriotism of the Duke was only a cloak for his own ambition.'—S. Brewer, *Ibid.*, introduction, pp. ccclxii–ccclxvi.

24. *Ibid.*, no. 3,512. A spy had confirmed Albany's departure from Eccles Abbey at midnight on Tuesday.

25. VV. 188 ff.

26. He had a private interview with the young reformer, during which he hoped to have brought him to better sentiments. He even gave him some pocket money before letting him go. *See* infra., p. 155.

27. V. 504–12.

28. *See* the description of Henry VIII's funeral: '. . . with Kings Chappell in theire surplesis and *grey ameces*, in like wise singinge.'—Brayley and Neale, *The History and Antiquities of the Abbey Church of St Peter*, vol. i, p. 52 B. The amice is a piece of linen which the priest places on his head or shoulders. It is thought to 'chasten the voice', *per quem designatur castigatio vocis*—X. Barbier de Montault, *Le costume et ses usages ecclesiastiques selon la tradition romaine*, Paris, 1899, vol. ii, pp. 226–231. Amice also denotes a fur hood, either black lined with violet or grey lined with black, worn mainly by prebendaries of cathedrals or the canons of collegiate churches.—*Ibid.*, vol. i, pp. 316–31.

29. Ed. Marshe (1568). *See* Dyce's objections (vol. i, pp. xl, xliv), which, in a new context, appear now out of date.

30. *L'Autre Envoi* is dedicated *ad serenissimam Majestatem Regiam, pariter cum Domino Cardinali, Legato a latere honorificatissimo.* It recalls the promise of a prebend:

> Et fiat memor ipse precare
> Prebendae, quam promisit mihi credere quondam . . .

In Marshe's edition this Envoi was placed at the end of *The Garland of Laurel*. But it does not figure in the 1523 edition published by Richard Faques in the author's lifetime.

CHAPTER IX

The Last Years, and the Struggle against the Lutherans *Page 150*

1. *A Hundred Merry Tales: the earliest English Jest-Book*, edited by W. C. Hazlitt, London, 1887.
2. Hazlitt finds analogies of detail with *The Four Elements*, an interlude printed by John Rastell, and suggests that its author was a member of Thomas More's circle—Rastell, his brother-in-law Heywood, or perhaps even More himself. The mediocrity of this compilation scarcely argues in favour of so great a talent.
3. *Joci ac Sales mire festiui, ab Ottomaro Luscinio Argentino partim selecti ex bonorum utriusque linguae authorû mundo, partim longis peregrinationibus uisi & auditi, ac in centurias duas digesti,* Augsburg, 1524. (The division into *Centuries* may have inspired the title of the *Hundred* Merry Tales.) It contains allusions to Thomas More, in stories no. cxxxi, cxlvii, clxv and clxviii. Ottomar Nachtgall was born at Strassburg *c.* 1487, and died *c.* 1535. A great traveller, he visited several regions of Europe and Asia, received holy orders, taught Greek at Strassburg in 1514, as well as in a convent at Augsburg. He fiercely opposed Luther and was forbidden to preach. He retired to Fribourg, whence he continually hurled his sarcasms at the partisans of the Reformation, Erasmus and Hutten.
4. 'How Scoggin was new christened and confirmed a knave by the French bishop', *Scoggin's Jests*, edited by W. C. Hazlitt, vol, ii, pp. 130–1.
5. *D.N.B.*
6. *D.N.B.*
7. *See* Charles Herford, 'The Ulenspiegel Cycle', *Studies in the literary relations of England and Germany in the sixteenth century*, Cambridge, 1886, pp. 242–322.
8. *Index Britanniae Scriptorum*, Oxford, 1902, p. 253.
9. *The Letter Book of Gabriel Harvey. A.D. 1573–1580*, edited by E. J. L. Scott, Camden Society LXXIV, 1800:

> And cause thou art a merry mate
> Lo Schoggin where he lawghes aloane

And Skelton that same madbrayne knave
Looke how he knawes a deade horse boane.

10. *The Fortunate Isles and their Union*, 1626, in *The Works of Ben Jonson*, edited by W. Gifford, 1816, vol, iii, p. 191 ff.

11. *Pastorals contayning, Eglogues with the Man in the moone*, 1619 (*To the Reader*), in *The Works of Michael Drayton*, Oxford, 1931.

12. Herford, *op. cit.*

13. Herford records a copy of the 'Parson of Kalenborow' in the Douce collection (Bodl.).

14. Robert Proctor, *Jan van Doesborgh, Printer at Antwerp, An Essay in Bibliography* (The Bilibographical Society. Illustrated Monographs, no. 2), London, 1894.

15. *Ibid.*, p. 31. Douce supposed that the English text of Van Doesborgh was by Richard Arnold, friend of Erasmus and Thomas More, which would confirm once again the active part taken by the English humanists in the process that led to the Skelton legend.

16. On the whole of this episode, *see* Henry E. Jacobs, *The Lutheran Movement in England during the reign of Henry VIII and its literary monuments*, London, 1892.

17. Cf. H. F. Westlake, *Westminster Abbey*, London, 1923, pp. 91–2; *L.P. H. VIII*, vol. iv. Part Feb. 1526, no. 1962(2): Wolsey's proceedings against heretics.

18. *D.N.B.*

19. Dyce, vol. i, pp. 206–24. Cf. J. B. Mullinger, *History of the University of Cambridge*, 1873, vol. i, pp. 607–8.

20. vv. 146–60.

21. Cf. Nelson, pp. 218–19.

22. *Dialogue against Heresies*, in *The English Works of Sir Thomas More*, London, 1931, pp. 193 ff. Cf. Nelson, p. 218; Edwards, pp. 248–9.

23. Skelton had apparently devoted to the subject of inspiration a work entitled *The Boke of Good Aduertysement*. Cf. Rep. v. 359 ff.

24. Noted by H.L.R. Edwards in *P.M.L.A.*, 1938, pp. 610–11. Cf. *L.P. H. VIII*, vol. iv, Part 2, p. 58, and Edwards, pp. 249 and 303.

25. *Churchwarden's Accounts (biennial)*. St Margaret's Westminster, 1512–1535, vol. E.2, Caxton Hall, 27 May 1528–2 June 1530.

26. Braynewode, quoted by J. Bale. 'In D. Margarete templo ante summum altare conditus est.' *Index Script. Brit.* His tomb has since disappeared.

27. Receipts by the sayde Wardens. Receyuyd in the second yere

of this ther accompte for buryalles obittes and lyghtis as perticuler(l)y folowyth.

—Item of Master skelton for iiij tapers   iis viijd
—Item of hym for iiij torches   iijs

Receipts of the belles for knylles and peales this second yere.

—Item of M. Iohn skelton for knyll and peales   vjs viijd

Paymentes leide oute by the said accomptantes this second yere ffor Ryngyng off knylls and pealles.

—Item paid to our lady brotherhed for M skelton   xxd
—Item for Ringyng of his knyll and peales   xijd

Cf. Nelson, p. 219, n. 21; Edwards, p. 304.

28. Peculiar Court of Westminster, fol. 6 'Bracy'. Nelson, p. 220, n. 23.

29. 'Per mortem naturalem magistri Johannis Skeltoune ultimi Rectoris eiusdem vacantem', *Norwich Institution Book*, vol. xvii, fol. 9. Nelson, *Ibid.*, n. 22.

CHAPTER X

Legend and Reputation *Page 164*

1. John Bale, on the authority of the antiquary Nicholas Brigan, attributes to Barclay a 'Contra Skeltonum'. Bibliography by T. H. Jamieson, *The Ship of Fools*, pp. xcvii–ci.
2. *The Ship of Fools*, loc. cit.
3. *The Lyfe of Saynt Radegunde*, printed by Pynson (s.d.), ed. F. Brittain, Cambridge, 1926, p. 37.

   In *The life of Saint Werburge of Chester*, 1513, printed by Pynson in 1521 and E.E.T.S. 1887. Bradshaw addresses his work to all poets, including:

   > Also to preignaunt Barkley/nowe beyng religious,
   > To inventive Skelton and poet laureate
   >
   > vv. 2024–6, p. 199.
4. Cf. supra, p. 150 ff.
5. *L.P. H. VIII*, 1530–1532, no. 923 (vii).
6. *Tales and quicke answeres, very mery, and pleasant to rede*, 4°, s.d. (*c.* 1535), printed by Thomas Berthelet. *Of the beggers answere to M. Skelton the poete*, in which the beggar remarks that there is no room for beggars in Hell, but only 'for such gentyl men as ye be'. Second edition by S. W. Singer, p. 9. *Mery Tales, Wittie questions and quicke answeres very pleasant to be reade*, H. Wykes, London, 1567.
7. Cf. Urry's edition of Chaucer.
8. Dyce, ii, pp. 400–13. MS. 2567, Cambridge Public Library.
9. Cf. Andrew Maunsell, *The First Part of the Catalogue of English printed Bookes*, London, 1545, p. 70. *Of Mariage of priestes, of Barnes Martyr, his works*, p. 7. *Strong defence of the mariage of Priestes against the Pope Eustachius and Papists of our time*, printed by Thomas Marshe (publisher of the first Complete Works of Skelton). *A very godly defence, full of learning, defending the mariage of Priestes, gathered by Phil. Melangton* [Melanchthon] *translated by Lewis Benchame*, printed 1541. *An epistle of much learning sent by S. Huldericus, Bishop of Augusta, vnto Nicholas, Bishop of Rome, the first of that name, against the vnmaried chastitie of Priestes.*

241

10. J. Bale, *Index Britanniae Scriptorum*, ed. R. Poole and M. Bateson, Oxford, 1902.

11. Bale, *Scriptorum Illustrium Maioris Brytannie Catalogus*, Basel, 1557–9.

12. Dyce, pp. *liii–lxxxviii*. Cf. Lardner's Cyclopedia, s.v. 'English Poets', vol. ii, pp. 111–14.

13. *Ibid.*, p. xxx.

14. *D.N.B.*

15. *Worthies*, vol. ii, p. 136.

16. *Pithy pleasaunt and profitable workes of maister Skelton, Poete-Laureate, Nowe collected and newly published. Anno 1568.* 12° Cf. Dyce, lxxvi–lxxix.

17. J. P. Collier, *Bibliographical Catalogue*. 'This Howleglasse, with Skoggin, Skelton and Lazarillo, given to me at London, of Mr Spensar, XX Dec. 1578, on condition that I would bestowe the reading of them on or before the first of January immediately ensuing: otherwise to forfeit unto him my Lucian in fower volumes, where upon I was the rather induced to trifle away so many howers as were idely overpassed in running thorowgh the foresaid foolish bookes; wherein me thought that not all fower togither seem'd comparable for false and crafty feates with Joe Miller, whose witty shiftes and practices are reported among Skelton's Tales.' Gabriel Harvey, *Marginalia*, ed. G.-C. More-Smith, Stratford upon Avon, 1913.

18. 'Skelton, a sharpe Satirist, but with more rayling and scoffery then became a Poet Laureat, such among the Greekes were called Pantomimi, with vs Buffoons, altogether applying their wits to Scurrillities and other ridiculous matters.' George Puttenham, *The Arte of English Poesie*; Haslewood, *Ancient Critical Essays*, London, 1811.

19. 'Since these I knowe none other tyll the time of Skelton, who writ in the time of Kyng Henry the eyght, who as indeede he obtained the lawrell Garland, so may I wyth good ryght yeelde him the title of a Poet: hee was doubtles a pleasant conceyted fellowe, and of a very sharpe wytte, exceeding bolde, and would nyppe to the very quicke where he once sette holde': William Webbe, graduate. *A Discourse of English Poetrie. Together with the Authors judgement, touching the reformation of our English Verse*, London, 1586: Haslewood, *op. cit.* p. 34.

20. Arthur Dent, *The Plaine Man's Pathway to Heaven, set forth*

dialogue-wise for the better understanding of the simple, ed. Robert Dexter, 1601, pp. 408–409.

21. 'As Sotades Maronites ye Iambicke Poet gave himselfe wholy to write impure and lascivious thinges: so Skelton (I know not for what great worthines, surnamed the Poet Laureat) applied his wit to scurrilities and ridiculous matters, such among the greeks were called Pantomimi, with us Buffoons.' Francis Meres, Maister of Artes of both Universities, *Palladis Tamia, wits treasury, (a comparative discourse of our English Poets, with the Greeke, Latine, and Italian Poets)*, London 1598, p. 149.

22. A condemnation which included the reading of Catullus and Ovid's *Ars Amoris;* William Vaughan (M.A.) *The Golden-grove, moralized in three bookes, a worke very necessary for all such as would know how to governe themselves, their houses, or their country*, 1599.

23. Orpheus Junior (William Vaughan), *The Golden Fleece*, 1st edition, Francis Williams, London, 1626.

24. Anthony Munday, *The Downfall of Robert Earl of Huntington.* Ed. in 1601 under the title *Robin Hood.* Cf. *The death of Robert Earl of Huntington*, Part II, by Henry Chettle and Anthony Munday.

25. Cf. Henslowe's Journal, 1600.

26. Michael Drayton, *Sir John Oldcastle*, in which appear Sir John, his manservant Hartlepool, the parish-priest of Wrotham and Doll his concubine. *The Works of Michael Drayton*, Tricentenary edition, Oxford, 1931, vol. i, lines 1991–6.

27. Michael Drayton, *Odes with other lyrick poesies*, 'A Skeltoniad', p. 370.

28. *The Works of Ben Jonson*, ed. W. Gifford, vol, iii, 1816, pp. 191 ff.

29. *Cynthia's Revels*, ed. Alexander C. Judson, Yale Studies in English, No. XLV, New York, 1912. Cf. Charles R. Baskerville, *English Elements in Jonson's Early Comedy*, Univ. of Texas Studies in English, No. 178, 1911.

30. *The Godly Queen Hester*, ed. W. W. Greg, London, 1904.

31. Described by Hall in his *Chronicle*, ed. 1809, p. 719, J. E. Bernard Jr, *The Prosody of the Tudor interlude*, New Haven, 1939.

32. Sir David Lyndsay, *The Poetical Works*, ed. D. Laing, Edinburgh, 1879, vol. ii.

33. *Respublica. A play on the social conditions of England at the accession of Queen Mary*, ed. Leonard A. Magnus, E.E.T.S., 1905; *Respublica, A.D. 1553. A drama of real life in the early days of Queen Mary*, ed. J. S. Farmer, 1907.

34. James A. S. MacPeek, *Catullus in strange and distant Britain*, Howard Studies in Comparative Literature, vol. xv, 1939; J. B. Emperor, *The Catullan Influence in English Lyric Poetry circa 1600–1650*, Univ. of Missouri Studies, vol. 3, 1928.

35. *The Life and Poems of William Cartwright*, ed. R. Cullis Goffin, Cambridge, 1918.

36. *Complete Poems of George Gascoigne*, ed. W. C. Hazlitt, London, 1869, p. 488, Cf. C. T. Prouty, *George Gascoigne, Elizabethan Courtier, Soldier and Poet*, New York, 1942. Skelton, pp. 281–4.

37. *The Complete Works of Sir Philip Sidney*, ed. A. Feuillerat, Cambridge, 1922, vol. ii, p. 216.

38. *Ibid.*, p. 275.

39. Richard Brome, *Dramatic Works*, London, 1873, vol, iii. p. 52.

40. W. C. Hazlitt, *Studies in jocular literature*, p. 149.

41. *The Poems of John Cleveland*, ed. John M. Berdan, New York, 1903, p. 109.

42. *The Familiar Letters of James Howell, Historiographer Royal to Charles II*, ed. Joseph Jacobs, London, 1892, vol. ii, book iv, letter XXVII, p. 605.

43. Abraham Cowley's *Complete Works*, 2 vols. 1881.

44. *Worthies*, vol. i, p. 238. *See* Dean B. Lyman, *The Great Tom Fuller*, California, 1935; also *Thomas Fuller, Selections with essays by Ch. Lamb, Leslie Stephen*, ed. E. K. Broadus, Oxford, 1928, pp. xii–xiv.

45. Anthony à Wood, *Athenae Oxonienses*, 1st edition, 1691–2.

46. 'The following poems having been lately recovered from the obscurity in which they had the fate to be concealed for many years.' The biographical details were taken from A. Wood.

47. The Will of a certain William S*h*elton (not S*k*elton), proved at Norwich on 7 November 1512 and making no reference to the poet.

48. *The Muses' Library or a series of English poetry*, London, 1741, pp. 48–9.

49. 'And heads of houses beastly Skelton quote'. *Epistle to Augustus* (Second Book of Horace), 1737, p. 38 (n.).

50. *The History of English Poetry*, London, 1774–81. Warton added to the Skeltonian canon the interlude entitled *The Nigramansir* (1504, imp. Wynkyn de Worde?) which he claimed to have seen at the house of his friend William Collins and of which he purports to give a summary (Cf. Dyce, pp. xcix–c). Unfortunately, that discovery has never been confirmed and

some think it may be just one of those puzzles in literary criticism which he was not above contriving. Cf. J. Ritson, *Observations on the three First volumes of the History of English Poetry in a familiar letter to the Author*, London, 1782, p. 360: 'If the existence of this before unheard of Morality rest entirely upon the dictum of the Author of the History of English Poetry, I had rather, if you please, withhold my belief till its production.' Also Ritson's *Bibliographica poetica*, 1802, p. 106; H. E. D. Blakiston, 'Thomas Warton and Machyn's Diary', *English Historical Review*, vol. XI, 1896, pp. 282–300; Edwards, p. 169. The fraud would not be an isolated instance. A. W. Pollard (*English Miracle Plays, Moralities and Interludes*, p. lxvi) pointed out that an interlude entitled *The Fyndyng of Troth*, attributed to Medwall and thought to have been performed before Henry VIII, flowed from the fertile pen of Payne Collier.

51. Eric Partridge, *The Three Wartons. A choice of their verse*, 1927.
52. *The Works of the English Poets, from Chaucer to Cowper; including the series edited, with prefaces, biographical and critical, by Dr Samuel Johnson: and the most approved translations*, London 1810, vol. ii, pp. 226–310.
53. Robert Southey, *Select Works of the British Poets from Chaucer to Jonson, with biographical sketches*, London, 1831.
54. Elizabeth Barrett, 'The Book of the Poets', *The Athenaeum*, 2 July 1842.
55. 'La renaissance sensuelle: Luther, Rabelais, Skelton, Folengo', in Revue des Deux-Mondes, 1st March 1842.

CHAPTER XI

Past and Present *Page 177*

1. Satire I, prologue.
2. Philip Henderson's 2nd (revised) edition, 1948, p. xii.
3. H. C. Andrews, 'Baldock, Herts, and John Skelton', *N. & Q.* 25 iv, 42.

CHAPTER XII

Satire and Poetry *Page 186*

1. The poet had his appointed place in the clerical hierarchy. A fifteenth-century Anglo-Latin vocabulary assigns the name 'poet' to thirteenth place in a list (*Nomina dignitatum clericorum*) beginning with the Pope. Cf. Thomas Wright, *Anglo-Saxon and Old English Vocabularies*, 2nd edition, London, 1884, vol. ii, pp. 675–744. In that list 'abbot' holds the seventeenth place, 'prior' the eighteenth, 'parish-priest' the twenty-seventh. The 'Versifyer' comes sixty-second, which agrees with Sir Thomas Elyot's distinction between a poet and a versifier, in *The Governour* (1531): '. . . sembably they that make verses, expressynge thereby none other lernynge but the craft of versifying, be nat of ancient writers named poetes, but onely called versifyers', ed. S. Laurie, Book I, Chap. xiii, p. 56.

2. Cf. G. R. Owst, *Literature and pulpit in medieval England—a neglected chapter in the history of English letters and the English people*, Cambridge, 1933, MS 29 of the Library of Jesus College, Oxford, ed. E.E.T.S.—O.S. No. 49, p. 189: 'Readers familiar with one of these poems . . . will realize how slight is the gap between metrical homilies for pulpit recitation and metrical satires for pulpit use,' p. 227.

3. B. D. Brown, *The Southern Passion*, E.E.T.S., p. 234.

4. Gaston Paris, *La littérature française au Moyen Age* (XI–XIVᵉ siècles), Paris, 1909 (4th edn.), p. 18.

5. Cf. *Le Livre des Manières*, by Etienne de Fougères, written in the seldom-used form of single rhymed octosyllabic quatrains. Ibid., p. 189. Cf. *Speke, Parrot* (vv. 442–511).

6. G. R. Owst, *op. cit.*

7. Text B., vv. 129–31. Owst claims to recognize Thomas Brunton behind the Angel of Heaven who descends from the clouds to intercede with the king, in Latin. Cf. 'The "Angel" and the "Golyardeys" of Langland, Prologue to Piers Plowman's Vision'. (B. Text) *M.L.R.* July 1925.

8. Colin Clout, however, is more concerned with attack than with defence, with denouncing Wolsey than with pleading on

behalf of a particular class of society. Reading the poem, one feels that Skelton created Colin Clout, a convenient double of himself, in order to ensure the manifold witness of a popular character capable of striking the imagination, but principally to strengthen the grounds of his campaign against the Cardinal.

9. Cf. G. R. Owst, *op. cit.* A monk, who was also a professor in the University of Paris, undertook to preach a synodal sermon in the presence of the King of France and numerous bishops. He began by taking a long look round at his audience and repeating several times: 'St Peter and St Paul, babimbado' (a derisive word used to idiots). When asked what he meant by speaking in this way, he explained: 'These bishops with their splendidly caparisoned mounts and their dainty dishes, with their rich vestments, their vices and their pleasures, are convinced they will go to heaven. So Peter and Paul, who endured poverty, tribulation, hunger, thirst and cold are silly fools.' A. Lecoy de la Marche, *Anecdotes Historiques, Légendes et Apologues tirés du recueil inédit d'Etienne de Bourbon, dominicain du XIIIᵉ siècle*, Paris, 1877, No. 257, p. 218. Bourbon's collection was entitled *Tractatus de Diversis Materiis praedicabilibus.*

10. Cf. the allusion to Cato in *Magnificence*, v. 1505: 'Of Cato the counte accountyd the cane,' where the word *cane* has nothing to do with *Khan* as suggested by R. L. Ramsay, p. 90, following Dyce, vol. ii, p. 260, but derives from O.F. *Cane*: the imposition of a tax.

11. Cf. *A Lawde and Prayse made for Our Souereigne Lorde the Kynge,* Dyce, vol. i, p. x.

12. *Speke, Parrot,* vv. 269–79. Cf. H. L. R. Edwards, 'The dating of Skelton's later poems', *P.M.L.A.*, 1938, vol. III, pp. 605–6.

13. Another cause of this natural coarseness of language may be traced to the extraordinary crudity of expression common in school books at that time. Cf. Stanbridge's *Vulgaria,* published by Wynkyn de Worde, 1519, pp. 6 and 7, where the vocabulary jibs at no aspect of reality. Other phrases likewise reveal the crudity and even the cruelty, of manners. For example:

I am almoost beshytten. *Sum in articulo purgandi viscera.*
Thou stynkest. *Male oles,* p. 17.
My heed is full of lyce. *Caput meum est plenum pediculorum.*
I shall kyll the with my owne knyfe, p. 20.

He is a kokolde. *Alter supponit uxorem suam*, p. 20.

He lay with a harlot al nyght. *Concubuit cum pellice tota nocte*, p. 23.

14. Vol. i, p. li, n. 3.

15. *WCYN* (vv. 1213–4) Juvenal, *Sat. I* (vv. 24–30).

   WCYN (v. 1224) Juvenal, *Sat. VIII* (v. 140).

16. S. M. Tucker, *Verse Satire in England before the Renaissance*, Columbia, 1908, p. 143.

17. Courthope, *History of English Poetry*, vol. i, pp. 382–5.

18. For latin warkis.

   Be good for clerkis (*G. of L.* 1542–3).

APPENDIX I

TWO VERSIONS OF A SINGLE POEM (cf. pp. 139–41)

A Ballade of the Scottyshe Kynge
(Ed. John Ashton, London, 1882)

Kynge Jamy/Jomy your Joye is all go
Ye sommnoed our kynge why dyde
[ye so
To you no thyng it dyde accorde
To sommon our kynge your soue-
[rayne lorde.
A kynge a somner it is wonder
Know ye not salte and suger asonder
In your somnynge ye were to mala-
[perte
And your harolde no thynge experte
Ye thought ye dyde it full valyaun-
[tlye
But not worth the skyppes of a pye/.
Syr squyer galyarde ye were to swyfte.
Your wyll renne before your wytte.
To be so scornefull to your alye /
Your counseyle was not worth a flye.
Before the frensshe kynge / danes /
[and other
Ye ought to honour your lorde and
[brother
Trowe ye Syr James his noble grace/
For you and your scottes wolde tourne
[his face
Now ye prode Scottes of gelawaye.
For your kynge may synge welawaye

Now must ye knowe our kynge for
your regent /
Your souerayne lorde and presedent /
In hym is figured melchisedeche /
And ye be desolate as ameleche
He is our noble champyon.
A kynge anoynted and ye be non
Thrugh your counseyle your fader was
[slayne
Wherfore I fere ye wyll suffre payne /
And ye proude scottes of dunbar
Parde ye be his homager.

Against the Scottes
(Ed. Dyce, 1843)

Kynge Jamy, Jemmy, Jocky my jo,
Ye summond our kynge,—why dyd
[ye so?
To you nothing it dyd accorde
To summon our kynge, your soueray-
[gne lord.
A kyng, a sumner! it was great
[wonder:
Know ye not suger and salt asonder?
Your sumner to saucy, to malapert,
Your harrold in armes not yet halfe
[experte.
Ye thought ye dyd yet valyauntly,
Not worth thre skyppes of a pye:
Syr skyrgalyard, ye were so skyt,
Your wyll than ran before your wyt.
Your lege ye layd and your aly
Your frantick fable not worth a fly,
Frenche kynge, or one or other;
Regarded ye should your lord, your
[brother.
Trowid ye, Syr Jemy, his nobul grace
From you, Syr Scot, would turne his
[face?
With Gup, Syr Scot of Galawey!
Now is your pride fall to decay.

Male vryd was your fals entent
For to offende your presydent,
Your souerayne lord most reuerent,
Your lord, your brother, and your re-
[gent.
In him is fygured Melchisedec,
And ye were disloyall Amalec.
He is our noble Scipione.
Anonynted kynge; and ye were
[none.
Thoughe ye vntruly your father haue
[slayne.

251

252   APPENDIX

And suters to his parlyment /
Ye dyde not your dewty therin.
Wyerfore ye may it now repent
Ye bere yourselfe somwhat to bolde /
Therfore ye have lost your copyholde.
Ye be bounde tenauntes to his estate.
Gyve up your game ye playe chek-
[mate.

For to the castell of norham
I understonde to soone ye cam.

For a prysoner there now ye be
Eyther to the deuyll or the trinite.
Thanked be saynte Gorge our ladyes
[knyght
Your pryd is paste adwe good nyght.
Ye have determyned to make a fraye
Our kynge than beynge out of the
[waye
But by the power and myght of god
Ye were beten with your owne rod
By your wanton wyll syr at a worde
Ye haue lost spores/cote armure/and
[sworde
Ye had bet better to have busked to
[huntly bankes
Than in Englond to playe ony suche
[prankes
But ye had some wyle sede to sowe.
Therfore ye be layde now full lowe
Your power coude no lenger attayne
Warre with our kynge to meyntayne.
Of the kynge of nauerne ye may take
[hede /
How unfortunately he doth now
[spede /
In double welles now he dooth dreme.
That is a kynge without a realme
At hem example ye wolde none take.
Experyence hath brought you in the
[same brake

His tytle is true in Fraunce to raygne;
And ye, proud Scot, Dunde, Dunbar,
Pardy, ye were his homager,
And suter to his parliament:
For your vntruth now ar ye shent.
Ye bare yourselfe somwhat to bolde,
Therfore ye lost your copyhold;
Ye were bonde tenant to his estate;
Lost is your game, ye are chekmate,
    Vnto the castell of Norram
I understande, to sone ye came.
At Branxston more and Flodden hyl-
[les,
Our Englysh bowes, our Englysh bylles,
Agaynst you gaue so sharpe a shower,
That of Scotland ye lost the flower.
The Whyte Lyon, there rampaunt of
[moode,
He ragyd and rent out your hart
[bloode;
He the Whyte, and ye the Red,
The Whyte there slew the Red starke
[ded.
Thus for your guerdon quyt ar ye,
Thanked be God in Trinite,
And swete Sainct George, our ladies
[knyght!
Your eye is out; adew, good nyght!
    Ye were starke mad to make afray,
His grace beyng out of the way:
But, by the power and might of God,
For your owne tayle ye made a rod.
Ye wanted wit, syr, at a worde;
Ye lost your spurres, ye lost your
[sworde.
Ye myght have buskyd you to Hunt-
[ley bankys;
Your pryde was peuysh to play such
[prankys:
Your pouerte coude not attayne
With our kynge royal war to mayn-
[tayne.
    Of the king of Nauerne ye might
[take heed,
Vngraciously how he doth speed:
In double delynge so he did dreme,
That he is kynge without a reme;
And, for example ye would none take,
Experiens hath brought you in suche
[a brake.
Your welth, your ioy, your sport,
[your play,

Your bragynge bost, your royal aray,
Your beard so brym as bore at bay,
Your Seuen Systers, that gun so gay,
All have ye lost and cast away.
Thus fortune hath tourned you, I dare
[well say,
Now from a kynge to a clot of clay:
Out of your robes ye were shaked,
And wretchedly ye lay starke naked.
For lacke of grace hard was your
[hap:
The Popes curse gaue you that clap.

Of the out yles ye rough foted
[scottes.
We have well eased you of the bottes
Ye rowe ranke scottes and droken
[danes
Of our englysshe bowes ye haue fette
[your banes.
It is not fyttynge in tour nor towne /
A somner to were a kynges crowne
That noble erle the whyte Lyon.
Your pompe and pryde hath layde a
[downe
His sone the lorde admyrall is full
[good.
His swerde hath bathed in the scottes
[blode
God saue kynge Henry and his lordes
[all
And sende the frensche kynge suche
[an other fall /
Amen / for saint charyte'
And god saue noble
Kynge / Henry /
The VIIJ.

Of the out yles the roughe foted
[Scottes,
We haue well eased them of the bot-
[tes:
The rude ranke Scottes, lyke dronken
[dranes,
At Englysh bowes haue fetched theyr
[banes
It is not fytting in tower and towne
A sumner to were a kynges crowne;
Fortune on you therfore did frowne;
Ye were to hye, ye are cast downe.
Syr sumner, now where is your crow-
[ne?
Cast of your crowne, caste vp your
[crowne!
Syr sumner, now ye haue lost your
[crowne.

Quod Skelton, laureate, oratoure
[to the
Kynges most royall estate.

APPENDIX II

AN UNPUBLISHED SOURCE OF THE POEM
ELYNOUR RUMMYNG

Thomas WRIGHT.—*Songs and Carols, now first printed from a Manuscript of the Fifteenth Century.* Percy Society, vol. XXIII. London 1847.

Nº LXXIV, pp. 91–5

I wyll you tell a full good sport
How gossyps gather them on a sort
Theyre syk bodes for to comfort,
    When thei mett in a lance ore stret.

But I dare not, fore ther displesaunce,
Tell off thes maters half the substaunce;
But yet sumwhatt off ther governaunce,
    As fare as I dare, I will declare.

Good gossipe myn, where have ye be?
It is so long syth I yow see.
Where is the best wyn? tell yow me.
    Can you ought tell full wele.

I know a drawght off mery-go-downe,
The best it is in all thys towne;
But yet wold I not, fore my gowne,
    My husbond it wyst, ye may me trust.

Call forth yowr gossips by and by,
Elynore, Jone, and Margery,
Margaret, Alis, and Cecely;
    For thei will come both all and sume.

And ich of them wyll sumwhat bryng,
Gosse, pygge, ore capons wyng,
Pastes off pigeons, are sum other thyng;
    Fore a galon off wyn thei will not
              [wryng.

Go befoore be tweyn and tweyn.
Wysly (that ye be not seen;
Fore I must home, and come ageyn,
    To witt i-wys where my husbond is.

ELYNOUR RUMMYNG

Tell you I chyll
If that ye wyll
A whyle be styll
             [v. 1–3

And sayeth, Gossyp, come hy-
                         [ther
                    v. 204

Some, lothe to be espyde
Hurt in at the backe syde
            v. 262–3

Elynour -halting Jone-
Margery Mylkeducke-
dronken Ales - Cysly-

Another brought two goslynges
            v. 459

Some, lothe to be espyde
          v. 262–3

254

A strype ore ij. God myght send me,
If my husbond myght her se me.
She that is aferd, lett her fle,
    Quod Alis than, I dred no man.

Now be we in tavern sett,
A drowght off the best lett hyme fett,
To bryng owr husbondes out off dett;
    Fore we will spend, tyll God more
                            [send.

Ech off them brought forth ther dysch;   Some brough . . .
Sum brought flesh, and sume fysh.
Quod Margaret mek, now with a wysh,   v. 437.
    I wold Ane were here, she wold mak
                            [us chere.

How sey yow, gossips, is this wyne good?
That it is, quod Elenore, by the rood;
It cherisheth the hart, and comfort the
                            [blood;
    Such jonckettes among shal mak us
                            [lyv long.

Anne, byd fill a pot of muscadell;
Fore off all wynes I love it well,
Swete wynes kepe my body in hele;
    If I had off it nought, I shuld tak gret
                            [thought.

How look ye, gossip, at the bordes end?   But some than sat ryght sad
Not merry, gossip? God it amend
All shalbe well, elles God it defend;   v. 607
    Be mery and glad, and sitt not so
                            [sadde.

Wold Gold I had don aftur yowr coun-
                            [sell!
Fore my husbond is so fell,
He betyth me lyk the devill off hell;
    And the more I cry, the lesse mercy.

Alys with a low voyce spak than,
I-wis, she seid, lytyll good he cane,
That betyth ore strykyth ony woman,
    And specially his wyff; God gyve him
                            [short lyve!

Margaret mek seid; So mot I thryffe,
I know no man that is alyffe,
That gyve me ij-strokes, but he shal
   [have fyffe;
 I ame not aferd, though I have no
   [berd.

On cast down her schott, and went her
   [wey.
Gossip, quod Eleonore, what dyd she
   [paye?
Not but a peny. Lo, therefore, I saie
 She shal be no more off owr lore.

Such gestes we maye have i-nowe,
That will not fore ther shott alow.
With whom cum she? gossipe, with
   [yow?
 Nay, quod Jone, I come alone.

Now rekyn owr shott, and go we hence,
What? cost it ich off us but iij. pence?
Parde, thys is but a smale expence,
 For such a sort, and all but sport.

Torn down the street where ye cum owt,
And we will compasse round abowt.
Gossip, quod Anne, what nedyth that
   [dowt?
 Yowr husbondes be plesyd, when ye
   [be reisyd.

What so ever ony man thynk,
We cum fore nowght but fore good
   [drynk.
Now lett us go hom and wynk;
 Fore it may be sen, where we have
   [ben.

Thys is the thought that gossips tak,
Ons in the weke mery will thei mak.
And all small drynd thei will forsak;
 But wyne off the best shall han no rest

Sum be at the taverne ons in a weke;
And so be sume every daie eke;
Ore ellis thei will gron and mak them
   [sek.
 For thynges usid will not be refusyd.

Some have no money
. . . .
Elynour swered, Nay,
Ye shall not beare away
My ale for nought.

      v. 160

Than cometh an other gest.

      v. 270

Who sey yow, women, is it no soo?
Yes suerly; and that ye wyll know;
And therfore lat us drynk all a row,
   And off owr syngyng mak a good
                           [endyng.

Now fyll the cupe, and drynk to me;
And then shal we good felows be.
And off thys talking leve will we,
   And speak then good off women.

I haue wrytten to mytche

Thus endeth the gest
Of this worthy fest.

APPENDIX III

APOCRYPHA

(a) *Of the Death of the Noble Prince, King Edward the Fourth*

— MS BM Harley 4011. Occurs, with no indication of author, following various works by Lydgate, fols. 169 v° and 170 r°–v°.
— MS BM. Add. 29,729, fol. 8 r°, various works of Lydgate copied by John Stow (1558).
— MS Richardson Currer (now lost) provided Dyce with supplementary stanza no. 4.

Attributed to Skelton by Richard Lant in the edition of 1542–8. This parable on the mediaeval theme of *Ubi sunt?* put into the mouth of this Yorkist king is neither in the style nor in the logic of Skelton, which were essentially Lancastrian. Disputed by F. Brie, *Skelton-Studien*, p. 27, 1907; W. Nelson, *John Skelton, laureate*, p. 65 (n. 26), 1939; Carleton Brown, *Religious Lyrics of the XVth Century*, p. 20, 1939. Ignored by H. L. R. Edwards, *Skelton*, 1949.

(b) *Prayer to the Father of Heaven—To the Second Person—To the Holy Ghost.*

— MS BM Add. 20,059, fols. 100 v° and 101 r°. *Registrum Cancellariae* on vellum, dating, according to Hunter, from the reign of Edward II, on the blank pages of which were transcribed, about the time of Henry VIII, several anonymous religious poems.
— MS Hunter, BM. Add. 24,542. Copied from the preceding. Attributed to Skelton by Richard Lant (*Ibid.*).

Rejected by Carleton Brown (*Ibid.*, no. 51, p. 80). The pieces attributed to Skelton are in the same excessively gallicized style as nos. 12, 38, 69 (*R.L. XVth*) which are not by Skelton.

(c) *On Time*

— Scottish MS Bannantyne, 1568, anonymous.
— MS Egerton, 2642 fol. 130, time of Elizabeth I or James I.

The stanzas attributed to Skelton by Richard Lant (*Ibid.*) are only a fragment corresponding to stanzas 6, 9, 10, and 11 of the

Bannantyne MS, with variants of form and metre. A supplementary stanza appears in the Egerton MS.

At best it is no more than a mediocre commonplace. Disputed by F. Brie (*op. cit.*) and by F. M. Salter, *T.L.S.*, 17 Jan. 1935.

(d) *Woefully Arrayed*

— MS Fairfax BM. Add. 5465, where it occurs twice, fols. 76 and 86.

— Version of the same poem copied on the fly-leaves of a vellum, a pseudo-Boethius: *Boetius: de discip. Schol.*, *cum Notabili commento*, Deventer, 1496 (Heber Collection) 4°, containing two stanzas which do not occur in the Fairfax MS. Ends. *Explicit qd Skelton.*

— MS Harley 4012, where it is presented as a prayer to be recited, preceded and followed by promises of indulgence.

— Refrain and second stanza on the last page of a fifteenth-century vellum MS, described in the Catalogue of the Quaritch Sale under no. 474, Lot 148. The conclusion differs markedly from the Harley MS.

This is a fine example of Christ's apologue on the Cross, a type of poem very common from the 13th to the 15th century. Christ *in articulo mortis* speaks with poignant bitterness to men forgetful of his sacrifice. The invocation of physical suffering, in particular, is well within the pathetic tradition of the 13th century.

Inspired by the words of Scripture *O vos omnes qui transitis per viam*, this theme is traceable to a Latin poem by Philippe de Greve, Chancellor of Paris (*ob.* 1236):

> Homo, vide
> Quid pro te patior . . .

which concludes with the reminder of man's ingratitude:

> . . . Planctus est gravior
> Dum te experior
> (Dreves, *Analecta Hymnica medii aevi*, XXI, p. 18)

Numerous imitations survive, notably in English and Scottish, and various dialects. (Cf. Carleton Brown, *R.L. XIIIth C.*, nos, 33–69; *R.L. XIVth* C., nos, 3, 4, 46, 47, 51, 70, 74, 77; *R.L. XVth* C., nos. 102, 104, 105, 108, 109). Lydgate composed on this theme the last part of his prolix *Testament*: 'Beholde, o man, lyft up thyn eye and see'. Stephen Hawes drew inspiration from the central section of the poem, *The Conversyon of Swerers* (ed. Dr Laing for the Abbotsford Club, 1854), where increasing and decreasing lines suggest the shape of a cross. It is true that John Skelton likewise wrote a *Woe-*

fully Arrayed. Cf. *The Garland of Laurel,* 1418–19: 'with, woefully arayd, and shamefully betrayed, of his makyng deuoute medyta-cyons'. It is by no means certain, however, that he refers to the text with which we are here concerned. Its authenticity has been questioned by F. Brie, J. Lloyd, H. L. R. Edwards, Carleton Brown (*R.L. XVth* C., no. 103, pp. 156–8) and, with some reservation, by E. K. Chalmers in *English Literature at the Close of the Middle Ages,* 1945–7, p. 107. If the words of *The Garland of Laurel* are reliable, the second version, or the second hemistich of Skelton's authentic poem must have been 'and shamefully betrayd', which is not the case in the Fairfax or in the Harley MSS.

(e) *Vexilla Regis Prodeunt*

— MS Arundel 285, anonymous Scottish, gives the best and most complete version.
— MS Makenlloch, transcribed in Scottish on blank pages of a course in logic (Faculty of Louvain, 1477); ed. G. S. Stevenson, Scottish Text Soc. XIX, 303, 1918. Very poor.
— B.M. Add. 37,049, fol. 27 v°.
— Ed. Kele, *Christmas Carolles, c.* 1546–52, reproduced in collotype from the only known copy, in the Huntington Library.

Printed by Bliss, *Bibliogr. Misc.* Oxford, 1813, pp. 48–57. Dyce took it from this work, attributing it to Skelton on the strength of a line in *The Garland of Laurel*: 'Vexilla Regis he devysid to be dis-playd'. But these words appear to allude, not to a poem, but to a spectacle.

In any case, Kele's *Vexilla Regis* has no connection with Skelton. It is not, as the refrain might suggest, a paragraph of the hymn by Venantius Fortunatus (Cf. Dreves, *Anal. Hymn.,* vol. i, p. 38), nor a Christmas carol. It is a very corrupt fragment, consisting of eleven stanzas, of an apologue of Christ on the Cross, an Easter theme of the sort described above, which contains twenty-three stanzas in the Arundel MS, and recurs, in part, in *The Resurrection of the Lord,* no. XXVI of the *Towneley Plays.* Cf. E. C. Taylor, 'The Relation of the English Corpus Christi Play to the Middle English Religious Lyric'. *Mod. Phil.,* Chicago, vol. v, 1907, pp. 1–38.

(f) *Good Order*

Fragment of a morality or interlude printed by William Rastell, 1533. Discovered by R. Nash and deposited in the Library of Dart-mouth College, U.S.A. Cf. George L. Frost and Ray Nash, '*Good*

Order, a Morality Fragment, *St. Ph.*', Baltimore, vol. XLI, 1944, pp. 483–601.

No work entitled *Good Order* appears in the *G. of L.* list. First attributed to Skelton by John Bale, who cannot be taken as reliable (Cf. MacCracken, *The Minor Poems of John Lydgate*, vol. ii, where the author names nineteen apocryphal titles in a list of forty-three works attributed by Bale to Lydgate, pp. xxvii–xxxviii).

This fragment, of very slight literary value, contains two details unusual in Skelton: (i) a reference to the New World; (ii) the advantages of mental over oral prayer—a theme familiar with the Reformers but striking a false note in Skelton, a parish-priest accustomed to vocal prayer.

Finally, this short passage betrays a carelessness in the matter of rhyme, not found in Skelton (Confessyon/acustome; come/pryson; deyntes/braunches).

(g) *Merie Tales, Newly imprinted and made by Master Skelton, Poet laureat, edited by Thomas Colwell*, 12mo, s.d. (*c.* 1567)

Reprinted in *The Poetical Works of John Skelton*, ed. Dyce, 1843; also in *Old English Jest Books alias Shakespeare's Jest Books: reprint of the early and very rare jest book supposed to have been made by Shakespeare*, edited by William Carew Hazlitt, vol. ii, London, 1864.

BIBLIOGRAPHY

A. TEXTS

I. Manuscripts

British Museum, London:

1.	Reg. 18 D. II, fol. 165	— *Vpon the doulourus dethe and much lamentable chaunce of the most honorable Erle of Northumberlande.*
2.	Cott. Vit. E. X, fol. 200	— *The Garlande of Laurell*
3.	Harl. 367, fol. 101	— *Poems against Garnesche*
4.	Harl. 2252, fol. 133	— *Speke, Parrot*
5.	Harl. 2252, fol. 147	— *Colyn Clout*
6.	Add. 4787, fol. 224	— *Salve plus decies*
7.	Add. 5465, Fairfax, fol. 109	— *Manerly Margery Mylk and Ale*
8.	Add. 26,787	— *Speculum Principis*
9.	Add. 28,504	— *Facsimile of an incunabulum of Elynour Rumming*
10.	Lansdowne 762, fol. 75	— Fragment of *Colin Clout* (v. 462–80) entitled *The Profecy of Skelton.*

Public Record Office, London:

11.	Records of the Treasury of the Receipt of the Exchequer, MS E 36–228	— *A Lawde and Prayse made for our Souereigne Lord the Kyng* (autograph).

Corpus Christi College, Cambridge:

12.	— MS 357	— Translation of the *Bibliotheca Historica* of Diodorus Siculus
13.	MS 432	— Codex in 4° of the 14th century entitled *Chronique de Rains*, containing autograph Latin dedications.

Bodleian, Oxford:

14.	Rawlinson C. 813	— Fragment of *Colin Clout*

II. Works Printed During the Author's Life

1. *The Bouge of Court,* printed by Wynkyn de Worde at Westminster, 4to s.d. (*c.* 1499). Advocates' Library, Edinburgh.
   The Bouge of Court, printed by Wynkyn de Worde at Fleet Street 'at the sygne of the sonne', 4to s.d. (*c.* 1500). University Library, Cambridge.

2. *A Ballad of the Scottish King,* printed by Richard Faques at London, 1513. British Museum C.39. e.I.

3. *A Garland of Laurel,* printed by Richard Faques or Fawkes 'in Powlis chyrche yarde at the sygne of the A.B.C.', 3 Oct. 1523, 4to. B.M. 82. d. 5.

   (The engraving, which represents 'Skelton Poeta' in the guise of an idealized poet, comes from a French edition by Guy Marchant of the *Sphera Mundi* of J. de Sacro-Busco or Bosco, in-fol. Goth, Paris, 1498.

   The engraving of an old man at his reading desk is reproduced in a later French book by La Salle, *Les Cent Nouvelles,* s.d. (*c.* 1530), Lyons. Cf. Olivier Arnoullet, *Bibliographie d'Editions Originales et Rares d'Auteurs Français des XVᵉ, XVIᵉ, XVIIᵉ, et XVIIIᵉ siecles,* A. Tchemarzine, Paris, 1933, vol. 7, p. 88.

4. *Agaynste a Comely Coistrown;*
   Contra Alium Cantitantem;
   Upon a Deadman's Head;
   Womanhood, wanton ye want.
   4 leaves, 4to s.d. (Pynson) Huntington Library.

5. *Dyuers Balletys and Dyties Solacious,* including:
   — *My darling dear, my daisy flower;*
   — *The Ancient Acquaintance, Madam;*
   — *Knowledge, acquaintance, resort, favour with grace;*
   — *Cuncta licet cecidisse putas* and its translation *Though ye suppose* . . .
   — *Go, piteous heart*
   4 leaves, 4to s.d. (Pynson), Huntington Library.
   (The engraving of the poet-laureate crowned was later taken to be a portrait of Dr Borde, in *The Boke of Knowledge c.* 1542).

6. *A Replicacion against Certain Young Scholars,* printed by Richard Pynson, King's Press, 4to s.d. (*c.* 1528), Huntington Library.

   (Anthony à Wood mentions also (*Athenae Oxonienses,* vol. i, p. 52, ed. Bliss, 1813) *Poetical Fancies and Satires,* London Oct. 1511. But the work remains unknown.)

III. LATER EDITIONS

7. *Magnificence*, in-fol. s.d. (Rastell *c.* 1533). University Library, Cambridge, British Museum. Bodleian (fragment).

8. *The Book of Philip Sparow*, impr. R. Kele, s.d. (*c.* 1545). B.M. Bod. Hunt. Chapin Library (Mass.); other editions by John Wyght (*c.* 1552), Anthony Kitson (*c.* 1565), Abraham Veale, John Walley, Robert Toy.

9. *Certain Books*, including:
   — *Speak, Parrot;*
   — *The Death of the Noble Prince King Edward the fourth;*
   — *A treatise of the Scots;*
   — *Ware the Hawk;*
   —*The Tunnyng of Elynour Rummyng.*
   Printed by John Kynge and Thomas Marsh, 12mo n.d.; other editions by John Day, 12mo s.d.; Richard Lant for Henry Tab, 12mo s.d.

10. *Colin Clout*, impr. R. Kele 12mo s.d. (*c.* 1545); other editions by Wyght, Kitson, Veale, Thomas Godfray.

11. *Why come ye not to court?* impr. R. Kele, 12mo s.d. (*c.* 1545); other editions by Wyght, Veale, Walley, Robert Toy, Kitson.

12. *Pithy, pleasant and profitable works of Master Skelton, Poet Laureate, now collected and newly published,* 12mo 1568.

13. *The Tunnyng of Elinor Rumming*, printed for J. Busbie and G. Loftis, 1609. Other editions by S. Rand, 4to 1624; Isaac Dalton, 1718; *The Harleian Miscellany*, vol. i, 1746.

14. Reprint of Marsh's edition by J. Bowle, London, 1736.

15. *The Muses Library*, London, 1737. (Extracts.)

16. *Complete Works*, ed. Chalmers from the 1736 edition, in *The Works of the English Poets*, vol. ii, 1810.

17. Extracts in *The Works of the English Poets*, vol. i, edited by Ezekiel Sandford, Philadelphia, 1819.

18. *Magnyfycence*. Facsimile edition by Sir Joseph Littledale for the Roxburghe Club, London, 1821.

19. *The poetical Works of John Skelton, with notes and Some Account of the Author and his writings*, ed. Alexander Dyce, 2 vols., Thomas Rodd, London, 1843. American editions: Cambridge (Mass.) 1855; Boston, 1856, 1864, 1871, 1887.

20. *The Earliest Known printed English Ballad: a Ballade of a Scottysshe Kynge*, ed. John Ashton, London, 1882; republished by John Ashton in *A Century of Ballads*, Boston, 1888.

21. *British Anthologies*, extracts from *Philip Sparrow* and *Why come ye not to court?*, London, 1901.

22. *A selection from the Poetical Works of John Skelton*, ed. W. H. Williams, Ibister (Tasmania) and London, 1902.

23. *Magnificence, a morality*, ed. Robert Lee Ramsay, E.E.T.S. (E.S.), vol. XCVIII, London, 1908; 2nd edition 1925. Also in Tudor Facsimile Texts, 1910; Students Facsimile, Amersham, 1914, and E.E.T.S., 1918.

24. *John Skelton: Poems*, ed. Richard Hughes, Heinemann, London, 1924.

25. *John Skelton (Laureate): Selected Poems*, Augustan Books of English Poetry, series 2, no. 1, 12 (ed. Robert Graves), 31 p. 8°, London, 1927.

26. *Elynour Rummynge*, illustrations by Pearl Binder, Fanfrolico Press, London, 1928; American edition, illustrated by Claire Jones, San Francisco, 1931.

27. *The Complete Poems of John Skelton, Laureate*, ed. Philip Henderson, Dent, London and Toronto, 1931; American edition, Dutton, New York, 1932; 2nd (revised) edition, London, 1948.

28. *Skelton's Speculum Principis*, ed. F. M. Salter in *Speculum, a Journal of Mediaeval Studies*, vol. IX, no. 1, January 1934, Cambridge (Mass.) pp. 25–37.

29. *Poems*, ed. Roland Gant, London, 1949 (Crown Classics), 64 pp.

30. *John Skelton. A Selection from his poems*, ed. Vivian De Sola Pinto, London, 1950 (A Series of English Texts), viii–127 pp.

31. *The Bibliotheca Historica of Diodorus Siculus, Translated by John Skelton. Now first edited by F. M. Salter and H. L. R. Edwards*, Oxford University Press, London, 1956–7, 2 vols. E.E.T.S. (O.S.) nos. 233, 239.

32. *Poems*, ed. R. S. Kinsman, 1970 (Clarendon Mediaeval and Tudor Series).

B. GENERAL WORKS

I. History

BACON, Francis. *The Reign of Henry VII*. London, 1622.

BARBIER de MONTAUT. *Le costume et ses usages ecclésiastiques selon la tradition romaine*. Paris, 1889.

BARONIUS. *Annales Ecclesiastici*. Ed. 1754.

BLORE. Th. *The History and Antiquities of the County of Rutland*. 1811.

BOISSONNADE, Paul. *Histoire de la réunion de la Navarre et de la Castille*. 1479–1521. Paris, 1893.

BRAYLEY and NEALE. *History and Antiquities of the Abbey Church of Saint Peter, Westminster.* London, 1818.

BREWERS, J. S. *The reign of Henry VIII, to the death of Wolsey,* Préface aux vol. 1–4 des *Letters and Papers of the reign of Henry VIII.* Ed. James Gairdner, 2 vols., 1884.

BROWN, Rawdon. *Four Years at the Court of Henry VIII, selection of despatches written by the Venetian Ambassador S. Giustinian,* 1854.

BUSCH, Wilhelm. *England under the Tudors.* (Trans. from German.) 1895.

CAMPBELL, William. *Materials for a history of the reign of Henry VII, from original documents preserved in the Public Record Office,* 1873–1877.

CAVENDISH, George. *The Negociations of Thomas Wolsey, the Great Cardinal of England, containing his life and death. Composed by one of his servants, being his gentleman-usher,* 1641.

CATHOLIC ENCYCLOPEDIA. 15 vols. New York, 1907–12.

CHILD, G. W. *Church and State under the Tudors,* 1890.

CHRIMES, S. B. *English Constitutional Ideas in the XVth Century.* 1936.

CHRONICLES and Memorials of Great Britain and Ireland. London, 1858–96.

CREIGHTON, Mandell. *Cardinal Wolsey.* London, 1888.

EKWALL,—. *The Oxford Dictionary of English Place-Names.* Oxford, 1936.

FISHER H. A. L. *The History of England,* 1906.

GAIRDNER, James. *Letters and Papers illustrative of the reigns of Richard III and Henry VII.* London, 1863.

GASQUET, F. A. *Eve of the Reformation.* 1900.

GROSE, Francis, Thomas ASTLE and other eminent antiquaries. *The Antiquarian Repertory.* 4 vols. London, 1807.

HORAE, Eboracences. *The prymer of hours of the blessed Virgin Mary, according to the use of the illustrious church of York with other devotions as they were used by the layfolks in the northern province in the XVth and XVIth centuries.* Surtees Society, 1920.

INDEX of wills in the York Registry—1389 to 1514—. The Yorkshire Archaeological and Topographical Association. V, 1888–9.

JACOBS, H. E. *The Lutheran Movement in England.* 1892.

JESSOPP. *Visitations of the Diocese of Norwich.* 1492–1522. Camden Society, N.S. XLIII, 1888.

KERN, F. *Kingship and Law in the Middle Ages.* 1939.

KINGSFORD, C. L. *Mediaeval London.* Hist. Assoc. no. 38, 1915.

LAW Ernest. *England's First Great war Minister. How Wolsey made a New Army and Navy and organised the English Expedition to Artois and Flanders in 1513.* London, 1916.

LEWIS. *Topographical Dictionary of England.* 4 vols. London, 1849.

LONDON. *Episcopal Register Hill, diocese of London.* 1489–1505.

LYTE, Sir H. C. M. *History of the University of Oxford.* 1886.

MACKIE, J. D. *The Early Tudors, 1485–1558.* Oxford, 1952.

MALLET, C. E. *History of the University of Oxford.* 1924.

MANUALE et processionale ad usum insignis ecclesiae Eboracencis. Surtees Society, 1875.

MEAD, W. E. *The English Medieval Feast.* 1931.

NICOLAS, Sir N. H. *The Controversy between Sir Richard Scrope and Sir Robert Grosvenor in the Court of Chivalry A. D.* 1385–90. London, 1832.

NORWICH. Consistory Court. *Registre Nix.* 1504–7.

PICKTHORN, Kenneth W. H. *Early Tudors' Government,* 1934.

PIRENNE et RENAUDET. *La fin du Moyen Age.* 1931.

POLLARD, A. F. *The reign of Henry VII,* 1913. *Henry VIII,* 1905. *Wolsey,* 1929. *Tudor Studies.* Ed. R. W. Seton-Watson, 1924.

RAIT, Sir Robert. *An outline of the relations between England and Scotland, 500–1707.* Blackie, London, 1901.

READ, Conyers. *The Tudors. Personalities and Practical Politics in XVIth Century England.* O.U.P. Ed. U.S.A., 1936.

RENAUDET, A. *Pré-réforme et Humanisme.* Paris, 1916.

RENAUDET et HAUSER. *Les débuts de l'âge moderne.* 1929.

RODOCANACHI, Emmanuel. *Histoire de Rome. Le Pontificat de Jules II, 1503–1513.* Paris, 1928. *Le Pontificat de Léon X, 1513–1521.* Paris, 1931.

ROSCOE, William. *The Life and Pontificate of Leo the Tenth.* London, 1842.

RYMER. *Foedera.* 20 tomes. London, 1704–32.

SALTER, E. G. *Tudor England through Venetian eyes.* 1930.

SALZMANN, L. F. *English Industries of the Middle Ages,* 1923; *England in Tudor Times,* 1926; *English Trade in the Middle Ages.* 1931.

SMITH, A. H. *The Place-Names of the North Riding of Yorkshire.* English Place-Name Society. Cambridge, 1928.

SMITH, George Gregory. *The days of James IV, 1488–1513. Scottish History by contemporary writers.* 1890.

STEELE, R. R. *Tudor and Stuart Proclamations, 1485–1714.*

STOWE Collections. *MS. Harleian* 540.

STRYPE. *Ecclesiastical Memorials.* London, 1822.

SYMONDS, J. A. *The Renaissance of Modern Europe.* 1872.

TAWNEY R. et POWER Eileen. *Tudor Economic Documents.* 3 volumes, 1924–51.

TEMPERLEY, Gladys. *Henry VII.* London, 1914–17.

TODD, Henry J. *The History of the College of Bonshommes at Ashrige.* London, 1823.

VERGIL, Polydore. *Anglica Historia.* Trad. Denys Hay. Camden Series. Vol. 74, 1950.

WALCOTT, M. E. C. *Westminster: Memorials of the City, Saint Peter's College, the Parish Churches, Palaces, Streets and Worthies.* Westminster, 1849.

WESTLAKE, H. F. *Westminster Abbey.* London, 1923.

WYATT, T. G. *The Part played by aliens in the social and economic life of England during the reign of Henry VIII.* Bull. Inst. of Hist. Research. Vol. 25, no. 72, Nov. 1952.

II. LITERATURE

ATKINS, John W. H. *English Literary Criticism: The Renaissance.* London, 1947.

BAILEY, C. *The legacy of Rome,* 1923.

BALDWIN, C. S. *Medieval Rhetoric and Poetic to 1400.* New York, 1928.

BALDWIN, Thomas W. *Shakespeare's Five Act Structure, on the background of Renaissance theories of five act structure from 1470.* University of Illinois, Urbana, 1947.

BARON, Hans. *Cicero and the Roman Civic Spirit in the Middle Ages and the Early Renaissance.* 1938.

BILLING, Anne H. *A Guide to the Middle English Metrical Romances.* Yale, 1901.

BONNEAU, Alcide. *L'Immaculée-Conception de la Vierge Marie, poème de Robert Gaguin, docteur en Sorbonne, général des Mathurins.* Paris, 1885.

BERNARD, J. E. Jr. *The Prosody of the Tudor interlude.* Newhaven (Mass.), 1939.

BOUCHET, Jean. *Un grand rhétoriqueur poitevin; Jean Bouchet 1476–1557,* par Auguste Hamon (with a bibliography), 1901.

BRANT, Sébastien. *The Ship of Fools.* Ed. T. H. Jamieson, 1874.

BROME, Richard. *Dramatic Works.* London, 1873.

BROOKE, C. F. T. *The Tudor Drama,* 1912.

BROWN, B. D. *The Southern Passion.* E.E.T.S., 1927.

BROWN, Carleton. *Religious Lyrics of the XVth Century,* Oxford, 1939.

BRUYANT, Jean. *Le Livre du Chastel de Labour.* Privately printed, 1909.

CARTWRIGHT, William. *The Life and Poems.* Ed. R. Cullis-Goffin, Cambridge, 1918.

CHAUCER, Geoffrey. Ed. J. Urry. London, 1687.

— *Complete Works.* Ed. W. S. Skeat, 1949.

CIMBER, M. L. et DANJOU F. *Archives curieuses de l'Histoire de France depuis Louis XI jusqu'à Louis XVIII.* Paris, 1835.

CLAUDIEN. *Invectives contre Eutrope.* Ed. Fargues, Paris, 1953.

CLEVELAND, John. *The Poems.* Ed. John M. Berlon. New York, 1903.

COLLIER, J. P. *A Catalogue, Bibliographical and Critical, of Early English Literature,* 1837.

CONLEY, C. H. *The First English translation of the classics.* 1927.

CREIGHTON, Mandell. *The Early Renaissance in England.* 1895.

CRÉTIN, Guillaume. *Oeuvres Poétiques.* Ed. Kathleen Chesney (with a bibliography). Paris, 1932.

CUSHMAN. *The devil and the vice in the English dramatic literature before Shakespeare,* Halle. 1900.

DESMOULINS, Laurent. *Le Catholicon des mal aduisez autrement dit le Cymetiere des malheureux.* Jean Petit et Michel le Noir. Paris, 1513. *Le dépucelage de Tournay.* Paris, 1513.

DESPOIS E. *Les Satiriques latins.* 1864.

DOBIACHE-ROJDESVENSKY, Olga A. *Les Poésies des Goliards,* 1931.

DRAYTON, Michael. *The Works.* Ed. J. William Hebel, Kathleen Tillotson et Bernard H. Newdigate. 5 vols. Oxford, 1931–41.

DUMERIL, Edelestand. *Poésies populaires latines du Moyen Age.* 1847.

DUNBAR, William. Ed. W. M. Mackenzie, 1st ed. Edinburgh, 1932.

EINSTEIN, Lewis. *Italian Renaissance in England.* 1902. *Tudor ideals.* 1921.

ELYOT, Sir Thomas. *The Gouernour.* 1st ed., 1531.

EMPEROR, J.-B. *The Catullian Influence in English Lyric Poetry, c.* 1600–1650. University of Missouri Studies, 1928.

ERASMUS. *Epistolae.* Ed. P. S. Allen. Oxford, 1913. *Apologia Erasmi ad E. Leeum.* Anvers, 1520. *Praise of Folly,* translated by Pierre de Nolhac, 1944. *Life of Erasmus* by John Jortin, 2 vols. London, 1758–1760. Marcel Bataillon: *Erasme et l'Espagne.* Paris, 1936.

FARAL, Edmond. *Les Arts poétiques des douzième et treizième siècles.* 1924.

FLOOD, Grattan. *Early Tudor Composers,* 1925.

FOLIGNO, C. *The legacy of the Middle Ages.* Oxford, 1926. *Latin thought during the Middle Ages.* Oxford, 1929.

FULLER, Thomas. *Selections with essays by Ch. Lamb, Leslie Stephen.* Ed. E. K. Broadus. Oxford, 1928. *Also* Dean B. Lyman: *The Great Tom Fuller.* California, 1935.

GASCOIGNE, George. *The Complete Poems,* Ed. W. C. Hazlitt. London, 1859.

GERTOPHIUS. *Recriminatio . . . adversus . . . E. Leeum qui ausus est primus Erasmus . . luto aspergere.* 1520.

GOWER. *Complete works.* Ed. G. C. Macaulay. Oxford, 1899–1902.

GODLY, Queen Hester. Ed. W. W. Greg. Louvain, 1504.

GREENE, R. L. *The Early English Carols.* Oxford, 1935.

GRINGORE, Pierre. *The Castell of Labour, translated from the French of Pierre Gringore by Alexander Barclay, 1501.* Ed. with French text by A. W. Pollard Roxburghe Club. Edinburgh, 1905. *La Chasse du Cerf des Cerfs.* Ed. Giraud et A. A. Veinant. Paris, 1513. Reissued 1829—*Oeuvres Complètes.* C. d'Héricault and A. de Montaiglon. Bibliothèque Elzévirienne. Paris, 1858.

GUY, Henri. *Histoire de la poésie française au seizième siècle.* Tome 4. l'Ecole des Rhétoriqueurs. Paris, 1910.

HARVEY, John H. *Gothic England. A survey of national culture, 1300–1550.* 1947.

HASKINS, Charles H. *Studies in Medieval culture, 1929.*

HAWKINS, Thomas. *The Origin of English Drama.* 3 vols., Oxford, 1773.

HAZLITT, W. Carew. *Shakespeares Jest Books.* 3 vols. London, 1864. *The English Drama and Stage under the Tudor and Stuart Princes.* 1543–1664. *The Roxburghe Library* (1869). *Studies in Jocular Literature.* 1890.

HEARNSHAW, F. J. C. *The social and political ideas of the Renaissance and the Reformation.* 1925.

HERFORD, C. H. *Studies in the literary relations of England and Germany in the XVIth Century,* 1836.

HORACE. *Satires.*

HOWELL, James. *The familiar letters of James Howell, Historiographer Royal to Charles II.* Ed. Joseph Jacobs. London, 1892.

HUIZINGA, Johan. *The waning of the Middle Ages.* 1927.

JAMES, M. R. *A Descriptive Catalogue of the Manuscripts in the Library of Corpus Christi College.* Cambridge, 1912.

JANELLE, P. *L'Angleterre catholique à la veille du schisme.* 1935.

JONSON, Ben. *The Fortunate Isles and their Union. Cynthia's Revels. Works.* Ed. W. Gifford, 1816. *English Elements in Jonson's Early Comedy.* Charles R. BASKERVILLE: University of Texas Studies in English no. 178. 1911.

JOHNSON, Dr Samuel. *The Works of the English Poets.* London, 1810.

JUVENAL. *Satires.*

LARDNER's Cabinet Cyclopoedia. *English Poets.* London, 1830–49.

LATHROP, H. B. *The First English printers and their patrons.* 1922. *Translations from the classics.* 1933.

LEACH. *The Schools of Medieval England.* 1915.

LECOY de la MARCHE, A. *Anecdotes Historiques, Légendes et Apologues tirés du recueil inédit d'Etienne de Bourbon, dominicain du XIIIᵉ siècle.* Paris, 1877.

LEE, Sidney. *The French Renaissance in England.* 1910.

LEMAIRE de Belges, Jean. *Oeuvres*. Ed. J. Stecher. Louvain, 1882–91. *Les Epitres de l'Amant vert*. Ed. Jean Frappier, Lille-Geneva, 1948. P. Spaak: *Jean Lemaire de Belges. Sa vie, son œuvre et ses meilleures pages*. 1926.

LILY, William. *Antibossicon*. R. Pynson, 1521.

LUPTON, J. H. *A Life of John Colet D.D.* London, 1909.

LYNDSAY, Sir David. *The Poetical Works*. Ed. D. Laing. Edinburgh, 1879.

MAUNSELL, Andrew. *Catalogue*. London, 1595.

MARTIAL d'AUVERGNE. *Les Vigiles de la Mort du Roy Charles VII*. Paris, 1493–1505–1528.

MÉNAGER de Paris (Le). Anon. *c.* 1392–4. Ed. Société des Bibliophiles français. Paris, 1846.

MOLINET, Jean. *Recueil de Chants historiques français*. Ed. Leroux de Lincy. Paris, 1841.

MONTAIGLON, A. de. *Recueil des Poésies Françoises des quinzième et seizième siècles*. Paris, 1855–78.

MORAWSKI, Jean (de). *Pamphile et Galathée par Jehan Bras-de-Fer de Dammartin-en-Goële, poème français inédit du XIVe siècle, précédé de recherches sur le Pamphilus latin*. Paris, 1917.

MORE, Thomas. *The English Works*. London, 1931.

NACHTGALL, Ottomar. *Joci ac Sales*. Augsbourg. 1524.

OWST, G. R. *Preaching in Medieval England*. Cambridge, 1926. *Literature and pulpit in Medieval England*. Cambridge, 1933.

PAMPHILUS, Maurilianus. *De amore*. Ed. Jean Prot. Paris, 1449. *Comédie latine du Xe siècle*. Ed. A. Baudoin. Paris, 1874.

PARIS, Gaston. *La littérature française au Moyen Age* (XIe XIVe siècles). Paris, 1909.

PASTON, LETTERS. Ed. J. Gairdner. 3 vols. Westminster, 1896.

PICOT, Emile et LACOMBE Paul. *Querelle de Marot et Sagon*. Société Rouennaise des Bibliophiles, Rouen, 1920.

PLUMPTON, CORRESPONDENCE. Ed. T. Stapleton. London, 1839.

POLLARD, A. W. *English Miracle Plays, Moralities and Interludes. Specimens of the pre-Elizabethan Drama*. Oxford, 1830.

QUICHERAT, A.-J. *Les Vers de Me Henri Baude, poète du quinzième siècle, recueillis et publiés avec les actes qui concernent sa vie*. Collection 'Le Trésor des pièces rares ou inédites'. 1856.

RABY, F. J. R. *A History of Christian latin Poetry from the beginnings to the close of the Middle Ages*. 1927. *A History of Secular Latin Poetry in the Middle Ages*. Vol. II, 1895.

RAND, E. K. *Ovid and his Influence*. London, 1926.

RASTELL, John. *A new interlude and a mery of the nature of the iv elements.* German edition by Julius Fisher, 1902.

RESNEL (Abbé du). *Recherches sur les Poètes Couronnés.* Histoire de l'Académie des Inscriptions et Belles-Lettres (Mémoire de Littérature), The Hague, 1719–71.

RESPUBLICA. *A play on the social condition of England at the accession of Queen Mary.* Ed. Leonard A. Magnus, E.E.T.S., 1905.

RESPUBLICA. A.D. 1553. *A drama of real life in the early days of Queen Mary.* Ed. J. S. Farmer. 1907.

REYHER, P. *Essai sur le doggerel.* Bordeaux, 1909.

ROBERT, Fernand. *L'Humanisme. Essai de définition*, 1946.

ROTHSCHILD, D. (de). *Recueil de Poésies Françoises des XVe et XVIe siècles.* Paris, 1878.

SAINTSBURY, George. *The Earlier Renaissance.* 1901.

SANDYS, J. E. *A History of classical scholarship from the 6th century to the end of the Middle Ages.* 1903.

SCHIRMER. *Der Englische Frühhumanismus.*

SEEBOHM, O. *Oxford Reformers.* 1867.

SIDNEY, Sir Philip. *The Complete Works.* Leipzig, 1931. Ed. A. Feuillerat. Cambridge, 1922.

SMITH, G. Gregory. *The Transition period.* Vol. IV, 1897.

SMITH, Preserved. *The Age of the Reformation.* 1921. *Erasmus*, New York, 1923.

SWAIN, Barbara. *Fools and Folly during the Middle Ages and The Renaissance.* Columbia Univ. New York, 1932.

TAYLOR, Archer, O. *The Classical heritage of the Middle Ages.* 1901.

THOMPSON, E. N. E. *The English Moral Plays.* Transactions of the Connecticut Academy of Arts and Sciences, 1910.

THUASNE, Louis. *Roberti Gaguini epistolae et orationes.* Bibliothèque Littéraire de la Renaissance. 2 vol. Paris, 1903.

VINAVER, E. *The Works of Sir Thomas Malory.* 1947.

VULGARIA (The) *of William Horman, reprinted with an introduction.* Ed. Montague Rhodes James. Oxford, 1931.—*The Vulgaria of John Stanbridge and the Vulgaria of Robert Whittinton.* Ed. Beatrice White, E.E.T.S. O.S., no. 187. London, 1932.

WALLACE, Charles W. *The Evolution of the English Drama up to Shakespeare.* Berlin, 1912.

WATSON, Foster. *The English Grammar Schools to 1660.* London, 1908.

WARTON. *The Three Wartons. A Choice of their Verse.* Ed. Eric Partridge 1927. *Thomas Warton and Machyn's Diary.* H. E. D. Blakiston. English Historical Review. Vol. XI, 1836.

WEISS, Roberto. *Humanism in England during the 16th Century.* 1941.

WELTER, J. I. L'exemplum *dans la littérature du Moyen Age.* 1927.

WESTON, J. L. *Romance, idiom and satire.* 1912.

WHITFIELD, J. *Petrarch and the Renascence.* 1943.

WOODWARD, W. H. *Studies in education during the Age of the Renaissance,* *1400–1600.* 1905.

WORKMAN, J. K. *15th Century translation as an influence on English Prose.* Princeton, 1940.

WRIGHT, Thomas. *Anglo-Saxon and Old English vocabularies.* London, 1884. *Songs and Carols, now first printed from a Manuscript of the Fifteenth Century.* Percy Society. Vol. XVIII. London, 1847.

C. WORKS RELATING TO THE AUTHOR

I. REFERENCES AND CRITICAL WORKS

AMES, Joseph. *Typographical Antiquities,* ed. Dibdin, vols. I–IV, London, 1810–19, 4to.

ASTLEY, H. J. D. *Memorials of Old Norfolk,* London, 1908.

ATKINS, John W. H. *English Literary Criticism: the medieval prose,* Cambridge, 1943, re-issued Methuen, 1952.

AUDEN, W. H. *The Great Tudors,* ed. Katharine Garvin, London, 1935.

AUSTIN and RALPH. *The Lives of the Poets Laureate, with an introductory essay on the title and office,* 1853.

BAKER, D. E. *Biographica dramatica, or a Companion to the Play-House,* vol. I, p. 672 (1812).

BALE, John. *Illustrium Maioris Britanniae Scriptorum, hoc est Angliae, Cambriae, ac Scotiae summariu,* 1548. Ed. subtitulo *Index Britanniae Scriptorum* by Reginald Poole and Mary Bateson, Oxford, 1902.

BALE, John. *Scriptorum illustrium Maioris Brytannie Catalogus.* Basel, 1557–9.

BALLARD, George. *Memoires of British Ladies.* London, 1775 (1st ed. 1762).

BARCLAY, Alexander. *The Ship of Fools* (1509). Ed. Jamieson, Edinburgh, 1874. *The Eclogues* (1514) from the original edition by John Cawood, ed. with an introduction and notes by Beatrice White E.E.T.S., 1928.

BASKERVILLE, Charles R. *English Elements in Jonson's Early Comedy.* Univ. of Texas Studies in English, 1911.

BERDAN, John M. *Early Tudor Poetry,* New York, 1920.

BERNARD, J. E., Jun. *The Prosody of the Tudor Interlude.* Yale Studies in English, vol. 90, 1939.

BLOMEFIELD, Francis. *A Topographical History of Norfolk*, London, 1805–10.

BLOXAM, J. R. *Register of the University of Oxford*. Ed. Boase, 1885.

BLUNDEN, Edmund. *Votive Tablets* (reprint from T.L.S., 1929). London, 1931.

BOLTON, Edmund. *Hypercritica or a Rule of Judgment for writing or reading our History*, *c.* 1610, ed. by Dr Anthony Hall, London, 1722.

BRADSHAW, Henry. *The Life of Saint Werburge of Chester*, printed by Pynson, 1521, ed. by C. Horstmann, E.E.T.S., no. 88, London, 1887. *The Lyfe of Saynt Radegunde* (Pynson, s.d.), ed. F. Brittain, Cambridge, 1926.

BRINK, Bernhard, Ten. *History of English Literature from the fourteenth century to the death of Surrey*, vol. III, 1892–1896.

BROWN C. and ROBBINS, R. H. *The Index of Middle English Verse*. The Index Society, Columbia Univ. Press, New York, 1943.

BROWNE, William. *The whole Works of William Browne, of Tavistock and of the Inner Temple*, 1614, Ed. W. Carew Hazlitt, *The Shepheardes pipe*, p. 19.

BRYDGES, Sir Egerton. *Censura Literaria*, vol. II. London, 1805. *British Bibliographer*, vol. IV, London, 1814.— *Restituta: or titles, extracts and characters of old books in English Literature, revived*, vol. I, 1814.

BULLEIN, William. *A Dialogue both pleasaunt and pitifull wherein is a godlie regiment against the Fever Pestilence, with a consolation and comfort against Deathe*, orig. *c.* 1564, ed. 1573, E.E.T.S., 1888.

Cambridge History of English Literature, 1909, vol. III, chap. IV.

CAMDEN, William. *Magna Britannia et Hibernia*, vol. III, 1724. Norfolk, p. 335. A and B.

CAMPBELL, Thomas. *Specimens of the British Poets*, London, 1841.

CAPTAIN COX. *His Ballads and Books*, ed. F. J. Furnivall, London, 1871.

CARTE, Thomas. *A general History of England*, 4 vol. London, 1747–1755.

CAXTON, William. *The Boke of Eneydos*, ed. W. T. Culley and F. J. Furnivall, E.E.T.S. E.S., no. LVII, 1890.

CHAMBER, John. *A treatise against judicial astrologie*, ed. *Censura literaria*, Sir Egerton Brydges, vol. IX, 1805.

CHAMBERS, E. K. *The Mediaeval Stage*, 2 vol. Oxford, 1903. *English Literature at the Close of the Middle Ages*, Oxford, 1945.— And SIDGWICK, F. *Early Lyrics, amorous, divine, moral and trivial*. London, 1907.

CHETTLE, Henry and MUNDAY, Anthony. *The Death of Robert, Earl of Huntington*, Part II, London, 1601.

276 BIBLIOGRAPHY

CHURCHYARD, Thomas. Cf. Preface in verse to the edition of Th. Marshe, 1568.

CIBBER, Thomas. *The Lives of the Poets of Great Britain and Ireland, to the Time of Dean Swift,* 1735.

COLERIDGE, Samuel. *Notes on Shakespeare's Plays from English History King John I,* I.

COLLIER, J. P. *Household Book of John, Duke of Norfolk,* 1844.

COLLINS, J. Churton. *The English Poets,* vol. I. *A treasury of Minor British Poets,* London, New York, 1896.

COOPER, Charles H. *Athenae Cantabrigienses,* 1898–1913.

COOPER, Elizabeth. *The Muses' Library, or a Series of English Poetry,* London, 1741.

CORSER T. *Collectanea Anglo-Poetica,* 1860–80.

COURTHOPE, W. J. *A History of English Poetry,* London, 1895, vol. I.

CRAIK, George. *A Compendious History of English Literature and of the English language from the Norman conquest, with numerous specimens,* 1864, vol. I.

DE FONBLANQUE. *Annals of the House of Percy,* 1887.

DELEPIERRE, J. O. *Macaroneana* or *Mélanges de la littérature macaronique des différents peuples de l'Europe.* Paris, 1852, p. 35.

DENT, Arthur. *The Plaine Man's Pathway to Heaven.* (Allusion to Elinor Rumming), *c.* 1590, ed. 1601, pp. 408–409.

Dictionary of National Biography. London, 1885.

D'ISRAELI, Isaac. *Curiosities of Literature,* 3 vol. London, ed. by Disraeli, 1886. *Amenities of Literature,* 3 vol. 1941. Vol. II, p. 19.

DRAYTON, Michael. *Odes with other lyrick poesies,* 1619. *Pastorales contayning Eglogues with the Man in the moon,* 1619. Tricentenary ed. 5 vol. Oxford, 1931–1941.

DUTT, William. *Some Literary Associations of East Anglia,* London, 1907, chap. XIII.

ELLIS, George. *Specimens of the Early English Poets,* 1790, re-issued. 3 vol. 1801.

ELLIS, Sir Henry. *Original Letters,* London. 1846.

EVANS, Thomas. *Old Ballads.* London, 1810.

FARNHAM, William. *The Medieval Heritage of Elizabethan Tragedy.* Berkeley Univ. of California Press, 1936.

FLUGEL, Ewald. *Neuenglisches Lesebuch.* Halle, 1895.

FRY, John. *Pieces of Ancient Poetry, privately printed,* Bristol, 1814.

FULLER, Thomas. *The History of the Worthies of England,* ed. Nichols, London, 1811.

GAYLEY, Charles M. *Representative English Comedies from the beginnings to Shakespeare. New York,* 1903.

GILFILLAN, W. George. *Specimens with Memories of the less-known British Poets.* Edinburgh, London, Dublin, 1860, vol. 1.

GRAESSE, Jean. *Trésor des livres rares et précieux ou Nouveau Dictionnaire bibliographique.* Tome IV, Dresde, Paris, 1805.

GRANGE, John. *The Golden Aphrodites,* ed. H. E. Rollins, 1934. *Biographical History of England from Egbert the Great to the Revolution,* 1769.

GREG, Walter W. *Pastoral poetry and pastoral drama.* London, 1906, p. 80.

HALL, Edward. *Chronicle,* ed. 1809.

HALL, Joseph. *Virgidemiarum. The Three Last Bookes of bytyng Satyres,* 1598, p. 83.

HALLAM, Henry. *Introduction to the Literature of Europe,* London, 1837–1839.

HAMILTON, W. *The Poets Laureate of England, being a history of the office of poet-laureate.* London, 1879.

HAMMOND, E. P. *English Verse between Chaucer and Surrey.* Duke Univ. Press, 1927.

HANNAY, James. *Satire and Satirists, six lectures.* London, 1854, lect. III.

HARINGTON, Sir John. *Nugae Antiquae,* 1749.

HARVEY, Gabriel. *Harvey's Letter-Book,* 1573? 1580, ed. J. L. Scott, Camden soc. 1884, p. 56–57. *Foure letters and certaine sonnets: Especially touching Robert Greene,* 1592, p. 7. *Pierces Supererogation or a New Prayse of the Old Asse,* 1593, p. 75. *Marginalia,* ed. G. C. Moore-Smith, Stratford-upon-Avon, 1913.

HAZLITT, W. Carew. *Remains of the Early Popular Poetry,* 1864–1866. *Studies in jocular literature.* London, 1890.

HEADLAM, Cecil. *British Satirist.* London, 1897.

HEARNE, Thomas. *Works,* London, 1810, vol. IV.

HENSLOWE, Philip. *The Diary of Philipe Henslowe from 1591 to 1609. Shakespeare,* Soc. 1845. 1600, *Scogan and Skelton,* the play by Richard Hathwaye and William Rankins.

HEYWARD, Thomas. *The British Muse,* 1738.

HILL, Nathaniel. *The Ancient Poem of Guillaume de Guileville entitled 'Le Pèlerinage de l'homme' compared with the Pilgrim's Progress of John Bunyan.* London, 1858, p. 11.

HOLINSHED, Ralph. *Chronicles of England, Scotland, Ireland,* London, 1807–8.

HOLLAND, Samuel. *Dom Zara del Fogo, A mock Romance,* 1656, book II, chap. IV, p. 101.

HOOPER, James. *Memorials of Old Norfolk,* 1907.

HOWELL, James. *The Familiar Letters*, 1658, ed. J. Jacobs, London, 1892, vol. II, b. IV, letter XXVII, pp. 604–605.

HUTCHINSON, William. *The History and Antiquities of Cumberland*, 1794, vol. I, pp. 495–496.

JAMES, Richard. *The Poems* 1625, ed. A. B. Grosart, 1880, p. 221. Cf. *The Jonson Allusion Book*, ed. J. F. Bradley and Quincey Adams, Newhavenvale, 1922, p. 137.

JOHNSON, Dr. *Dictionary of Johnson and English Poetry before* 1660. W. B. C. Watkins, Princeton, 1936, p. 6.

JONSON, Ben. *The Fortunate Isles and their Union*, 1626, ed. Gifford, vol. III, 1816.

JOHNSTON, George Burke. *Ben Jonson: Poet.* Columbia Univ. Press, New York, 1945.

JUSSERAND, J. J. *Histoire littéraire du peuple anglais des origines à la Renaissance*, 2 vol. Paris, 1894–1904.

KRAPP, George Philip. *The Rise of English Literary Prose.* Oxford, New York, 1915.

LAW, Ernest. *A short History of Hampton Court.* London, 1906, p. 28.

LEGOUIS, Emile and CAZAMIAN, Louis. *Histoire de la Littérature anglaise*, 1st edition, 1921.

LOWELL, J. R. *Conversations on some of the old poets.* Cambridge (Mass.), 1845.

MAC PEEK, Jame A. S. *Catullus in strange and distant Britain.* Harvard Studies in Comparative Literature, vol. XV, 1939.

MAGNUS, Laurie. *A Dictionary of European Literature, designed as a companion to English Studies.* London, 1927.

MAITLAND, S. R. *A list of some of the early printed books in the Archiepiscopal Library at Lambeth.* London, 1843.

MERES, Francis. *Palladis Tamia or Wits' Treasury. A comparative discourse of our English Poets, with the Greeke, Latine and Italian Poets*, London, 1598.

MILTON, John. *Areopagitica, with a commentary by Sir Richard C. Jebb.* Univ. Press, Cambridge, 1940.

MISCELLANEA. *Antiqua Anglicana*, 1816, *The Life of Long Meg of Westminster*, 1635, chap. II and IV.

MULLINGER, J. B. *History of the University of Cambridge.* Cambridge, 1873.

MUNDAY, Anthony. *The Downfall of Robert, Earl of Huntington*, 1597, 1601. English Plays, London, 1828.

NASH, Thomas. *The Works.* Lenten Stuff, 1595, ed. 1904–1910.

NEVE, Philip. *Cursory Remarks on some of the Ancient English Poets*, 1789.

NICHOLS. *Literary Anecdotes of the Eighteenth Century.* 9 vol., London, 1812–15. Vol. II, p. 660.

NICOLSON, J. and BURN, R. *The History and Antiquities of the Counties of Westmoreland and Cumberland*, London. 1777, vol. II, p. 384.

OLDYS, William. *British Librarian*, London, 1738.

PARKHURST, John. *Ludicra siue Epigrammata Juvenilia*, 1573. *De Skeltono vate et sacerdota*, p. 103.

PEACHAM, Henry the younger. *The Compleat Gentleman*, 1st ed. 1612, 2nd ed. 1634, p. 161.

PHILLIPS, Edward. *Theatrum Poetarum, or a compleat collection of the Poets, especially the most eminent of all Ages*, 1675.

PITS, John. *Joannis Pitsei angli, s. theologiae doctoris, Liverduni in Lotharingia, decani, relationum historicarum de rebus anglicis.* Paris, 1619.

POLLARD, Alfred W. *Fifteenth Century Prose and Verse.* London, 1903.

POMPEN, Aurelius. *English versions of the Ship of Fools.* London, 1925.

POPE, Alexander. *Second Book of Horace*, Epistle to Augustus 1737, n. 38 (n.).

PROUTY, Charles C. T. *George Gascoigne, Elizabethan Courtier, Soldier and Poet.* New York, 1942.

PUTTENHAM, George. *The Arte of English Poesie, c.* 1580, ed. Haslewood, Anc. Critical Essays, 1811.

QUICHERAT. *Trésor des pièces rares.* 1856.

RENWICK, L. and ORTON, H. *The Beginnings of English Literature to Skelton*, 2 vols., 1939.

RIMBAULT, E. F. *A little book of Songs and Ballads, gathered from Ancient Music Books, MS. and printed.* London, 1851.

RITSON, Joseph. *Observations on the three first volumes of the History of English Poetry* (by Th. Warton), 1782. *Bibliographia Poetica: a catalogue of English poets of the twelfth, thirteenth, fourteenth, fifteenth, and sixteenth centuries, with a short account of their works*, London, 1802.

RIX, S. WILTON. *Norfolk Archaeology: or miscellaneous tract relating to the antiquities of the County of Norfolk.* Ed. Norfolk-Norwich Archaeol. Soc., 1949, vol. II.

ROBINSON, Richard. *The Rewarde of Wickednesse*, 1574.

RUBEL (Vera L.). *Poetic Diction in English Renaissance from Skelton through Spenser.* New York, 1941.

SHAFER, Robert. *The English Ode to 1660.* Princeton, 1918.

SMITH, Preserved. *Erasmus, A study of his life, ideals and place in history*, XIV, 479. New York and London, 1923.

SNELL, F. J. *The Age of Transition.* Handbooks of English Literature, 1905, vol. I.

SOUTHEY, Robert. *Select works of the British Poets from Chaucer to Jonson, with biographical Sketches,* London, 1831.

SPENCE, Joseph. *Observations, Anecdotes and Characters of Books and Men,* 1744, ed. Malone, 1820, p. 8.

SPENSER, Edmund. *The Shepheardes Calendar,* 1579, ed. Selincourt, Oxford, 1910.

STANLEY, Arthur P. *Historical Memorials of Westminster Abbey,* London, 1882.

STRICKLAND, Agnes. *Lives of the Queens of England,* vol. I, p. 104, 1840–1848.

SWEETING, Elisabeth J. *Early Tudor Criticism, Linguistic and Literary.* Oxford, 1940.

TAINE, Hippolyte. *Histoire de la Littérature anglaise.* 4 tomes, Paris, 1863–4.

TANNER, Thomas. *Chaucer, Animadversions upon Chaucer's Works,* 1598, ed. G. H. Kingsley, E.E.T.S., 1865.

TUCKER, Samuel Marion. *Verse Satire in England before the Renaissance.* Columbia Univ. Studies in English, 1908.

VAUGHAN, William (ORPHEUS JUNIOR). *The Golden Fleece,* ed. Francis William, London, 1626.

VENN, J. A. *Alumni Cantabrigienses.* Cambridge, 1926.

WALKER, Thomas A. *A Biographical Register of Peterhouse Men and Some of their Neighbours, from the earliest days, 1284, to the commencement, 1611, of the first Admission Book of the College.* Cambridge, 1927.

WARD, A. William. *A History of English Dramatic Literature to the death of Queen Anne.* 1st ed. 1875.

WARTON, Thomas. *The History of English Poetry,* 1744–81.

WEBBE, William. *A discourse of English Poetrie Together withe Authors judgment touching the reformation of our English verse,* London, 1586, ed. Sir Egerton Brydges. *Cens. Lit.* 1805 and Haslewood, *Anc. Critical Essays,* 1811.

WEEVER, John. *Ancient Funerall Monuments.* London, 1631, p. 476.

WILLIAMS, Dr R. Vaughan. *Five Tudor Portraits, a Choral suite founded on Poems by John Skelton (laureate),* 1460–1529. Oxford, 1935.

WOLFE, Humbert. *Notes on English Verse Satire,* 1929.

WOOD, Anthony-à-. *Athenae Oxonienses,* ed. 1691–2, ed. 1813, vol. I.

II. Works Concerned Exclusively with the Author

KRUMPHOLZ, H. *John Skelton und sein Morality Play 'Magnificence'*. Prossnitz, 1881.

SCHÖNEBERG, G. *Die Sprache John Skeltons in seinen kleineren Werken*. Marburg Dissertation, 1888.

REY, Albert. *Skelton's Satirical Poem in their relation to Lydgate's Order of Fools, Cock Lorell's Bote and Barclay's Ship of Fools*. Bern, 1899.

BISCHOFFBERGER, E. *Einfluss John Skeltons auf die Englische Literatur*. Freiburg, 1914.

KOELBING, A. *Zur Charakteristik John Skeltons*, 1904.

THUMMEL, B. A. *Studien über John Skelton*. Leipzig, 1905.

LLOYD, L. John. *John Skelton, laureate*. London, 1938.

EDWARDS, H. L. R. *The humanism of John Skelton with special reference to his translation of Diodorus Siculus*. Phil. Diss. no. 944 (typescript). Cambridge University Library.

NELSON, William. *John Skelton, laureate*. Columbia University Studies in English and Comparative Literature no. 139, 1939, vi–266 p.

GORDON, Ian A. *John Skelton, poet laureate*. Melbourne and London, 1943, 223 p.

EDWARDS, H. L. R. *Skelton. The Life and Times of an Early Tudor Poet*. London, 1949, 325 p.

HEISERMAN, A. R. *Skelton and Satire*. The University of Chicago Press. 1961, 326 p.

FISH, S. R. *The Poetry of Awareness: A Reassessment of John Skelton*. Unpublished Doctoral Dissertation. Yale, 1962.

FISH, S. R. *John Skelton's Poetry*. Yale Studies in English no. 157, 1965.

SCHULTE, Edvige. *La poésia di John Skelton*. Naples, 1963.

HARRIS, William. *Skelton's Magnyfycence and the Cardinal Virtue Tradition*. University of North Carolina Press, 1965.

GLASSCO, W. G. *Against Wolsey: A Critical Edition of John Skelton's 'Why come ye Nat to Court?' and 'Colyn Cloute'*. Unpublished Doctoral Dissertation. University of Toronto, 1966. Dissertation Abstracts. XXVIII, 1395A–6A.

III. Reviews and Periodicals

Academy, The, Aug. 1896—Henry Bradley, 'Two Puzzles in Skelton'.
Academy, The, 8 Mar. 1903—'A Lippo Lippi of Poetry'.
Antiquary, The, Oct. 1905, vol. 41—Article by C. V. Manning.
Archiv für Studium der reveren Sprachen und Literatur, 1919, N.S.

282   BIBLIOGRAPHY

XXXVIII—Friedrich Brie, 'Zwei Verlorene Dichtungen von John Skelton'.

Athenaeum, 2 July 1842, no. 763—Elizabeth Barrett, 'The Book of the Poets. Skelton'. Reprinted in *The Greek Christian Poets and the English Poets*, London, 1863.

Athenaeum, 4 May 1881—G. Barnett Smith, Skeat, A. Williamson, 'A Ballad of the Scottishe King'.

Athenaeum, 2 May 1914, no. 4514—C. C. Stopes, 'A laureate poem by Skelton'.

Criterion, I, 1932—W. Auden, critical review of Henderson's edition.

Critical Essays on English literature, Madras, 1965—S. Kandasarami, 'Skelton and the Metaphysicals'.

English Language Notes, June 1967—M. J. Tucker, 'Skelton and Sheriff Hutton'.

Englische Studien, XXXVII, Heilbronn, 1907—Fr. Brie, 'Skelton Studien'.

Englische Studien, LXXI—Fr. Brie, 'Thomas More der Heitere'.

English Review, May 1925—L. Lloyd, 'John Skelton, a forgotten poet'.

English Studies. A Journal of English Letters and Philology, Groningen, Oct. 1946—Th. Tillemans, 'John Skelton, a Conservative'.

Etudes anglaises, Feb. 1952—Maurice Pollet, 'Skelton et le Yorkshire'.

Everybody, 7 Oct. 1950—Roland Gant, 'no dry and dusty scholar'.

Explicator, The, XXV, no. 42, Jan. 1967—D. V. Harrington, 'Skelton's *Mannerly Margery Mylk and Ale*'.

Fortnightly Review, Nov. 1931—C. H. Warren, critical review of Henderson's edition.

Gentleman's Magazine, Sept. 1844—Critical review of Dyce's edition. Sept. 1897—Article by James Hooper.

Hispania, XLVII, 1964—O. T. Myers, 'Encina and Skelton'.

Huntington Library Quarterly, XXVI, Aug. 1963—R. S. Kinsman, 'The Voices of Dissonance: Pattern on Skelton's *Colyn Cloute*'. XXIX, Feb. 1966—R. S. Kinsman, '*A Lamentable of Kyng Edward the IIII*'.

Journal of English and Germanic Philology, LXV, Jan. 1966—Norma Phillips, 'Observations on the Derivative Method of Skeltons' Realism'.

Journal of English letters and Philolopgy, A, Vol. XLV, Amsterdam, 1964—Zandvoort Studies. English Studies presented to R. W. Zandvoort on the occasion of his seventieth Birthday. J. Swart, 'John Skelton's *Philip Sparrow*'.

Modern Language Notes, 1901 no. 16—E. S. Hooper, 'Skelton's Magnificence and Cardinal Wolsey'.

1913, no. 28—G. E. DeBoyne, 'Skelton's Replycacion'.

1915, no. 30—John Berdan, 'Speke, Parrot, an interpretation'.

1928, no. 158—Helen S. Sale: (1) 'The date of the Garland of Laurel'; (2) 'John Skelton and Christopher Garnesche'.

1937, no. 52—Helen S. Sale-Stearns, 'The date of Skelton's Bowge of Court'.

Modern Language Review, Cambridge, 1916, vol. IX—'A. S. Cook, Skelton's Garland of Laurel and Chaucer's House of Fame'.

1917, vol. XII—R. L. Dunbabin: (1) 'Skelton's Birthplace'; (2) 'Skelton's relation to humanism'.

1929, vol. XXIV—Leslie J. Lloyd, 'John Skelton and the New Learning'.

1934, vol. XXIX—A. Gordon, 'Skelton's Philip Sparrow and the Roman Service-Book'.

1937, vol. XXXII—H. L. R. Edwards, 'Robert Gaguin and the English Poets, 1489–1490'.

Modern Philology, 1950, 158—Alan Swallow, 'The Pentameter Lines in Skelton and Wyatt'.

Nation, 8 Nov. 1933, 136—I. Schneider, critical review of Henderson's edition.

New Studies, 16 Jan. 1932—E. J. Scovell, critical review of Henderson's edition.

Notes and Queries, 10 Nov. 1849—'Joseph Barnes and the Armada'.

4 Feb. 1893—Walter Hamilton, 'The Poets Laureate of England'.

1936, 171—Pyle, 'The origin of the Skeltonics'.

1938, 174—'Heywood's The Foure PP's: a debt to Skelton'.

29 Jul. 1939—Hibernicus, 'Skelton's Reputation'.

25 Apr. 1942—H. C. Andrews, 'Baldock, Herts, and John Skelton'.

1 May, 1948—R. G. Howarth, 'Note on Skelton'.

6 Jan. 1951—H. H. Huxley, 'Philip Sparrow'.

31 Mar. 1951—James MacManaway, 'An uncollected poem of John Skelton'.

Nov. 1963—A. D. Deyermond, 'Skelton and the Epilogue to Marlowe's Dr Faustus'.

June 1964—Beryl Rowland, 'Bone Ache in Skelton's *Magnyfycence*'.

Publications of the Modern Language Association of America, Baltimore, 1914, 29 N.S. 22—John Berdan, 'The dating of Skelton's satires'.

1936, vol. 51—William Nelson: I. 'Skelton's Speak, Parrot'; II. 'Skelton's Quarrel with Wolsey'.

Jun. 1938, 53—H. L. R. Edwards and William Nelson, 'The dating of Skelton's later poems'.

66—Robert S. Kinsman, 'Skelton's Colyn Cloute: The Mask of vox populi'.

Quarterly Review, London, 1844, 73—Critical review of Dyce's edition.

Retrospective Review, London, 1822, 6—'Pithy, Pleasant and Profitable Works of Maister Skelton, Poet Laureate to Henry VIII'.

Review of English Studies, 1929, 5—Leslie J. Lloyd, 'A note on Skelton'.

1934, 40—H. L. R. Edwards, 'John Skelton: a genealogical study'.

Revue des Deux-Mondes, 1 Mar. 1842—Philarète Chasle, 'La Renaissance sensuelle: Luther, Rabelais, Skelton, Folengo'.

Saturday Review, 1931, 152—O. Burdett, critical review of Henderson's edition.

1922, 133—Louis Golding, 'Merie Skelton'.

Spectator, The, 14 Nov. 1931, 147—A. Clarke, critical review of Henderson's edition.

Speculum, a Journal of Mediaeval Studies, Cambridge (Mass.), 1934–9. —F. M. Salter, 'Skelton's Speculum Principis'.

Studies in English Literature 1500–1900—Rice University—W. O. Harris, 'The Thematic importance of Skelton's Allusion to Horace in *Magnyfycence*'.

Studies in Philology, 1944, 41—Frost and Nash, 'Good Order: a morality fragment'.

7, 1950—Robert S. Kinsman, 'Phyllyp Sparow = Titulus'.

Oct. 1917—Elaine Spina, 'Skeltonic Meter in *Elynour Rummyng*'.

April 1966—R. S. Kinsman, 'The Strategy of the Olde Sayde Sawe'.

Times Literary Supplement, 27–40, 1921—H. F. Westlake, 'Skelton in Westminster'.

1 Jan. 1925—'The Poems of John Skelton'.

20 Jun. 1929—Edmund Blunden, 'John Skelton'.

24 Sept. 1931—Critical review of Henderson's edition.

7 Jan. 1932—'Elynour Rummyng'.

1 Feb. 1934—Ian A. Gordon, 'Skelton's Speke, Parrot'.

15 Mar. 1934—G. L. Apperson, 'Epigrammes'.

19 Jul. 1934—Robert Graves, 'English Epigrams'.

2 Aug. 1934—E. Bensly, 'Epigrammes'.

9 Aug. 1934—H. L. R. Edwards, 'Syr Capten of Catywade'.

16 Aug. 1934—B. Redstone, 'Syr Capten of Catywade'.

30 Aug. 1934—H. L. R. Edwards, 'Syr Capten of Catywade'.

20 Sept. 1934—Ian A. Gordon, 'New Light on Skelton'.

27 Sept. 1934—L. John Lloyd, H. L. R. Edwards and E. Ellam, 'New Light on Skelton'.

15 Nov. 1934—Ian A. Gordon, 'A Skelton Query'.

13 Dec. 1934—Weitzman, 'Philip Sparrow's Elegy'.

20 Dec. 1934—W. Kerr, 'Note on Philip Sparrow and Politian's De Angeli puella'.

27 Dec. 1934—H. L. R. Edwards, 'Pereles Pomegranet'.

17 Jan. 1935—F. M. Salter, 'New Light on Skelton'.

7 Dec. 1935—Thomas Wolsey, 'Wolsey and French Farces'.

9 May 1936—Harry Levin, 'Skelton and Oxford'.

16 May 1936—H. E. Salter, 'John Skelton'.

12 Sept. 1936—H. L. R. Edwards, 'Pleris cum musco'.

19 Sept. 1936—G. P. C. Sutton and E. A. Bunyard, 'Pleris cum musco'.

3 Oct. 1936—Phyllis Abrahams, 'Pleris cum musco'.

24 Oct. 1936—H. L. R. Edwards, 'Hermoniake'.

19 Dec. 1936—H. L. R. Edwards, 'A Skelton emendation'.

22 May 1937—H. L. R. Edwards, 'Skelton at Diss'.

2 Nov. 1944—J. G. Tilney-Bassett, 'John Skelton and the Tilneys'.

10 Feb. 1950—J. C. Maxwell, 'A Skelton Ascription'.

Transactions of the Royal Society of Canada, 1946, 3rd series, vol. 39 (sect. 2)—F. M. Salter, 'John Skelton's Contribution to the English Language'.

University Review, Kansas City, XXXII, Oct. 1965—Barry Targan, 'Irony in John Skelton's *Philip Sparrow*'.

INDEX